Intimate Citizenships

Routledge Research in Gender and Society

Intimate Citizenships

Gender, Sexualities, Politics

Edited by Elżbieta H. Oleksy

Routledge
Taylor & Francis Group
New York London

First published 2009
by Routledge
270 Madison Ave, New York, NY 10016

Simultaneously published in the UK
by Routledge
2 Park Square, Milton Park, Abingdon, Oxon OX14 4RN

Routledge is an imprint of the Taylor & Francis Group, an informa business

© 2009 Taylor & Francis

Typeset in Sabon by IBT Global.
Printed and bound in the United States of America on acid-free paper by IBT Global.

Library of Congress Cataloging in Publication Data

Intimate citizenships : gender, sexualities, politics / edited by Elzbieta H. Oleksy.
  p. cm. — (Routledge research in gender and society ; 18)
Includes bibliographical references and index.
  1. Gender identity. 2. Sex role. 3. Citizenship. I. Oleksy, Elzbieta H., 1946–
  HQ1075.I68 2009
  306.701 — dc22
  2008020572

ISBN10: 0-415-99076-9 (hbk)
ISBN10: 0-203-88789-1 (ebk)

ISBN13: 978-0-415-99076-9 (hbk)
ISBN13: 978-0-203-88789-9 (ebk)

In memory of Mateusz,
my son, philosopher, and alpinist

Contents

Acknowledgments

My deepest thanks go to the contributors to this book for their reliability and commitment. I would like to express gratitude to Benjamin Holtzman for his patience, encouragement, and understanding during the editing process and to the production manager, Terence Johnson, during the project's finale.

I would also like to thank Dorota Golańska and Kaja Zapędowska for their advice and constructive conversations. Without the support of the staff of Women's Studies Centre—especially Marta Kotwas, Ewa Pikała, and Dorota Szafrańska—it would have been much harder to accomplish this project.

My biggest thanks—as usual—go to Wiesiek Oleksy.

Citizenship Revisited

Elżbieta H. Oleksy

In Zora Neale Hurston's metaphorical novel, *Their Eyes Were Watching God* (1978), Janie—a Mulatta also known as Alphabet for the different names white folks have been giving her—discovers her identity while looking at a photograph. Gazing at the picture of all white children but one, taken on the farm where she has been living with her grandma, Janie cannot find her own image and asks: "[W]here is me? Ah don't see me." The white folks laugh and someone points to the dark face on the photograph and says: "Dat's you, Alphabet, don't you know yo' ownselfe?" And Janie exclaims: "Aw, aw! Ah'm colored!" (1978, p. 21).

Hurston seems to have thus invented, in the mid-1930s, the concept, which has been the backbone of contemporary identity theories and can be found in recent publications on race, ethnicity, nationality, sexuality, gender, age, class, and so forth, the work that sees these social differentials not as isolated or cumulative but as intertwining, intersecting, and interlocking—in Janice Radway's phrase, as "intricate interdependencies" (1999, p. 9) or as "intersectionalities," a term more commonly used in Europe. Much of this work deals with the social and cultural construction of the subject as it is discussed in feminist and pro-feminist work on gender (inclusive of discussions on men and masculinities), queer studies, and antiracist studies of race and ethnicity. By detaching the issue of difference from various essentialisms, be they biological, national, or cultural, it marks a critical theoretical departure from previous definitions of identity and explores, in the words of Radway, "the complex, intersecting ways in which people are embedded within multiple, conflicted discourses, practices, and institutions" (1999, p. 9).

Intersectionality theories came in the wake of multiculturalism and replaced the modernist emphasis on identity with a postmodernist, poststructural concept of subjectivity (i.e., a person's sense of self). The latter perception embraces both stability and change and signifies an endless process of becoming. With such a change of emphasis came the shift from identities in common, that is to say, from commonality and inclusion, from shared experience to its opposite: exclusiveness and taking subject positions. In feminist theory, for example, the emphasis on commonality of women's experience worldwide brought the questioning of the second wave of women's rights activism.[1] As Elizabeth Spelman (1988) argues, humorously metonymizing Iris Murdoch's usage of "pebblehood" in *The Nice and the Good* (1977) for womanhood, the "manyness" of women and "all the differences among us are disturbing, threatening to the sweet intelligibility of the tidy and irrefutable fact that all women are women" (1977, p. 2). From such a perspective, adds Spelman, "this fact about women is more important than those facts about us that distinguish us from one another" (p. 2).

Women of color, in particular, have challenged those varieties of feminism, which perceive the roots of women's predicament exclusively in their disproportionate access to the means of production, characteristic of wealthy Western civilizations. Disclosing material foundations of women's social submission, as well as the relationship between the mode of production and women's status—goals advocated by Marxist feminism—fails to embrace the experience of women of color, who, similarly to women in numerous Eastern European countries, traditionally had access to the means of production (see Oleksy, 2000).

This collection of chapters takes an intersectional approach, which has recently become a useful research tool in feminist and postcolonial theory. Since its inception, political settings have been instrumental to intersectionality because of its interest in examining the complexities of social hierarchization and practices of disciplining the human experience. Intersectional analysis is always confronted with challenges resulting from the inherent complexity of the concept. Leslie McCall argues that "despite the emergence of intersectionality as a major paradigm of research in women's studies and elsewhere, there has been little discussion of how to study intersectionality, that is, of its methodology" (2005, p. 1771). The chapters in this volume, through their application of intersectional perspectives to the analysis of current theoretical and empirical understandings and practices of citizenship, directly address this challenge.

This book responds to the need to reevaluate the concept of citizenship from different theoretical, practical, and critical perspectives, for the most part offered by contemporary feminist debates. Recent years have witnessed the process of departing from the standard definitions of citizenship, particularly those developed by T. H. Marshall in the 1940s and the 1950s, but influential until the early 1990s and still used in the analyses of citizenship in postcommunist countries. Marshall studied the development of political, civil, and social rights in Great Britain from a historical perspective and with an emphasis on class, the welfare state, the nuclear family with full male employment, and the clear cut division between low and high culture—all under the impact of the nation-state. He traced the formation of civil and political rights to the 18th and 19th centuries and social rights—to the 20th. Since 1992, when Marshall's *Citizenship and Social Class* was published, his ideas have been undermined for a number of reasons. Migration flows in Europe and beyond, globalization and postmodernization of cultures, and the opening up of many societies to issues of difference throughout the various intersections accelerated the creation of new categories and new theories. The brands of citizenship that came in the wake of all these questionings centered, *inter alia*—on multicultural, cultural, sexual, and intimate aspects of the nation, while, at the same time, querying the very concept of the nation-state. In the words of Judith Butler,

> Given the complexity and heterogeneity of modes of national belonging, the nation-state can only reiterate its own basis for legitimation by literally producing the nation that serves as the basis for its legitimation. . . . modes of national belonging designated by "the nation" are thoroughly stipulative and criterial: one is not simply dropped from the nation; rather, one is found to be wanting and, so, becomes a "wanting one" through the designation and its implicit and active criteria. (2007, p. 31)

Since the early 1990s, citizenship scholarship has focused on the "wanting ones." Marion Young (1989, 1990), Will Kymlicka (1995), Homi Bhabha (1992), and Jeremy Waldron (1999), to mention just a few, promote— partly in disagreement with one another—brands of multicultural citizenship focusing on national, ethnic, and racial minority group rights. Critical of Marshall's insistence on class, Jan Pakulski returns to the concept of social community and makes an appeal for full inclusion in culture of the excluded in previous critiques of citizenship: from children to the disabled. Cultural rights, to Pakulski, are "a new breed of claims for unhindered representation, recognition without marginalization, acceptance and integration without normalizing distortion" (1997, p. 80). Central in Nick Stevenson's *Cultural Citizenship. Cosmopolitan Questions* (2003) are issues of visibility and recognition. His is an interdisciplinary project that takes inspiration from political theory, sociology, and cultural studies.

The chapters in this book tag along the track identified by two of these recently formulated brands of citizenship studies: cultural and intimate, with an emphasis on the latter. Both the subject matter of the various "schools" of citizenship research and their methodologies have followed the same trajectories and are, therefore, very well matched. Intersectionality theories grew out of the critique of multiculturalism with its emphasis on group solidarities and identities just as cultural and intimate brands of citizenship research followed the transfer from group identities to the study of subjectivities. The chapters in this volume very well document this transformation.

The term "intimate citizenship," first elaborated by Ken Plummer in 2003 (see also Plummer 1995, 2001), describes a range of emerging concerns over the right to choose what people do with their lives, their bodies, identities, feelings, relationships, representations, and so on. Not only can this type of citizenship research lend itself to intersectional analysis, but the very term intimate citizenship implies an intersection between the private and the public realms of individual life. Plummer convincingly argues that in our turbulent actuality permeated by all kinds of "intimate troubles," such as new kinds of bonding either publicly recognized or publicly held in disdain; debates around gender/s and sexualities; and medical debates over new reproductive technologies, to mention just a few, we need new discourses to ponder over the practices of these new intimacies. Intimate citizenship theory describes how our private decisions and practices have become intertwined with public institutions and state policies, such as public discourse on sexuality, legal codes, medical system, family policy, and the media, to name just a few.

Crucial in Plummer's discussion of intimate citizenship is the notion of storytelling inherent in literature, everyday conversation, and the media. Nick Stevenson's study of cultural citizenship has already touched upon the controversial nature of the new media: "Are the new media technologies," Stevenson asks, "responsible for undermining a sense of community by robbing people of participatory public spaces, or are they sites where more diversified relations of solidarity can be made?" (2003, p. 108). He gives consideration to both sides of this question, but importantly notes that the new media, especially the Internet, open up possibilities of an exchange of voices that were formerly excluded from public spaces. The reciprocity and interactivity of the various underground networks, the MUDs (Multi User Dungeons), and so forth, develop communicative skills, bind people together, and often imbue life with art. Here, Plummer's discussion of the role of storytelling in intimate citizenship is especially worthy of note. In the absence of meta-narratives, argues Plummer, people use their own stories and those of others to "construct" themselves. He makes an important reference to Richard Rorty, whose critique of the pretentiousness of traditional epistemology led him to conclude that no belief is more essential than any other. The implication of this inference is that—since philosophy cannot determine anything—it can only be understood as an "edifying" conversation on a par with discussions of literary or cultural scholars: "the novel, the movie, and the TV program have, gradually but steadily, replaced the sermon and the treatise as the principal vehicles of moral change and progress" (Rorty 1989, p. xvi). Though "edifying" is a somewhat negatively tainted term that goes back to Søren Kierkegaard and such Catholic writers as Walker Percy, here it is understood as the practice of experimenting with channels of communication in order to create "social hope, not universal knowledge" (Rorty, 1987, p. 12). Plummer concludes with the words that constitute one of the main facets of feminist ways of knowing: "we need to hear new stories and anticipate how they might change our lives" (2003, p. 100).

From personal narratives of slave women in the United States South (see Oleksy, 1998, pp. 84–91), through Charlotte Perkins Gilman's short story "The Yellow Wallpaper" (1892), and Mary Shelley's oft-discussed in the context of "intimate troubles" novel *Frankenstein* (1831), to Jeannette Winterson's work *Oranges Are Not the Only Fruit* (1990), storytelling bridges the private with the political. "Stories of intimate citizenship" or "public identity narratives" (Plummer, 2003, p. 104) are told in all kinds of texts: literary, visual, and academic. They are told to family and friends, to audiences; they are told to researchers. This volume wholly documents these ways of "practicing" intimate citizenship. The chapters focus on the empirical analyses of particular cases in specified national and international contexts, and they fully reveal the complex nature of intimate citizenship, which includes not only political and social status but also private decisions, choices, and practices. This book argues that processes appearing at the overlap of the public and the private realms have an immense impact on the redefinition of the concept of citizenship. The case studies included in this volume make the theoretical discussion of citizenship more palpable. Situated perspectives, as well as application of the theoretical concept to real experience, constitute important new avenues of research. Moreover, such a broad approach to the concept of citizenship makes it clear that it is no longer possible to theorize citizenship in universal and abstract terms, but that it should always be situated in the context of an individual lived experience. Seen from this perspective, citizenship's territory must be extended beyond the conventional public sphere and, consequently, located at the intersection of many axes of social, political, and cultural stratification.

Collectively and individually, the authors argue that although usually constructed in a universal way, it is impossible to interpret and articulate citizenship without always situating it in a lived experience. The emphasis in this book is on the urgent need to both pluralize and contextualize the public and private realms of human experience. Following recent feminist criticism, the overall objective of this collection is to stress the need to broaden the traditional understanding of citizenship to include intimate practices and entertain new approaches to the concept. While all chapters in the collection take a complex approach to the issue of intimate citizenship in its different manifestations, they are divided into three thematic and partially overlapping sections. Such a structure emphasizes the multilayered understanding of the volume's key concept and offers different dimensions of the practices of "doing" citizenship.

PART I: GENDER POLITICS—TOWARD A NEW VISION OF THE SUBJECT

Part I revisits some contemporary dilemmas, which feminist debates have to face in the context of present discussions related to identity politics. The issue is of central importance in view of the increasing globalization of cultures and simultaneous reemergence of master narratives. The aim of this section is to make a plea for the revision of identity and subjectivity theories in order to liberate them from the normative constraints of traditional and humanistic thought. The focus here is on the need to develop new ethics connected to new forms of political agency. The important claim to go beyond the binary system of thinking, related to the negatively understood notions of difference and otherness, paves the way for new forms of solidarities and alliances stemming from lived experiences, which occur not only at the intersection of different social and political axes of differentials but also at the overlap of the public and private spheres.

The three chapters gathered in this section have a general character and provide an important global, political, and philosophical context for the book's remaining chapters. The processes of dissolving and decentering the stable identity in favor of a nomadic and fluid vision of the subject constitutes an important point of departure for discussions of citizenship in its different—intimate above all—dimensions.

Social marginalization and political exclusion constitute a critical leitmotif in Chapter 1 by Judith Butler. Butler engages with recent sociopolitical phenomena such as gay parenting, Dutch immigration policy, and islamophobia in selected geographical locations (France, the Netherlands, and the United States), considering them in a broader theoretical context of time and "modernity." Who gets defined as "modern," and who does not, emerge as highly problematic, ideologically charged cultural processes, wherein sexuality and otherness become a major axis of intersection. This inevitably raises issues of freedom and progress which must, as Butler evinces, never be accepted uncritically. Continuous proximity of theological dogmatism, state policy, and culture render objectionable or, at least, ambiguous, a claim of secular time. Ubiquitous cruelty and torture (war, discrimination, persecution) exercised upon *abjected* bodies make us carry on revising old and new conceptions of civilizational progress and social liberties in order to unravel their hidden exclusionary mechanisms and discursive limitations. Postsecular time, in Butler's view, emerges as far more invested in religion than one might think.

As Rosi Braidotti argues in Chapter 2, politics is out of favor today, whereas public debates tend to emphasize ethics. Her chapter examines three aspects of the so-called "postsecular" turn: a reactionary angle of religious and political extremism and neoconservatism, what she calls "a new political economy of affects," and the transformative character of postsecular ethics that accommodates present time contradictions and intricacies and their implications for feminist politics. The stress on ethics in this contribution indicates the return of the master narrative of religious fundamentalisms of different kinds and a global clash of civilizations energized by "The Project for a New American Century," all of which put European feminism in a precarious situation. Braidotti's chapter proposes an oppositional strategy, one that she finds in alternative models of ethical accountability. Firmly grounded in Braidotti's former research, this chapter argues that a postsecularist and nomadic vision of the subject can provide an alternative foundation for ethical and political subjectivity.

In the same vein and inspired by Nietzsche's and Deleuze's thought, Marek Wojtaszek's Chapter 3 argues for a novel, more vitalistic, understanding of the socio-political changes and cultural development than the ones offered by psychoanalysis or Marxism. Problematizing gender(ed) character of the dualistic positioning of conflicting forces, the text aims to expose such reliance on systemic categories as entangled in the maintenance of the oppressive patriarchal regime. In setting a new political agenda, an emphasis is placed on creativity and affirmation, which by engendering new concepts, helps avoid a prior critical acceptance of the status quo. This new framework, it is believed, appears effective in accounting for production and velocity of changes and, most crucially, in enabling men and women to realize that no ethico-political cha(lle)nge has ever been made by *non*-wishes.

PART II: NEGOTIATING CITIZENSHIP— GENDER, SEXUALITY, POLITICS

This section focuses on sexuality and gender politics in their different national, social, and political contexts. Public discourses and their critiques constitute an important background for empirical analyses of particular cases. The alleged division of the public and private sphere is also an object of critical analysis as related to different practices situated in diverse places and spaces. The chapters gathered in this section aim to contest the taken-for-granted normative claims and postulates and to demonstrate how private decisions translate into public debates and vice versa. They argue for a need to find new forms of negotiating the most intimate dimensions of subjectivity in the world in which people's private choices are often subject to political debate and public scrutiny.

In Chapter 4, Sally Hines examines changing concepts and practices of gendered citizenship in relation to transgender. The chapter charts the ways in which transgender has become a topic of growing social, political, and cultural interest. She focuses her analysis on the United Kingdom, where altering attitudes toward transgender people brought about such legislative changes as the Gender Recognition Act (2004). She notes that all these changes have resulted in a greater visibility of gender diversion and higher degrees of social acceptance and inclusion of trans people. However, Hines sees transgendered citizenship as still vulnerable because a persistent, normative binary perception of "gender" as distinct from "sex" gives the discussion of transgender a medical perspective, the consequence of which is marginalization of gender diversity. Drawing on recent qualitative research on transgender practices of identity, the chapter examines citizenship debates within United Kingdom transgender communities and explores the subjective understandings and experiences of concepts and practices of citizenship for transgender men and women.

In Chapter 5, Karin Lenke examines the ways in which social policy and (step)family discourse are constituted by the cultural and legal priority granted to biological kinship ties. The discourses that perpetuate the primacy of biological kinship are gathered under the label of the politics of biology. She scrutinizes the ways in which this politics is constituted, expressed, and challenged in contemporary Sweden. Lenke's methodological framework is inspired by discourse theory in which struggles over meaning are central to the two-fold analysis in this study . She first traces the politics of biology in social policy and family law and argues that even though late modern family forms come in a multitude of different constellations, the heterosexual, nuclear, first marriage family stands as a model, and biological ties between parents and children are privileged over social ties. She subsequently examines the tensions over the meaning of family and parenthood present in interviews conducted with four young adults brought up in stepfamilies, with one or more social parents.

Lisa Smyth argues in Chapter 6 that infant feeding policies address women's citizenship from specific cultural perspectives. Building on recent feminist work on breastfeeding, this chapter argues that frequently breastfeeding is approached through fixed cultural norms, which construct women's breasts in sexual terms. Focusing on health promotion work in the field of infant feeding in Northern Ireland, Smyth argues that, in the absence of broader discussion on and questioning of cultural norms, an individualized and moralistic policy approach has had the effect of privatizing the practice of breastfeeding. Situating breastfeeding in the context of debates concerning care ethics and rights, Smyth argues that it could promote women's autonomy and be considered as a reproductive right. Conversely, the lack of state recognition for a right to breastfeed on the basis of "cultural norms" raises doubts about women's full social inclusion.

The next three chapters situate the discussion of "intimate troubles" in East-Central Europe. With a few exceptions (notably, Heinen, 1997, 2006; Štulhofer & Sandfort, 2005), most citizenship scholarship has been written from the Western perspective. This collection includes voices from some of the new European Union member states, ones characterized by the same communist past and presently grappling with similar social dilemmas. As a result of opening up to the free market and the processes of democratization and globalization, issues of gender equality and freedom of sexual orientation have moved to the very center of public discourse in the countries of East-Central Europe. Paradoxically, the political and economic liberalization taking place in the region is counterbalanced by conservatism in the area of gender norms and acceptable sexual behaviors and identities as if—argues Agnieszka Graff in Chapter

7—"the area of gender became a depositary of national pride." Situating her analysis on the broader spectrum of criticism on gender and nation, Graff discusses several instances of gendered nationalist rhetoric in Poland. She notes a "striking overlap" between ideologies of gender and nationalism. Nations, she argues, are often allegorically represented as female figures in which women's role in relation to the nation-state is primarily metaphorical (see also Oleksy, 2005), whereas that of men tends to be metonymic. Drawing on the analysis of recent media coverages of these issues, her chapter investigates the rhetorical and political consequences of this "peculiar division of labor" in the context of Poland's recent surge into nationalist sentiment and revival of national mythology.

Through attempts to define pornography, Czech discourses of criminology and sexology effectively contribute to the production of a normalizing and marginalizing regime of sexual citizenship. The continuum of approaches is defined by an uncompromising deprecation of pornography. On one side, the use of pornography results in increased aggressiveness and general sociopathy. On the other side of the Czech scientific continuum of porn, sexologists do not hastily condemn porn users but instead stress the naturalness of hard, promiscuous, predator-like bodily oriented sexuality for men, and softer, relationship, and love-oriented sexuality for women, thus reproducing and reinforcing the gender binary. An important issue in Chapter 8 by Kateřina Lišková is finding the extent to which these conservative scientific discourses overlap with feminist antipornography rhetoric. The "liberal" sexologists presenting reconciliatory notions of porn are indiscriminate in their negative depiction of feminists. Thus, while positioning themselves as the liberal alternative to the standard, scientific antiporn discourse, they at the same time maintain deeply conservative views. The irony here is that the "conservative" antiporn writers use *quasi*-feminist discourse, whereas the "liberal" wing espouses an explicitly antifeminist agenda.

In Chapter 9, Anikó Imre examines how such meanings of representation as mimetic and performative, on one hand, and political and artistic, on the other, intertwine in postcommunist countries. She takes the Budapest-based organization Labrisz Society as her main case study and points out how its visual practices are essentially performative, following transnational trends of lesbian representation. Their regular social events gain support from foreign, rather than local, institutions. They ridicule the issue of identity politics based on mimetic essentialist ideas and define national citizenship as inherently obsolete. Drawing on feminist theories of duality of representation, Imre analyzes how the Labrisz Society and its Lesbian Film Committee negotiate national and transnational tensions inherent in their efforts to include lesbianism in citizenship as well as the frequently challenging relationships they attempt to sustain with feminist and male gay organizations.

PART III: MEN AND MASCULINITIES—
NEW IDENTITIES, EMERGING SUBJECTIVITIES

This section continues the debate raised in previous chapters but with a more particular focus on men and masculinities. The chapters gathered here trace how people's most private decisions and choices have become increasingly bound up with public institutions, on one hand, and emerging discourses, on the other. The issues at stake in this section are the pluralized and contested contemporary public sphere and the new ideas to navigate through a world in which people's private spheres get increasingly conflated with politics and public debates. The plurality of experiences and stories about how to live one's personal life is seen here as the most intimate dimension of citizenship understood as both status and practice. The intersectional approach is instrumental in analyzing the particular contexts and serves to dilute the monolithic understanding of identity in favor of emerging unstable subjectivities.

Although a relatively new field of research, masculinity studies have developed very rapidly around the globe. In Europe, much of the research on men, masculinities, and men's practices was initiated, in 1999, by the Critical Research on Men in Europe (CROME) Network, as well as stemming out of its first European Union Framework 5 project "The Social Problem of Men: The Social Problem and Societal Problematization of Men and Masculinities." Some of the chapters of this section draw on the findings of these new European initiatives.

Basing his discussion on feminist and profeminist criticism of patriarchy as too monolithic, ahistorical, ethnocentric, biologically over-determined, and dismissive of women's resistance and agency, Jeff Hearn, in Chapter 10, revisits the notion of patriarchy. He points out two aspects of the patriarchy debate: (1) the historical periodization of patriarchy and other gender systems, inclusive of the intersectionality debates (e.g., family/generation, work/class, sexuality), and (2) the discussion on global or world patriarchy, which—in Hearn's view—has been too monolithic. He refers to patriarchy in transnational contexts as transpatriarchies (i.e., as a way of talking about patriarchies, intersectionalities, and transnationalization at the same time). Examples that Hearn analyzes include transpatriarchies in international business corporations, the sex trade, information and communication technologies, and militarism.

In Chapter 11, Iva Šmídová questions constructions and reproductions of certain types of contemporary masculine identities in the Czech Republic in relation to equal opportunity debates. Drawing on two studies of men employed in environmental protection related occupations, and on fathers on parental leave, she acknowledges new societal developments in that country geared toward generating more gender-sensitive arrangements. Šmídová points to clashes between individual men's actions and the presence of societal gendered structures. These structures of masculine domination are critically reviewed based on two examples: (1) alternative life-course trajectories in the narratives of the interviewed men, and (2) the absence of any direct connection between environmental protection and/or paternal leave with gender equality in individual actions. Environment-friendly men and fathers on parental leave present a challenge to exploitative misogynist forms of masculinities, but they also often reproduce forms, which strongly support conventional, mainstream essentialist approaches to, *inter alia*, housework and child care.

Chapter 12 by Iwona Chmura-Rutkowska and Joanna Ostrouch presents the findings of five focus group and biographical interviews with men aged 35 to 40, in the context of important developmental imperatives of middle adulthood and in different realms of life: private, public, and in the sphere of symbolic patterns and models. These interviews demonstrate how masculinity is being redefined in contemporary Poland and how men respond to new forms of masculinity. The authors draw attention to their interviewees' trepidation of their new roles. The principal strategy of managing this fear are all kinds of withdrawal strategies. An analysis of the group discussions shows that men lack ideas about how to create their own roles in contemporary Poland. The authors consider the ways in which interviewees experience masculinity, locating them in the context of a situation of crisis, a strategy of withdrawal, and the necessity of change.

Michael Flood claims in Chapter 13 that new formations of sexuality are emerging among heterosexual men, ones informed by constructions of "queer" and "metrosexual" masculinities and other alternatives. Some straight men express solidarity with gay men, question the binary of heterosexual and homosexual, take up egalitarian or even subordinate roles in their heterosexual relations, or adopt a feminized preoccupation with personal grooming. Such developments signal a weakening of longstanding constructions of heterosexual masculinity, and as a result there is significant diversity in the contemporary sexual cultures of young heterosexual men. Drawing on empirical research in Australia and a review of international scholarship, this chapter maps the shifting sexual and social relations of young heterosexual men. On one hand, there are signs of a growing acceptance of norms of gender equality, gender convergence in young heterosexual men's and women's sexual and intimate practices and understandings, as well as an increased assertion of young female sexual desire and agency. On the other hand, there are persistent gender inequalities and "pornographication" of mainstream culture, which offer only narrow constructions of female sexuality.

The chapters in this book, with their thematic and disciplinary diversity, present new theoretical approaches applied to the empirical studies, respond to the complex nature of contemporary social and political changes, and give a better understanding of challenges posed by the return of master narratives, on one hand, and the emergence of new diversity discourses, on the other. This volume's ambition is partly to bridge this gap and open a vast debate, which society has to face vis-à-vis new phenomena connected to, among others, globalization, mediatization, and biotechnology. The inclusion of the intimate realm explicitly exposes the overlap of the public and the private as well as demonstrates the importance of the consequences that these intersections have for the redefinition of the concept of citizenship. The approach to the overlap of politics, culture, identity, and subjectivity that the book takes constitutes an important voice in the debate on the notion of citizenship, which urgently needs revision and theoretical reevaluation.

NOTES

1. It should be admitted, however, that arguments sceptical of feminist theories of intersectionality have also recently been made. Naomi Zack (2005) points out that "divisions of human beings by race, class, and sexuality in society are not taxonomies of mere variety but. . . components of the hierarchies." Such categorizations diminish the chances for democratic change and preclude the commonality of experience among women across social differentials (p. 11). Earlier on, Nancy Frazer (1997) critiqued the pluralistic version of multiculturalism, which replaced the essentialist perception of women as a homogenous category with an equally essentialist view about generalized cultural categories. She postulates an antiessentialist version of multiculturalism, in which cultural differences are not essentialized and thus able to enhance feminist politics to oppose fundamentalisms. See also Oleksy (2007).

REFERENCES

Bhabha. H. (1992). *The location of culture.* London: Routledge.
Butler, J., & Charkravorty Spivak, G. (2007). *Who sings the nation state? Language, politics, belonging.* London, New York, Calcutta: Seagull.
Frazer, N. (1977). *Justice interruptus: Critical reflexions on the "postsocialist" conditions.* New York: Routledge.
Heinen, J. (1997). Public/private, gender, social and political citizenship in Eastern Europe. *Theory and Society, 26(4),* 577–597.
———. (2006). Clashes and ordeals of women's citizenship in Central and Eastern Europe. In J. Lukic, J. Regulska, & D. Zavirsek, *Women and citizenship in Central and East Europe* (pp. 95–114). .Aldershot: Ashgate.
Hurston, Z. N. (1978). *Their eyes were watching God.* Urbana: University of Illinois Press.
Kymlicka, W. (1995). *Multicultural citizenship: A liberal theory of minority rights.* Oxford: Clarendon Press.
McCall, L. (2005). The complexity of intersectionality. *Signs: Journal of Women in Culture and Society, 30(3),*1771–1802.
Murdoch, I. (1977). *The nice and the good.* Frogmore, St Albans: Triad/Panther Books.
Oleksy, E. H. (1998). *Kobieta w krainie Dixie. Literatura i film.* Łódź: Wydawnictwo Uniwersytetu Łódzkiego.

———. (2000). American feminism and pedagogy: The case of Poland. *American Studies International, xxxviii*(3), 36–46.

———. (2005). "Women, don't interfere with us; we're fighting for Poland": Polish mothers and transgressive others. In M. Mikula (Ed.), *Women, activism and social change.* London: Routledge.

———. (2007a). Intricate interdependencies and female buddy movies. In J. Maszewska & Z. Maszewska (Eds.), *Walking on a trail of words. Essays in honor of Agnieszka Salska* (pp. 345–356). Łódź: Łódź University Press, 2007.

———. (2007b). Women's commonality and social change. . In N. Lykke, S. Adrian, & M. Gustavson (Eds.), *GEXcel Work in Progress Report, Vol. 1. Proceedings from GEXcel Kick-off Conference.* Linköping: LiU Press.

Pakulski, J. (1997). Cultural citizenship. *Citizenship Studies, 1*(1), 73–86.

Plummer, K. (1995). *Telling sexual stories: Power, change and social worlds.* London: Routledge.

———. (2000). Intimate choices. In G. Browning, A. Halcli, & F. Webster (Eds.), *Theory and society: Understanding the present.* London: Sage.

———. (2003). *Intimate citizenship: Private decision and public dialogues.* Seattle: University of Washington Press.

Radway, J. (1999). What's in a name? Presidential address to the American Studies Association, November 20,1998. *American Quarterly, 51*(1), 8–18, 23–24.

Rorty, R. (1987, September 3). Posties. *London Review of Books,* p. 12.

———. (1989). *Contingency, irony and solidarity.* Cambridge: Cambridge University Press.

Spelman, E. (1988). *Inessential woman: Problems of exclusion in feminist thought.* Boston: Beacon Press.

Stevenson, N. (2003). *Cultural citizenship: Cosmopolitan questions.* Maidenhead: Open University Press.

Štulhofer, A & Sandfort, T. (Eds.). (2005). *Sexuality and gender in postcommunist Easten European and Russio.* New York: The Haworth Press.

Waldron, J. (1999). Minority cultures and the cosmopolitan alternative. In W. Kymlicka (Ed.), *Minority cultures.* Oxford: Blackwell.

Winterson, J. (1990). *Oranges are not the only fruit.* New York: Grove Press.

Young, I. M. (1989). Polity and group difference: A critique of the ideal of universal citizenship. *Ethics,* 99,250–274.

———. (1990). The ideal of community and the politics of difference. In L. J. Nicholson (Ed.), *Feminism/postmodernism.* London: Routledge.

Zack, N. (2005). *Inclusive feminism: A third wave of women's commonality.* New York: Rowman & Littlefield.

Part I

Gender Politics

Toward a New Vision of the Subject

1 Sexual Politics, Torture, and Secular Time

Judith Butler

If one wants to commence with the most common of beginnings, namely, with the claim that one would like to be able to consider sexual politics during this time, a certain problem arises. It seems clear that one cannot reference "this time" without knowing which time, where that time takes hold, and for whom a certain consensus emerges on the issue of this time. So, if it is not just a matter of differences of interpretation about which time this is, then it would seem that we have already more than one time at work in this time, and that the problem of time will afflict any effort I might take to consider some of these major issues. It might seem odd to begin with a reflection on time when one is trying to speak about sexual politics. My suggestion here, however, is that the way in which debates within sexual politics are framed are already imbued with the problems of time, of progress in particular, and in certain notions of what it means to unfold a future of freedom. That there is no one time, that the question of what time this is already divides us, has to do with which histories have turned out to be formative, how they intersect—or fail to intersect—with other histories, and so with the question of how temporality is organized along spatial lines. I am not suggesting here that we return to a version of cultural difference that depends on cultural wholism. The problem is not that there are different modalities of time articulated in different cultural locations. Of course, at some level, that is true, but it does not quite approach the problem of temporality at issue here, since politically, the question of what time we are in, and of who is modern and who is not, is raised in the midst of very serious political contestations. It is my view that sexual politics, rather than operating to the side of this contestation, is in the middle of it, and that very often claims to new or radical sexual freedoms are appropriated precisely by that point of view which would try to define Europe and the sphere of modernity as the privileged site where sexual radicalism can and does take place.

In this way, the problem is not that there are different temporalities in different cultural locations (and, that, accordingly, we simply need to broaden our cultural frameworks to become more internally complicated and capacious). Rather, the problem is that certain notions of relevant geopolitical space are circumscribed by this story of a progressive modernity, and that certain notions of what "this time" can and must be are similarly construed on the basis of circumscribing the "where" of its happening. I should make clear at the outset that I am not opposing all notions of "moving forward" and am certainly not against all versions of "progress," but only that I am profoundly influenced, if not dislocated, by Walter Benjamin's graphic means of rethinking progress and the time of the now, and that that is part of what I am bringing to bear on a consideration of sexual politics. I want to say: a consideration of sexual politics *now*; of course, that is true, but perhaps my thesis is simply that there can be no consideration of sexual politics without a critical consideration of the time of the now. My claim will be that thinking through the problem of temporality and politics in this way may well open up a different approach to cultural difference, one that eludes the claim of pluralism and intersectionality alike.

One can see already in the very terms of the thesis I propose that there is not only a problem of time and, in particular, one pertaining to the conceit of progress. Time is already of the essence here, since I think that a common understanding left within the United States of what it means to be progressive is to be in the progress of developing new movements that follow upon prior ones, with the new ones establishing more radical claims for justice or more copious notions of equality. Perhaps most importantly, the idea of progress has been linked with the historical unfolding of freedom, such that when we assess the sequence of movements that form the recent history of feminist and sexual politics, as well as civil rights struggles, in the United States, we tend to assume that greater freedoms are being achieved, that coercion is being qualified or diminished, and that a certain emancipatory potential is being realized, perhaps in fits and starts, but progressively, over time. In fact, I think we proceed too quickly, fail to take enough time, when we track the evolution of lesbian and gay into queer, and then the movement from queer into transgender, or the politics of intersex as interceding in the transition from queer to transgender. This is perhaps most clear when, within the United States, certain people proclaim that the AIDS crisis is over. That utterance concedes that the United States borders supply the taken-for-granted spatial and imaginary parameters for this discourse. Such an utterance dismisses the fact that more than 30 million people are infected with the virus in Sub-Saharan Africa alone and that nearly 3 million have lost their lives to the disease on the African continent. Nearly 64% of all new HIV infections take place in Sub-Saharan Africa, which houses 10% of the world's population. So there is obviously the question of "for whom" the AIDS crisis is over, if it is, as well as where and on the conditions of what kind of available healthcare. Thus, at whose expense do we claim the "now" in the story of progress?

The point is not just to become mindful of the temporal and spatial presuppositions of some of our progressive narratives, the ones that inform various parochial, if not structurally racist, political optimisms of various kinds. Rather, it is to show that our understanding of what is happening "now" is bound up with a certain geo-political restriction on imagining the relevant borders of the world and even a refusal to understand what happens to our notion of time if we take the problem of the border (what crosses the border, and what does not, and the means and mechanisms of that crossing or impasse) to be central to any understanding of contemporary political life. Even if those who reside in the United States were to remain restricted within its borders (which would be odd, given that the "United States" is now virtually defined by the means and mechanisms by which it exports itself both economically and politically), such a restriction would ratify a set of borders that are part of a new security state, one that is mired in the monitoring of immigration, especially from the southern border. Therefore, we cannot take either the spatial or temporal frame for granted, and we are also under some serious pressure to think anew how they structure and affect one another. The contemporary map of sexual politics is crossed, I would say, with contentions and antagonisms, ones that define the time of sexual politics as a fractious constellation; the story of progress is but one strand within that constellation, one that has, for good reason, come into crisis. [1]

My interest is to focus on how certain secular conceptions of history and of what is meant by a "progressive" position within contemporary politics rely on a conception of freedom that is understood to emerge through time, and which is temporally progressive in its structure. [2] I want to suggest that this link between freedom and temporal progress is often what is being indexed when pundits and public policy representatives refer to concepts like *modernity* or, indeed, *secularism*. I do not mean to say that this is all they mean, but I do want to say that a certain conception of freedom is invoked precisely as a rationale and instrument for certain practices of coercion, and this places those of us who have conventionally understood ourselves as advocating a progressive sexual politics in a rather serious bind.

In this context, I want to point to a few sites of political debate involving both sexual politics and anti-Islamic practice that suggest that certain ideas of the progress of "freedom" facilitate a political division between progressive sexual politics and the struggle against racism and discrimination against religious minorities. I consider in this regard the Dutch civic integration exam, some French debates on gay parenting whose ideological underpinnings dovetail with anti-immigration politics, and recent papal engagements with the topic of homosexuality as well as with Islam. Or, if we ask about the way that misogyny and homophobia figure in the cultural logic of sexual torture documented in outsourced United States war prisons, we see yet another permutation of these trends that suggest how domestic debates might be reconstellated yet again within a global frame. One of the issues that follows from such a reconstellation is that a certain version and deployment of "freedom" can be used as an instrument of bigotry and coercion. This happens most frightfully when women's sexual freedom or the freedom of expression and association for lesbian and gay people is invoked instrumentally to wage cultural assaults on Islam, which reaffirm United States sovereign violence. Must we rethink freedom and its implication in the narrative of progress, or must we resituate? My point is surely not to abandon freedom as a norm, but to ask about its uses, and to consider how it must be rethought if it is to resist its coercive instrumentalization in the present and have another meaning that might remain useful for a radical democratic politics.

Consider, then, the following way in which claims for sexual freedom have become bound up with state coercion and state-induced forms of abjection. In the Netherlands, for instance, new applicants for immigration are asked to look at photos of two men kissing and report whether those photos are offensive, whether they are understood to express personal liberties, and whether the viewers are willing to live in a democracy that values the rights of gay people to open and free expression. The test became compulsory in March 2006 and was made available at 138 Dutch embassies around the world. The Dutch immigration ministry called this "the civic integration examination."[3]

Those who are in favor of the new policy claim that acceptance of homosexuality is the same as the embrace of modernity. We can see in such an instance how modernity is being defined as sexual freedom, and the particular sexual freedom of gay people is understood to exemplify a culturally advanced position as opposed to one that would be deemed premodern. It also would seem that the Dutch government has made special arrangements for a class of people who are considered presumptively modern. The presumptively modern includes the following groups, who are exempted from having to take the test: European Union nationals, asylum-seekers, and skilled workers who earn more than 45,000 Euros per year. Also exempt are citizens of the United States, Australia, New Zealand, Canada, Japan, and Switzerland, where presumably homophobia is not to be found or where, rather, importing impressive income levels clearly preempts concerns over importing homophobia.[4]

In the Netherlands, of course, this movement has been brewing for some time. The identification of gay politics with cultural and political modernity culminated with the career and death of Pim Fortuyn, the gay and overtly anti-Islamic politician, who was gunned down by a radical environmentalist in the winter of 2002. A similar conflict was also dramatized in the work and the death of Theo van Gogh, who, in this instance, came to stand not for a set of cultural norms articulated only for sexual freedom, but for principles of political and artistic freedom. Certainly I am in favor of such freedoms, but it seems that I must also ask whether these freedoms for which I have struggled and continue to struggle are being instrumentalized to established a specific cultural grounding, secular in a particular sense, that functions as a prerequisite for admission into the polity as an acceptable immigrant. In what follows, I will elaborate further on what this cultural grounding is, how it functions as both transcendental condition and teleological aim, and how it complicates any firm distinctions we might have between the secular and the religious. In this instance, a set of cultural norms is being articulated as preconditions for citizenship. We might accept the view that there are always such norms, and even accept that full civic and cultural participation for anyone, regardless of gender or sexual orientation, be included among such norms. However, are such norms not only articulated differently, but also instrumentally, in order to shore up particular religious and cultural preconditions that effect other sorts of exclusions? One is not free to reject this cultural grounding since it is the basis, even the presumptive prerequisite, of the operative notion of freedom, and freedom is articulated through a set of graphic images, figures that come to stand for what freedom can and must be. Thus, a certain paradox ensues in which the coerced adoption of certain cultural norms becomes a requisite for entry into a polity that defines itself as the avatar of freedom. Is the Dutch government engaging in civic pedagogy through its defense of lesbian and gay sexual freedom, and would it impose such a test on the right-wing white supremacists, such as *Vlaams Blok*, who are congregated on its border with Belgium and who have called for a *cordon sanitaire* around Europe to keep out non-Europeans? Is it administering tests to lesbian and gay people to make sure they are not offended by the visible practices of Muslim minorities? If the civic integration exam were part of a larger effort to foster cultural understanding about religious and sexual norms for a diverse Dutch population, one that included new pedagogies and funding for public arts projects dedicated to this purpose, we might then understand cultural "integration" in a different sense, but certainly not coercively. In this case, though, the question raised is: Does the exam becomes the means for testing tolerance, or does it carry an assault against religious minorities, part of a broader effort on the part of the state to demand coercively that they rid themselves of their traditional religious beliefs and practices in order to gain entry into the Netherlands? Is this a liberal defense of my freedom for which I should be pleased, or is my "freedom" freedom, or is my freedom being used as an instrument of coercion, one that seeks to keep Europe white, pure, and "secular" in ways that do not interrogate the violence that underwrites that very project? Certainly, I want to be able to kiss in public—do not get me wrong. However, do I want to require that everyone watch and approve before they acquire the rights of citizenship? I think not.

If the prerequisites of the polity require either cultural homogeneity or a model of cultural pluralism, then either way, the solution is figured as assimilation to a preestablished and presumptively common set of cultural norms. These norms are not in conflict, open to dispute, in contact with other norms, contested, or disrupted in a field in which a number of norms converge—or fail to converge—in an ongoing way. The presumption is that culture is a uniform and binding groundwork of norms, and not a field of contestation; this groundwork only functions if it is uniform or integrated, and that desideratum is required, even forcibly, for something called modernity to emerge and take hold. Of course, we can already see that this very specific sense of modernity entails an immunization against contestation, that it is maintained through a dogmatic grounding, and that already we are introduced to a kind of dogmatism, which belongs to a particular secular formation. Within this framework, the freedom of personal expression, broadly construed, relies upon the suppression of cultural difference, and the issue makes clear how state violence invests in cultural homogeneity as it applies its exclusionary policies to rationalize state policies toward Islamic immigrants.

Although theories of modernity are, in my view, for the most part too general and sketchy to be useful, and people from different disciplines mean very different things by "modernity," it makes sense to trace its discursive uses—which is something other than supplying a theory. As for the discursive uses of modernity, it seems to function not as a signifier of cultural multiplicity or of normative schemes that are dynamically or critically in flux. To the extent that both artistic expression and sexual freedom are understood as ultimate signs of this version of modernity, and they are conceived as rights that are supported by a particular formation of secularism, we are asked to disarticulate struggles for sexual freedom from those against racism and anti-Islamic sentiment. There is presumably no solidarity among such efforts within a framework such as the one I have just outlined. Indeed, the struggles for sexual expression depend on the restriction and foreclosure of rights of religious expression (if we are to stay within the liberal framework), and so we can see something of an antinomy within the discourse of liberal rights itself. Nevertheless, it seems that something more fundamental is occurring, namely, that liberal freedoms are understood to rely upon a hegemonic culture, one that is called "modernity" and relies on a certain progressive account of increasing freedoms. This uncritical domain of "culture," which functions as a precondition for liberal freedom, in turn becomes the cultural basis for sanctioning forms of cultural and religious hatred and abjection. My point is not to trade sexual freedoms for religious ones, but, rather, to question the framework that assumes there can be no political analysis that tries to analyze homophobia and racism in ways that move beyond this antinomy of liberalism. At stake is whether or not there can be a convergence or alliance between such struggles, or whether the struggle against homophobia must contradict the one against cultural and religious racisms. If this framework of mutual exclusion holds—one that is derived, I would suggest, from a restrictive idea of personal liberty—then it would appear that there are no points of cultural contact between sexual progressives and religious minorities that are not encounters of violence and exclusion. If, in the place of a liberal conception of personal freedom, however, we consider the importance of a political analysis that has as its focus the critique of state violence and the elaboration of its coercive mechanisms, we may well arrive at an alternative political framework, one that implies not only another sense of modernity, but also of the time, the "now," in which we live.

It was Thomas Friedman who claimed in the *New York Times* that Islam has not yet achieved modernity, suggesting that it is somehow in a childish state of cultural development and that the norm of adulthood is represented more adequately by critics such as himself.[5] In this sense, then, Islam is conceived as not of *this* time or *our* time, but *another* time, one that only anachronistically emerged in this time. However, is not such a view precisely the refusal to think this time not as one time, as one story, developing unilinearly, but as a convergence of histories that have not always been thought together, and whose convergence or lack thereof presents a set of quandaries that might be said to be definitive of our time?

A similar dynamic is to be found in France, where questions of sexual politics converge in some unhappy ways with anti-immigration politics. There, of course, ideas of "culture" and of *"laïcité"* (or secularism) work differently, and one can see how a certain ostensibly progressive sexual politics is sanctioned, again, as the logical culmination of a secular realization of freedom at the same time that the very same conception of secular freedoms operates as a norm to exclude or to minimize the possibility of ethnic and religious communities from North Africa, Turkey, and the Middle East from attaining legal membership. Indeed, the situation is even more complex, because the idea of culture, bound up with a conception of symbolic law, is regarded as founding the freedom to enter into free associations, but is also invoked to limit the freedom of lesbian and gay people from adopting children or gaining access to reproductive technology, thus avowing the rights of contract but refusing challenges to the norms of kinship. The arguments that secured the legislative victory for the Pacte Civil de Solidarité (PACS)—those legal partnerships into which any two people, regardless of gender may enter—are based on an extension of those rights to form contracts on the basis of one's own volition.[6] And yet, once the cultural preconditions of that freedom are abrogated, the law intervenes to maintain—or even mandate—that cultural integrity.

One can rather quickly conclude, on the basis of a variety of opinions published in French journals and newspapers, that there is a widely held belief that, for instance, gay and lesbian parenting runs the risk of producing a psychotic child. The extraordinary support among French republicans for the PACS has depended from the start on the separation of the PACS from any rights to adoption or to parenting structures outside the heterosexual norm. In the newspapers and throughout public discourse, one hears that lesbian or gay parenting—and this would include single-mother parenting as well—threatens to undermine the very framework a child requires in order to (1) know and understand sexual difference, and (2) gain an orientation in the cultural world. The presumption is that if a child has no father, that child will not come to understand masculinity in the culture, and if it is a boy child, that child will have no way to embody or incorporate his own masculinity. This argument assumes many things, but chief among them is the idea that the institution of fatherhood is the sole or major cultural instrument for the reproduction of masculinity. Even if we were to accept the problematic normative claim that a male child ought to be reproducing masculinity (and there are very good reasons to question this assumption), any young person has access to a range of masculinities, which are embodied and transmitted through a variety of cultural means. The "adult world," as Jean Laplanche puts it in an effort to formulate a psychoanalytic alternative to the Oedipal triad, impresses its cultural markers on the child from any number of directions, and the child, boy or girl, must fathom and reckon with those norms. However, in France, as you may know, the notion of a "framework of orientation"—called *"le repère"*—is understood to be transmitted uniquely by the father. Moreover, this symbolic function is ostensibly threatened or even destroyed by the presence of two fathers, of an intermittent father, or of no father at all. One has to struggle not to get lured into this battle on these terms, since the fight misconstrues the issue at stake. Nevertheless, if one *were* to get lured into it, one could, of course, make the rejoinder that masculinity can certainly be embodied and communicated by a parent of another gender. But if I argue that way, I concede the premise that the parent is and must be the unique cultural site for the communication and reproduction of gender, and that would be a foolish point to concede. It is crucial to remark that in France the lines of patrilineality are secured in the civil code through rights of filiation. To the extent that heterosexual marriage maintains its monopoly on reproduction, it does so precisely through privileging the biological father as the representative of national culture.[7]

Thus, the debates on sexual politics are bound up with the politics of new immigrant communities. Here it becomes clear that the theories of psychological development that produce the patrilineal conditions of national culture constitute the "norms of adulthood" that precondition the substantive rights of citizenship. It is a direct result of this view that the father underwrites the national culture. Thus, Ségolène Royal, the 2006 Socialist party presidential nominee, can join Nicolas Sarkozy, the winning candidate, in arguing that *les émeutes*, the riots, of 2005 in the *banlieu* were the direct consequence of deteriorated family structures, represented by new immigrant communities.[8] The theme of certain childishness remerges in this context as well, such that we are to understand the political expressions of Islamic minorities as failures of psycho-cultural development. These kinds of arguments parallel the parent/child relation that Thomas Friedman articulated in relation to secular modernity and anachronistic Islam. Family politics, even the heterosexual ordering of the family, function to secure the temporal sequence that establishes French culture at the forefront of modernity. This modernity involves an odd situation in which an intractable developmental law sets limits on volitional freedom, but the contract form extends freedom almost limitlessly. In other words, contracts can be extended to any pair of consenting adults—the legal achievement of the PACS, which has become relatively normalized for both straight and gay couples. Such partnerships, however, have to be rigorously separated from kinship which, by definition, precedes and limits the contract form. These norms of kinship are referenced by the term *l'ordre symbolique*, which actually functions in public discourse; it is this order that underwrites contract relations even as it must be immunized against a full saturation by contract relations. Whether or not such an order is unambiguously secular is, in my view, an open question, but there are many reasons to ask whether it transmits and maintains certain theological notions, predominantly Catholic. This becomes explicitly clear, for instance, in the work of anthropologist Françoise Heritier, who argues on Catholic grounds that the symbolic order is both theologically derived and a prerequisite of psycho-social development.

The refusal to grant legal recognition for gay parenting works in tandem with anti-Islamic state policies to support a cultural order, *l'ordre symbolique*, which keeps heterosexual normativity tied to a racist conception of culture. This order, conceived as pervasively paternal and nationalist, is equally, if differently, threatened by those kinship arrangements understood to be operative in new immigrant communities that fail to uphold the patriarchal and marital basis of the family, which in turn produces the intelligible parameters of culture and the possibility of a "knowing orientation" within that culture. Of course, what is most peculiar about this critique of the absent father in the *banlieu* is not only that it can be found among socialists and their right wing foes, but also that it fails to recognize contemporary immigration law as itself being partially responsible for reforging kinship ties in certain ways. After all, the French government has been willing to separate children from parents, to keep families from reunifying, and to maintain inadequate social services for new immigrant communities. Indeed, some critics have suggested that social services constitute the emasculation of the state itself.

One can see such a view articulated, for instance, by psychoanalyst Michel Schneider, who registers his views on cultural affairs and has publicly maintained that the state must step in to take the place of the absent father, not through welfare benefits (conceived as a maternal deformation of the state), but through the imposition of law, discipline, and uncompromising modes of punishment and imprisonment (Schneider, 2005). In his view, this is the only way to secure the cultural foundations of citizenship, that is, the cultural foundations required for the exercise of a certain conception of freedom. Thus, state policies that create extreme class differentials and pervasive racism in employment practices, separate families in order to save children from Islamic formations, and sequester the *banlieu* as intensified sites of racialized poverty are exonerated and effaced through such explanations. Antiracist demonstrations such as those that happened in 2005 took aim at poverty, not persons, yet they were widely interpreted as the violent and arelational acts of young men whose family structures were lacking firm paternal authority.[9] A certain prohibitive "no" was absent from the family and culture, and the state thus acts as a compensatory paternal authority in such a situation. That the state then develops a host of rationales for regulating family and school in the *banlieu* is further proof that it responds to such insurgency through consolidating and augmenting its power in relation to biopolitics and kinship arrangements at every level. Thus, we might conclude that at a basic level, the entitlement to a notion of freedom, which is based on contract, is limited by those freedoms that might extend the contract too far, in other words, to the point of disrupting the cultural preconditions of contract itself. Said otherwise, disruptions in family or in kinship arrangements that do not support the lines of patrilineality and the corollary norms of citizenship rationalize state prohibitions and regulations that augment state power in the image of the father, that cultural fetish signifying a maturity based upon violence.

The rules that define culture as supported by the heterosexual family clearly are also those that set the prerequisites for entering into citizenship. Although in France this is the basis of *laïcité,* and the grounds for state intervention to maintain a certain cultural grounding for the rights of men, it is not far from the clearly theological view of the current Pope, who voices his condemnation of gay parenting and Islamic religious practice on common grounds. This parallelism raises the question of the status of this idea of culture as part of secular modernity and, in particular, whether the symbolic order is finally a secular concept (and if so, what this tells us about the impurity of secularism). In particular, it raises the question of whether this symbolic order, understood as a binding and uniform set of rules that constitute culture, function in alliance with theological norms governing kinship. This view, interestingly enough, is not far from the Vatican's stance that the heterosexual family is what secures gender in its natural place, one that inscribes a divine order. Whereas in France, the notion of "culture" is precisely what communicates the universal necessity of sexual difference, understood as the unequivocal difference between masculine and feminine, in present-day Catholic theology, we find that the family not only requires two discrete sexes, but has as its duty the embodiment and reproduction of sexual difference as both a cultural and theological necessity.

In his 2004 "Letter to the Bishops of the Catholic Church in the Collaboration of Men and Women in the Church and the World,"[10] Ratzinger (then Cardinal, now Pope) considers two approaches to women's issues. The first, he maintains, sustains an oppositional relationship to men. The second one seems to pertain to the new gender politics, which takes gender to be a variable social function. Ratzinger characterizes this second strand of feminism with the following language:

In order to avoid the domination of one sex or the other, their differences tend to be denied, viewed as mere effects of historical and cultural conditioning. In this perspective, physical difference, termed sex, is minimized, while the purely cultural element, termed gender, is emphasized to the maximum and held to be primary. The obscuring of the difference or duality of the sexes has enormous consequences on a variety of levels. This theory of the human person, intended to promote prospects for equality of women through liberation from biological determinism, has in reality inspired ideologies which, for example, call into question the family, in its natural two-parent structure of mother and father, and make homosexuality and heterosexuality virtually equivalent, in a new model of polymorphous sexuality. (Ratzinger, 2004)

He goes further to suggest that this second approach to women's issues is rooted in a motivation understood as "the human attempt to be freed from one's biological conditioning. According to this perspective, human nature in itself does not possess characteristics in an absolute manner: all persons can and ought to constitute themselves as they like, since they are free from every predetermination linked to their essential constitution."[11]

In France, the view that culture itself is carried by the heterosexual family, patrilineally defined, is communicated clearly through the notion that a child without heterosexual parentage will not only be without cognitive orientation, but will be precluded from the cultural and cognitive prerequisites of citizenship. This explains in part why France was able to extend rights of contract through the passage of the PACS, but to oppose every effort to legalize gay parenting. It is, as I argue elsewhere, linked to the conviction that new immigrant communities lack a strong paternal figure, and that full rights of citizenship require subjection to an embodiment of paternal law. For some French politicians, this analysis leads to the conclusion that the state must enter into the regulation of the family where it is perceived that strong fathers do not exist. This has actually led to the forced separation of parents and children through new immigration policy (i.e., one that works in favor of the father and so, the symbolic family, even if it means destroying existing ones).

If the Pope refers to the natural laws of culture when he opposes gay and lesbian sexuality and nonheterosexual parenting arrangements, he refers to civilization when he makes his indirect denunciations of Islam. In late 2006, of course, we had new proclamations from the papal authority. The Pope publicly cited a document that contained the following denunciation of Islam: "Show me just what Mohammad brought that was new, and there you will find things only evil and inhuman, such as his command to spread by the sword the faith he preached."[12] Ratzinger claimed that this statement was not his, that he was only citing it, but if one looks closely, it becomes clear that he cites it, takes distance from it, and then mobilizes it to issue a warning about the current threat to civilization that, in his view, Islam represents. Of course, there are many ways to approach this rather astonishing declaration, most obviously by pointing to the bloodshed by which Christianity sought to spread its own faith over the last many centuries. However, I want to note the word "inhuman," since it is coupled with "evil," and we have already considered what the Pope thinks about the cultural foundations of the human as such.

Additionally, the sword, which is explicitly prohibited as a means of coercing faith in the Qur'an, is surely a term of transference in this scenario, since to whom did the sword belong, by whom was it wielded, and how is it wielded today? Because swords are not the weapons of choice in a contemporary sense, they evince a mythical time, a tribalist archaism, and also become precisely the nexus of fantasy. I could go on at length, but I want here only to point out the extraordinary inversions of history that the word "sword" permits, and the enormous ideological force of distinguishing between the human, as that which is presumably only supported by a Judeo-Christian culture, and the "inhuman" and "evil," which follows from a departure from that culture. Let us remember, as Uri Avnery points out, that Islam was never forced upon the Jews; when Spain was conquered by Catholics and the Muslims were dispossessed of power, the Inquisition was turned against both Muslims and Jews, and Sephardic Jews found hospitality in Arab countries for 50 generations.[13] So when the Pope refers to this "sword" wielded by those who are less than human, we have to wonder what inversion, displacement, and effacement of history is congealed in this strange proposition, a kind of dream-speak at best, which manifests its profound alliance with what it proclaims to disdain and disavow.

Indeed, the entire sequence of proclamations enacted this disavowal and displacement in plain view. It is as if he was saying: I said it, I did not say it; I cited it; others said it, and so it has authority; this is their aggression, this is my aggression circuited through their aggression, though I have no aggression. The figure through which he names the aggression of Islam is a figure of Christianity's own aggression, at which point the figures converge, and the ability to sustain the distinction between Islam and Christianity founders. Of course, it is that distinction that the Pope seeks to underscore, to make certain, to establish without a shadow of a doubt. But his language upends his argument, starting with the strange way he appropriates and disavows the citation. The paradox has a social and even psychoanalytic valence, but it seems also to proceed from a certain idea of development and civilizational progress (noting here that one has to distinguish between culture and civilization for all kinds of reasons, but that the latter, despite its origin in the replacement of ecclesiastical authorities by civic courts of law, functions discursively at the present moment to effect a syncretism of religious and secular ideals).

Now it may be in relation to the previous sorts of arguments that we try to make a case for a purely secular resistance. I am less sure, however, that our ideas of secularism do not already carry religious content, and that we are, with any of these positions, invoking an unalloyed secularism (it may be that secularism can only be defined by its implication in the very religious traditions from which it seeks to distinguish itself, but that is a broader question that I can only gesture toward in this context). Provisionally, I would suggest that secularism has a variety of forms, and many of them involve forms of absolutism and dogmatism, if not fundamentalism, that are surely as problematic as those that rely on religious dogma. In fact, a critical perspective does not line up perfectly with the distinction between religious and secular thinking.

Let us remember that it is the idea of culture in the French instance, a notion that understands itself as "secular," which clearly works in tandem with the papal argument. Although the Pope argues on religious grounds, there are clearly religious opponents to his views, a situation suggesting that we ought not to understand secularism as the sole source of critique, and religion as the sole source of dogmatism. If religion functions as a key matrix for the articulation of values, and if most of the people in this global condition look to it to guide their thinking on such matters, we would make a political error in claiming that religion ought to be overcome in each and every instance. There are a number of secularisms, and sometimes they gain their definition by the nature of the break they make with specific religious inheritances, but sometimes secularism achieves its meaning through the disavowal of a religious tradition that inchoately and continuously informs and supports its own ostensibly postreligious claims. I think the noncontradictory status of the secular Jew, for instance, explicitly makes this point. We can also see this at work, for instance, in the differential treatment of religious minorities within an ostensibly secular framework, since "*laicité*" in France is defined precisely over and against the intrusion of Church authorities into matters of state. The debate on whether girls should be prohibited from wearing the veil in public schools seemed to bring this paradox into relief. The ideas of the secular were invoked to consolidate ignorant and hateful views of Islamic religious practice (i.e., the veil is nothing other than the communication of the idea that women are inferior to men, or the veil communicates an alliance with "fundamentalism"), at which point "*laicité*" becomes a way not of negotiating or permitting cultural difference, but of consolidating a set of cultural presumptions that effect the exclusion and abjection of cultural difference.

If I opened this chapter by wondering about the implications of secular progress as a temporal framework for thinking about the sexual politics during this time, I suggest now that what is at issue is less any and all ways of looking forward (I hold out for those—I look forward to those!), but an idea of development in which secularism does not so much succeed religion sequentially, but reanimates it as part of its ideas of culture and civilization. The kind of secularism we are witnessing in France denounces and surpasses the very religious content that it also reanimates in the very terms by which culture is defined. In the case of papal authority, we see a different recourse to a framework, presumptively timeless and binding, that is at once cultural and theological, suggesting an invariable implication of one sphere in the other. These are not quite the same as the idea of Dutch civic integration, but perhaps there are parallelisms, even phantom resonances, which are worth exploring further. The problem is, of course, not progress per se, nor surely the future, but specific developmental narratives in which certain exclusionary and ever persecutory norms become at once the precondition and teleology of culture. Thus, framed both as a transcendental condition and as teleology, culture in such instances can only produce a monstrous specter of what lies outside its own framework of temporal thinkability. Outside of its own teleology exists a ruinous and foreboding sense of the future, and what lies before its transcendental condition lurks an aberrant anachronism, threatening, and intruding upon, the political present to become the grounds for general alarm within the secular frame.

I write this as one who is trying to come to a critical understanding and a political opposition to the discourse on Islam currently propagated by the United States. This leads us to yet another discourse, that of the civilizing mission, and there is not much time to try to delineate its logic here or trace its resonance with these other developmental patterns I have been trying to discern. It is probably worth noting in brief, however, that the United States takes its own civilizing mission to be a cross of secular and nonsecular perspectives. After all, President George W. Bush tells us he is guided by God, and for whatever reason, this is the discourse that he mobilizes at times to rationalize his extralegal, if not criminal, actions. It would appear that the civilizational mission is an effort to bring notions of democracy to those who are characterized as premodern, who have not yet entered into the secular terms of the liberal state, and whose notions of religion are invariably considered childish, fanatic, or structured according to ostensibly irrational and primitive taboos. The civilizational mission, as it has been described by Samuel Huntington, is itself a self-avowed mix of religious and secular ideals: the notion that the United States, representing what he calls, somewhat wildly, "the West," is considered to have undergone modernization, to have arrived at secular principles that transcend and accommodate religious position, that are more advanced and finally more rational and, hence, more capable of democratic deliberation and self-governance.[14] Yet the ideals of democracy espoused by Huntington are also those that express the values of a Judeo-Christian tradition, a view suggesting that all other religious traditions are outside the trajectory of modernization that constitutes civilization and its "missionary" claim to the future.

As a kind of postscript, then, let me offer a final discussion on the violence that this temporal account of the instatement of progressive freedoms implies. If the Islamic populations destroyed in the recent and current war are considered less than human or "outside" the cultural conditions for the emergence of the human, then they belong either to a time of cultural infancy or to one that is outside time as we know it. In both cases, they are regarded as not yet having arrived at the idea of the rational human. It follows from such a viewpoint that the destruction of such populations, their infrastructures, housing, and religious and community institutions, constitutes the destruction of what threatens the human, but not the human itself. It is also precisely this particular conceit of a progressive history that positions "the West" as articulating the paradigmatic principles of the human—humans worth valuing, whose lives merit safeguarding and protecting, yet are precarious, and worth public grieving as well. This civilizational mission implies a clear racism in this regard, and it also champions a "secularism," which values certain religious traditions over others and makes the formation within certain religious traditions presuppositional to achieving the status of a rational man. I suggest that this particular conceit is also at work in the torture and sexual humiliation of women and men belonging to the Islamic faith in the prisons outsourced by the United States, Abu Ghraib and Guantánamo, to name the ones we know about.

Let me suggest first that the United States made use of bad anthropology when it devised its protocols of torture. The Department of Defense assigned a text from the 1970s called "The Arab Mind," which assumed that there was such a mind, that it could be characterized in general ways with respect to the religious beliefs and specific sexual vulnerabilities of people from Arab descent.[15] The text subscribed to that form of cultural anthropology that treated cultures as self-sufficient and distinctive, which refused the global mixing of cultural and social formations, and which considered itself beyond moral judgment and more generally in the service of cultural tolerance. I suggest that the massive reduction of Arab life to "the Arab mind" produced a ready object for the United States military and for the protocols of torture enacted under the direction of General Geoffrey Miller. Since, of course, there is no one "Arab mind," and it is not possible to attribute the same fears and anxieties across the Arab world in its geographical complexity and its cosmopolitan formulations, the text constructed an object that it could then manipulate. Strategies for extracting information from this mind were devised, and they were applied in the various scenes of torture that have become visually available to us as well as those that remain unrepresented in any media form.

Those who devised these schemes of torture sought to understand the specific vulnerabilities of a population formed within Islam and developed their plans as a kind of sexual targeting that was at once a form of religious bigotry or hatred. But what we have to remember is that the subject of Islam was also constructed through the torture, and the anthropological text, as well as the protocols, were part of the production of that subject within the discourse of the military. I want to be careful here, so let me repeat this formulation: the torture was not merely an effort to find ways to shame and humiliate the prisoners of Abu Ghraib and Guantánamo on the basis of their presumptive cultural formation. The torture was also a way to coercively produce the Arab subject and the Arab mind. That means that regardless of the complex cultural formations of the prisoners, they were compelled to embody the cultural reduction described by this anthropological text. Let us remember that the text does not have an epistemically privileged relation to its subject. It is part of the project to compel the production of that subject, and we will have to ask why.

This perspective has not been considered in most of the debates that have predominated on this issue within the mainstream media. There have been, broadly speaking, two ways to approach this issue within a liberal framework. The first is an argument on the basis of cultural rights and cultural violations, whereby these orchestrated scenes of sexual and physical humiliation exploit the specific sexual vulnerabilities of these populations. The second position is that one requires a normative condemnation of this torture that makes no reference to culture, since clearly these actions would be wrong and punishable no matter against whom they were perpetrated or who was perpetrating them. The first view, which emphasizes cultural rights, is espoused by the United States journalist Seymour Hersh,[16] and the argument maintains that specifically cultural violations occurred in the course of these tortures, ones that have to do with modesty, taboos on homosexuality, and conditions of public exposure and shame. The torture also broke down social codes of sexual difference, forcing men to wear women's lingerie, and debasing women through forced nudity.

I suggest that both of these frameworks for understanding the torture are necessary, but finally insufficient. Yes, there were clearly specific cultural violations at work, and these acts of torture were patently wrong according to any normative framework, not only the one tied to the specific cultural violations at issue here. However, we must include both of these views within a larger framework if we are to understand how the scenes of sexual debasement and physical torture are part of the civilizing mission linked to the bombings and general lawlessness of United States war efforts and, in particular, its efforts to seize absolute control over the construction of the subject of torture. Neither of the previous frameworks on their own can take account of the centrality of homophobia, misogyny, and sexual hatred to the culture of the army, and neither can they describe or explain how the civilizational mission can be seen to act upon the body of the other through the means of torture. If we ask what is at stake in producing the Arab subject as a distinctive locus of sexual and social vulnerability, we must find out what subject position is being staked not only by the United States military, but by the war effort more generally. If we want to speak about "specific cultures," then it would make sense to begin with *the specific culture of the United States army,* its emphatic masculinism and homophobia, and ask why it must, for its own purposes, cast the predominantly Islamic population against which it wages war as the site of primitive taboo and shame. I mean to suggest that a civilizational war is at work in this context that casts the army as the more sexually progressive culture. The army considers itself more sexually "advanced" because they read pornography or impose it upon their prisoners, because they overcome all inhibition in exploiting and breaking down the inhibitions of those they torture.

This constitutes an example of the violence legitimated by the kinds of developmental logics that I sketched earlier. The ostensible "superiority" of the army consists in its capacity to wage war not against military subjects, and not only against the putative sexual and moral codes of Islam, but in their ability to coercively construct the Arab subject through the enacted protocols of torture. The point is not simply to break down the codes, but to construct a subject that would break down when coercively forced to break such codes—and I suppose we have to ask—which subject would *not* break down under those conditions? It may be that the torturer postures as one whose impermeability is won at the expense of the radical permeability of the tortured, but that posturing cannot deny a fundamental permeability that traverses all corporeal life. More specifically, for the army to break down those codes is itself an act of domination, but it is also a way of exercising and exemplifying a freedom that is at once lawless and coercive, one that has come to represent and enact the civilizing mission. After all, there can be no civilization with Islam on the "inside," according to the avatars of Huntington and theorists of the so-called "Arab mind." And yet, if we look closely at what is being represented as the civilizing mission, it consists of unbridled homophobic and misogynist practices. Thus, we must understand the torture as the actions of a homophobic institution against a population that is both constructed and targeted for its own shame about homosexuality, the actions of a misogynist institution against a population in which women are cast in roles bound by codes of honor and shame, and so not "equal" in the way that women ostensibly are in the West. In this way, we can see the photographs that the United States army distributed of women without the veil as a sign of the United States "triumph" in Afghanistan as prefiguring the digital capture and coerced stripping and violation that United States soldiers perpetrated in Abu Ghraib and Guantánamo.

In addition, we can see here the association of a certain cultural presumption of progress with a license to engage in unbridled destruction. More specifically, at work in this mode of implicit rationalization is a crude deployment and exploitation of the norm of "freedom" as it operates in contemporary sexual politics, one in which "freedom" becomes not only the means of coercion, but what some might call "the *jouissance* of torture." If we ask what kind of freedom this is, it is one that is free of the law while at the same time coercive, and it is an extension of the logic that establishes state power—and its mechanisms of violence—as beyond the law. This is not a freedom that belongs to a rights discourse, unless we understand the right to be free of all legal accountability as the right in question.

There are at least two countervailing trends at work in the scenes of torture. The Iraqi prison population is considered precisely as premodern to the extent that it is understood to embody certain prohibitions and inhibitions in relation to homosexuality, exposure, masturbation, and nudity. Thus, the torture can be understood in this regard as a technique of modernization. Unlike those disciplinary regimes of subject formation that would seek to transform the tortured into exemplary modern subjects, mistreatment of this kind seeks to expose the status of the tortured as the permanent, abased, and aberrant outside to subject-formation as such. Because these are coercive techniques of modernization, however, the question of a barbarity specific to secular modernism is also at stake. In this regard, we can see that the civilizational mission effected by the military in its acts of torture complicates the progressive narrative, which would rationalize the war against Islam. We also see in abbreviated form the "deployment" of a position of sexual freedom to coerce capitulation to sexual humiliation, at which point the "coercive" dimension of this historical version of the modern secularization project makes itself graphically available. It should be clear that I see the torture neither as aberrant individual acts nor as fully conscious and strategic goals of the United States military. Rather, I understand the coercive nature of these acts of humiliation and torture as making explicit *a coercion that is already at work in the civilizational mission* and, most particularly, in the forced instatement of a cultural order, which figures Islam as abject, backward, a foreboding ruination, and, as a consequence, requiring subordination within and exclusion from the culture of the human itself. This logic is not far from the disavowal and displacement that marked the Pope's rhetoric on Islam. If Islam is figured as definitionally violent yet encumbered by inhibiting rules, to the extent that it is violent, it requires new disciplinary rules; to the extent that it is rule-bound, it requires an emancipation, which only modernity can bring.

I am not saying that denying someone rights of immigration is the same as subjecting that person to sexual torture. But I am suggesting that the rigorous exclusion of norms in Islamic communities pose a threat to culture, even to prevailing norms of humanization. When some group of peoples comes to represent a threat to the cultural conditions of humanization and of citizenship, then the rationale for their torture and their death is secured.

In the case of sexual torture, a noxious deployment of the notion of sexual freedom is at work: "we embody that freedom, you do not; therefore, we are free to coerce you, and so to exercise our freedom, and you, you will manifest your unfreedom to us, and that spectacle will serve as the visual justification for our onslaught against you." Of course, this is different from the unveiling of Afghani women that took place on the front page of the *New York Times*, but is there a common presupposition at work? Has feminism and the struggle for sexual freedom become, horrifyingly, within these contexts a "sign" of the civilizational mission in progress? Can we even begin to understand the scenes of torture if we cannot account for the homophobia *in the military* as it acts on populations formed religiously through a taboo on homosexuality? What kind of encounter is this, then, at the scene of torture, in which a violent homophobia and misogyny exploit the presumptive homophobia and misogyny of its victims? If we focus on the latter, even within a framework of tolerance or cultural rights or specific cultural violations, we lose sight of the precise exploitation at work in the scene of torture: Homophobia and misogyny seem more central to the scene of torture than any homophobia and misogyny one may have attributed to the tortured population, or indeed, that one might understand as the specific liability or backwardness of Islam itself. Whatever the relation is between Islam and the status of women, let us begin with the proposition that it is complex, historically changing, and not available to a quick reduction (I would suggest that Suad Joseph's edited collection on *Women in Islamic Cultures*, four volumes of which have already been published by Brill, might be a good place to start for an English-speaking audience).

What is at issue in the scene of torture is the nexus of violence and sexuality that belongs to the civilizational thesis as it has been formulated in the context of this war. After all, the United States is bringing civilization to the ostensibly "backward" or premodern Islamic "Other." And what it brings, most clearly, is torture as the instrument and sign of civilization. These are not aberrant moments of a war, but rather the cruel and spectacular logic of United States imperial culture as it operates in the context of its current wars.[17] The scenes of torture are conducted in the name of civilization against barbarism, and we can see that the "civilization" at issue is part of a dubious secular politics, no more enlightened or critical by virtue of its secularism than the worst forms of dogmatic and restrictive religion. In fact, the historical, rhetorical, and logical alliances between them may be more profound than we know. The barbarism at issue here is the barbarism of the civilizational mission, and any counter-imperialist politics, especially a feminist and queer one, must oppose it at every turn. The point is to establish a politics that opposes state coercion and violence, and to build a framework that can see how the violence done in the name of preserving a certain modernity and conceit of cultural homogeneity or integration is the most serious threat to freedom. If the scenes of torture are the apotheosis of a certain conception of freedom, it is one that is free of all law and free of all constraint precisely in order to impose law and to exercise coercion. The fact that there are competing notions of freedom at stake is obvious, although it is probably worth noting that the freedom to be protected from coercion and violence is among the meanings that have been lost from view.

The same is the case regarding the ability to think time, this time, outside of that teleology, which violently installs itself as both origin and end of the culturally thinkable. The possibility of a political framework that opens up our ideas of cultural norms to contestation and dynamism within a global frame would surely be one way to begin to think a politics that reengages sexual freedom in the context of allied struggles against racism, nationalism, and the persecution of national and religious minorities. I am not at all sure that we need to gather those struggles within a unified framework. As I hope I have shown, at least in preliminary form, to insist on a unified cultural framework as a precondition of politics, whether secular or religious or both, is to preclude from political contestation precisely such a framework. If, as Marx insists, the point of departure for our analysis must be the historical present, then it seems to me that a new way of understanding how temporalities conflict and converge will be necessary for any complex description of that present. This means, I think, resisting unified frameworks that would distill the antagonisms in question into equivalent rights claims, but also refusing those developmental narratives that know in advance of what a just view of human flourishing consists. It is always possible to show the various ways in which Islam is modern, and this is important to do—including the demonstration of how certain secular ideals could not have been developed without their transmission and elaboration through Islamic practices. Nevertheless, the point is not to show that we are all modern. It is rather to take account of the present in a different way, one that does not presume anyone's modernity. If modernity seeks to constitute itself through a continuous and unfolding idea of time, and if some of our personal liberties are conceptualized within that notion of a continuous and unfolding realization, then perhaps we would do well to remember Nietzsche's quip from *The Will to Power:* "Mankind does not advance, it does not even exist" (Nietzsche, 1968, p. 55). More salient, perhaps, is Walter Benjamin's insistence in the thirteenth of his *Theses on the Philosophy of History* "that the concept of the historical progress of mankind cannot be sundered from the concept of its progression through a homogenous, empty time. A critique of the concept of such a progression must be the basis of any criticism of the concept of progress itself" (Benjamin, 1968, p. 261). He notes in a subsequent thesis that "the awareness that they are about to make the continuum of history explode is characteristic of the revolutionary classes at the moment of their action" (p. 261). The historian who understands how the past flashes up, how the past is not past but continues in the present, is one who understands "the time of the now" as "shot through with chips of Messianic time" (Benjamin, 1968, p. 263). Benjamin's emphatically nonsecular reference here does not rely on an ideal future to come, but rather on the interruptive force of the past on a present that effaces all qualitative differences through its homogenizing effect. The "constellation" which is one's own era is precisely the difficult and interruptive scene of multiple temporalities, ones that cannot be reduced to cultural pluralism or a liberal discourse of rights. For Benjamin, in the final line of those theses, "every second of time was the strait gate through which the Messiah might enter," an historical condition under which political responsibility for the present exists precisely "now." It is not by accident that Benjamin understands the revolutionary action as the strike, as the rejection of coercive state power. That power relies on a certain taken-for-granted notion of historical progress to legitimate itself as the ultimately modern achievement. To separate the "now time" from these claims of modernity is to undercut the temporal framework that uncritically supports state power, its legitimating effect, and its coercive instrumentalities. Without a critique of state violence, our claims to freedom risk an appropriation by the state, which can make us lose sight of all our other commitments. Only with such a critique of state violence do we stand the chance of finding the sites of contact, however antagonistic, with other minorities in order to consider systemically how coercion seeks to divide us and to keep attention deflected from the critique of violence itself.

Over and against such a politics, we have to renew our understanding of nonviolence, cultural translation, solidarity across difference and by virtue of difference. We cannot ask for cultural homogeneity without refusing the present moment, a moment that is narrated in no one way and serves as a nexus of competing and converging histories. It is only by coming to terms with the epistemic shifts among critical perspectives, both secular and religious, that any of us stand a chance of taking stock of the time and place of politics. If freedom is one of the ideals we hope for, perhaps it will be important to start by remembering how easily freedom can become deployed in the name of state self-legitimation—one whose coercive force gives the lie to its claim to safeguard humanity. Maybe then we can rethink freedom, even freedom from coercion, as a condition of solidarity among minorities, and how necessary it is to formulate sexual politics in the context of a pervasive critique of this war.

NOTES

1. See Brown, W. (2001). *Politics out of history*. Princeton: Princeton University Press.
2. See Jakobsen, J,. & Pellegrini, A. (2004). *Love the sun: Sexual regulation and the limits of religious tolerance*. New York: New York University Press; Mahmood, S., (2005). *The politics of piety*. Princeton: Princeton University Press; Asad, T. (2003). *Formations of the secular.*Palo Alto: Stanford University Press; Connolly, W. (2000). *Why I am not a secularist*. Minneapolis: University of Minnesota Press,.
3. As reported on http://www.msnbc.msn.com/id/11842116/. The statement can be found on the website of the Dutch Immigration and Naturalization Service (IND) at http://www.ind.nl/en/inbedrijf/actueel/basisexamen_inburgering.asp.
4. As reported on http://sweetness-light.com/archive/dutch-make-gay-acceptance-litmus-test-for-immigrants.
5. See Friedman, T. "Foreign affairs: The real war" *New York Times*, November 27, 2001, Opinion Page, A19. Retrieved from http://query.nytimes.com/gst/fullpage.html?res=9C02E1D6113AF934A15752C1A9679C8B63&sec=&spon=.
6. See Borillo, D., Fassin, E., & Iacub, M. (1999). *Au-delà du PACS: l'expertise familiale à l'épreuve de l'homosexualité*. Paris: Presses universitaires de France.
7. See Fassin, E. (2005). *L'inversion de la question homosexuelle.*Paris: Éditions Amsterdam; Fassin D., & Fassin, E. (2006). *De la question sociale à la question raciale?* Paris: La Découverte.

8. *Libération*, June 1, 2006. Retrieved from http://www.liberation.fr/actualite/evenement/evenement1/371.FR.php.

9. See Guénif-Souilamas, N. (Dir.). (2006). *La République mise à nu par son immigration*. Paris: La fabrique éditions.

10. See Cardinal Joseph Ratzinger. (2004). *Letter to the Bishops of the Catholic Church on the collaboration of men and women in the church and in the world.*

11. I would like to position myself in neither way, but what way is then left? Ratzinger characterizes positions here, without citation, so whereas it appears that he may have read some of them, he is not beholden to any textual evidence in making his claims. The scripture, of course, is cited, but the positions that defy or threaten scripture are clearly not (as far as my research has yielded).

Ratzinger goes on to make clear how the doctrine of sexual difference he defends is rooted in the story of Genesis, a story that establishes the "truth" of men and women. His opposition to gay marriage, which seeks to "destroy" that truth, is thus linked with his implicit creationism. One could simply reply by saying, yes, the truth of man and woman that you outline is no truth at all and we seek to destroy it in order to give rise to a more humane and radical set of gender practices. But to speak this way is simply to reiterate the cultural divide that makes no analysis possible. Perhaps one needs to start with the status of the story, of Genesis itself, and to see what other readings are possible. Perhaps one needs to ask which biology Ratzinger actually accepts, and whether the biological theories he supports are ones that consider homosexuality to be a benign part of human sexual variation. It seems that his remark that social constructionists seek to deny and transcend biological differences commits him to a theological reading of social construction, since that "transcendence" is, presumably, what is to be sought for the "sacralization" of sexuality in terms of its transcendent function. Can it be shown that the biological differences to which he refers are actually consonant with the transcendent meanings he reserves for heterosexual sexuality in the service of reproduction? In addition to finding out which biological account Ratzinger has in mind, it would be important to understand whether the social practices he seeks to curb, including civil unions for same-sex partners, are either prescribed or proscribed by any ostensible biological function. The point is not to deny biology and to embrace a voluntaristic self-making, but to ask whether and how biology and social practice are understood in relation to one another.

12. Pope Benedict XVI. (2006). *Faith, reason and the university: Memories and reflections*. Speech given at the University of Regensburg, September 12, 2006. The speech and the subsequent explanations can be found electronically at the Vatican's website: http://www.vatican.va/holy_father/benedict_xvi/speeches/2006/september/documents/hf_ben-xvi_spe_20060912_university-regensburg_en.html.

13. Avnery, U. *Muhammad's sword*. Uri Avnery's column, Gush-Shalom.org.

14. See, for example, Huntington, S. *The clash of civilizations: The debate* (Foreign Affairs, 1996) and *Who are we: The challenges to America's national identity* (New York: Simon & Schuster, 2005).

15. See Patai, R. (2002). *The Arab mind*. Long Island City: Hatherleigh Press.

16. See Hersh, S. M. (2004, May 25). The grey zone: How a secret pentagon program came to Abu Ghraib." *The New Yorker*; Hersh, S. M. (2004). *The chain of command: The road from 9/11 to Abu Ghraib*. New York: Harper-Collins.

17. Although some religious constituencies have supported the Bush wars, there are others that have strongly opposed it, including a number of African-American evangelical churches, and Jewish groups, such as Tikkun, Jews Against the Occupation, and Jewish Voice for Peace.

REFERENCES

Asad, T. (2003). *Formations of the secular.* Palo Alto: Stanford University Press.

Avnery, U. [Column]. Retrieved from Gush-Shalom.org. http://zope.gush-halom. org/home/en/channels/avnery.

Benedict XVI, Pope. (2006). Vatican: the Holy See. Retrieved from http://www. vatican.va/holy_father/benedict_xvi/speeches/2006/september/documents/hf_ ben-xvi_spe_20060912_university-regensburg_en.html.

Benjamin, W. (1968). *Illuminations* (H. Arendt & H. Zohn, Ed. & Trans.). New York: Schocken Books.

Borillo, D., Fassin, E., & Iacub, M. (1999). *Au-delà du PACS: l'expertise familiale à l'épreuve de l'homosexualité.* Paris: Presses universitaires de France.

Brown, W. (2001). *Politics out of history.* Princeton: Princeton University Press.

Connolly, W. (2000). *Why I am not a secularist.* Minneapolis: University of Minnesota Press.

Fassin, E. (2005). *L'inversion de la question homosexuelle.* Paris : Éditions Amsterdam.

Fassin, D., & Fassin, E. (2006). *De la question sociale à la question raciale?* Paris : La Découverte.

Friedman, T. (2001, November 27). Foreign affairs: The real war *.New York Times,* p. A19. Retrieved from http://query.nytimes.com/gst/fullpage.html?res=9C02E 1D6113AF934A15752C1A9679C8B63&sec=&spon=.

Guénif-Souilamas, N. (Dir.). (2006). *La République mise à nu par son immigration.* Paris: La fabrique éditions.

Hersh, S. M. (2004, May 25). The grey zone: How a secret pentagon program came to Abu Ghraib. *The New Yorker.* .

Huntington, S. (1996). The clash of civilizations: The debate. In *Foreign Affairs.*

———. (2005). *Who are we: The challenges to America's national identity.* New York: Simon & Schuster.

Jakobsen, J., & Pellegrini, A. (2004). *Love the sin: Sexual regulation and the limits of religious tolerance.* New York: New York University Press.

Joseph, S. (Ed.). (2005). Encyclopedia of women in Islamic cultures (Vols. I & II). Boston: Brill Publishing.

Mahmood, S. (2005). *The politics of piety.* Princeton: Princeton University Press.

Nietzsche, F. (1968). *The will to power* (W. Kaufman, Ed., W. Kaufman & R. J. Hollingdale, Trans.). New York: Vintage.

Patai, R. (2002). The *Arab mind.* Long Island City: Hatherleigh Press.

Ratzinger, Cardinal Joseph. (2004). Vatican: The Holy See. Retrieved from http:// www.vatican.va/roman_curia/congregations/cfaith/documents/rc_con_cfaith_ doc_20040731_collaboration_en.html.

Schneider, M. (2005). Big mother: Psychopathologie de la vie politique. Paris: Odile Jacob.

2 Postsecular Feminist Ethics

Rosi Braidotti

The public debate at the end of the postmodernist era shows a decline of interest in politics, whereas discourses about ethics, religious norms, and values triumph. Some master-narratives circulate, which reiterate familiar themes: One is the inevitability of capitalist market economies as the historically dominant form of human progress (Fukuyama, 1989, 2002). Another is a contemporary brand of biological essentialism, under the cover of "the selfish gene" (Dawkins, 1976) and new evolutionary psychology. Yet another resonant refrain is that God is not dead. Nietzsche's claim rings hollows across the spectrum of contemporary global politics.

In this chapter, I explore the so-called "postsecular" turn from three different angles. The first is the reactive or downright reactionary angle of religious extremism and neoconservative politics. The second concerns a change of emotional temperature, or a new political economy of affects—the pathos of the early third millennium. The third is transformative in that it calls for a postsecular ethics attuned to the complexities and contradictions of our era. After touching briefly on the first two, I will concentrate on the third aspect: the move towards an affirmative postsecular ethics and its implications for feminist politics.

THE REGRESSIVE ASPECTS OF THE POSTSECULAR CONDITION

God is not dead at all. The monotheistic view of the Divine Being merely slipped out the back window during the passionately secularized second half of the 20th century, only to return through the front door, with the clash of civilizations in the third millennium.

The postsecular defined as a neoreligious revival both supports and is enhanced by political restoration. This is clearly evidenced by the militant comeback of Christian and religious activism all over the world, in the public arena, beyond the boundaries of the private spiritual domain. When he was still only Cardinal Ratzinger, Pope Benedict XVI had already declared

Nietzsche his own personal enemy. Today, he joins forces with the Evangelical Protestants' "born again" fanaticism in leveling the charge of moral and cognitive relativism against any project that challenges the traditional, Christian, and humanistic view of the moral subject. This *doxa* or common belief stresses the necessity of strong foundations as the basic points of reference that guarantee human decency, moral and political agency, and ethical probity.

Solidified in these beliefs, the religious hard-line offensive operates a number of disjunctions: It separates women from mothers and rewards the latter, but also subjugates them to the rights of the embryo and the child. It also separates gays from humanity, depriving us of the right to have rights—which is the basic definition of Human Rights. It forcefully collapses human sexuality with reproduction, thereby demonizing all forms of homo and transsexuality. This translates into a campaign against contraception, family planning, and nonmarital sex of all kinds. It also produces the absurd proposal that abstinence is the cure for the HIV epidemic, which is spreading not only in sub-Saharan Africa, as everyone knows—but also in former Eastern Europe and especially the Baltic states, as most choose to ignore. Furthermore, Christian and other religious militants attack contemporary science on two fronts, bio-genetics or genetic technologies and evolutionary theories, to which they oppose contemporary variations on the theme of creationism and obscurantism, disguised as a return to tradition.

The politically conservative return of God, however, is not a linear, but rather a multilayered process, which works by racializing and naturalizing differences, thereby turning them into pillars to support structural inequalities (Braidotti, 2006). Phenomena that entail this degree of complexity cast a methodological challenge for the politically motivated social critic in that they call for nonlinear, intersectional analytic methods to deal with their inherent contradictions. Let me illustrate this with reference to gender. The current political situation positions women's bodies as markers of authentic cultural and ethnic identity and as indicators of the stage of development of their respective civilization fault lines. Sexual difference has returned on the world stage in a fundamentalist and reactionary version, reinstating a worldview based on colonial lines of demarcation. The dominant discourse nowadays is that "our women" (Western, Christian, white, or "whitened" and raised in the tradition of secular Enlightenment) are already liberated and thus do not need any more social incentives or emancipatory policies. "Their women" (non-Western, non-Christian, mostly not white, and not whitened, as well as alien to the Enlightenment tradition), however, are still backwards and need to be targeted for special emancipatory social actions or even more belligerent forms of enforced "liberation."

This is the line cynically run by archconservative and antifeminist politicians, like President George W. Bush, to justify their wars on terror through the theory of "Full Spectrum Dominance," also known as "Project for a New American Century." Paradoxically enough, the same arguments are reiterated, with distressing regularity, by their non-Western opponents. This type of polarization results in mutual and respective claims about authentic and unitary female identity on the part of the "liberated" West and of its traditionalist critics. Each fails to take into account the patient and pragmatic work accomplished by the women's movements over the last 30 years, also and especially in the non-Western world.

One can only guess where this play of specular fundamentalisms leaves the sophisticated, feminist theoretical discussions about nonunitary, deconstructive, queer, or nomadic subject positions. Anything related to postmodernist theory or deconstructive methods is a "soft target" for the conservative and religious right and its crusaders. Moreover, the White House wasted no time in declaring, in the aftermath of the attacks on the World Trade Center, that academics are the "weak link" in the war against terror, suspected of disloyalty to their culture and lacking patriotism, which leaves the century-old tradition of "academic freedom" in tatters. In such a context, academic debates have become simultaneously less relevant to the public sphere and infinitely more important as a statement of freethinking and a political gesture of resistance.

A NEW POLITICAL ECONOMY OF NEGATIVE PASSIONS

As for the second aspect of the postsecular turn, the affective economy, we now live in a militarized social space, under the pressure of increased enforcement of security and escalating states of emergency. The Cold War doctrine of Mutually Agreed Destruction (MAD) mutated into the global notion of Self-Assured Destruction (SAD). Nuclear paranoia has given way to viral politics, hence the need for total coverage against any eventuality: Accidents are imminent and certain to happen—weapons of mass contamination are in store everywhere, starting from the food we eat. The epidemics or catastrophe will definitely break out; it is only a question of time. Graffiti on the walls of the Tate Modern Gallery, London, says it all: "After Cold War, Global Warming!"

In this context, mass political activism was replaced, especially after September 11, 2001, by public collective mourning. The politics of melancholia became dominant; "after being MAD, we're all SAD," or, as another popular saying goes, "God is dead, Marx is dead and I am not feeling too well myself!"

There is, of course, much to be mournful about, given the pathos of our global politics; our social horizon is war-ridden and death-bound. We live in a culture where religious-minded people kill in the name of "the Right to Life." Moreover, bodily vulnerability is increased by the great epidemics: some new ones, like HIV, Ebola, SARS, or the bird flu; others more traditional, such as TB and malaria. Health has become more than a public policy issue; it is a human rights and a national defense concern.

While new age remedies of all sorts proliferate, our political sensibility has taken a forensic shift: "bare life," as Agamben (1999) argues, marks the liminal grounds of probable destitution—infinite degrees of dying. Hal Foster (1996) describes our schizoid cultural politics as "traumatic realism"—an obsession with wounds, pain, and suffering. Proliferating medical panopticons produce a global patho-graphy (Seltzer, 1997).

Political philosophy reflects this mood—rediscovering with Derrida (2002) the mystical foundations of Law and political authority, or, turning towards Schmidt's political theology (Schmidt, 1996), we have definitely moved away from high secularism. I choose to pass on the popularity of Leo Strauss (Norton, 2004) in American neotheological conservative political thought. Now that even Francis Fukuyama has come out as an "ex-neo-con," that seems like yesterday's news.

I do not want to suggest that the politics of mourning and the political economy of melancholia are intrinsically reactive or necessarily negative. A number of critical theorists argue forcefully the case for its productive nature and potential for creating solidarity (Butler, 2004a; Gilroy, 2004). I am also convinced that melancholia expresses a form of loyalty through identification with the wound of others and hence promotes the ecology of belonging by upholding the collective memory of trauma or pain. My argument is rather that the politics of melancholia has become so dominant in our culture that it ends up functioning like a self-fulfilling prophecy, which leaves very small margins for alternative approaches; therefore, I want to argue for the need to experiment with other ethical relations as a way of producing a postsecular ethics of affirmation.

The Feminist Dilemma

The bulk of European feminism is justified in claiming to be secular in the structural sense of the term: to be agnostic if not atheist and to descend from the Enlightenment critique of religious dogma and clerical authority. As the secular daughters of the Enlightenment, raised in rational argumentation and detached self-irony, our belief-system is civic, not theistic. In other words, we have only paradoxes to offer, as Joan Scott (1996) so eloquently put it.

Anticlericalism and critique of the Christian church, especially the dogmatic attitude of the Catholic Church, is an integral element of feminist secularism. Because the idea of a clash of civilization is Islam-phobic in character, it contains an explicit message about the status of women and gays as well as the degrees of tolerable emancipation. Feminists, however, cannot be simply secular, or be secular in a simple or self-evident sense. An automatic and unreflective brand of normative secularism runs the risk of complicity with anti-Islam racism and xenophobia. This position was taken up by significant European feminists, such as Elizabeth Badinter (2002) in France, Ciska Dresselhuys and Ayaan Hirsi Ali in the Netherlands, and

Oriana Fallaci in Italy (2002), often striking a strident and aggressive note. This is an objectionable stance not only because it is racist, but also in terms of its failure to acknowledge the historical specificity of the phenomenon of postsecularism in the world today.

The crisis of secularism amidst both second and third generation Muslim immigrants, as well as born again and born-that-way Christians, is a phenomenon that takes place within the social and political horizon of late globalized postmodernity, not in premodern times. It is of here and now. Even Samuel Huntington (1996) recognizes this important aspect. This means that the feminists' visceral reaction against the postsecular turn is a serious misreading: It is as if some of us had fallen into some bad dreams of our own, as if we were reliving the memories of our own struggles against the Christian and mostly Catholic Church on the back of the Muslim headscarves debate, or the never-ending discussions about the veil. We need to reconsider this.

The fact is that, in spite of our secular claims, if there is one philosopher who has singularly failed to affect European feminism to any significant degree, that would have to be the anti-Christ, Nietzsche. His critique of the Christian God and the obscene power of the Church have somehow fallen on deaf ears, or maybe they were deafened by the excessive noise made around the Nietzsche case in relation to national-socialism and Hitler's misappropriation of the Übermensch theory: the post-human man of the postmetaphysical era. It is one of the lasting paradoxes of the history of European philosophy how Nietzsche, the anti-Christian, has been accused of links to Nazism—though he effectively died long before any of that happened—whereas Heidegger, a self-declared and unrepentant Nazi, escaped any serious criticism. But then, the whole chapter of European philosophy's relationship to fascism and the Holocaust is something that nobody seems to want to confront openly.

Many argue that the value-system of European secular Humanism, that is to say respect for Human Rights, the modern notion of equality and democracy, which lie at the core of the emancipatory project of the Enlightenment, is implicitly religious. This position rests on the notion that a secular distillation of Judeo-Christian precepts is responsible for producing the notion of contractual agreements or respect for the law. In turn, this entails regard for the intrinsic worth of the individual person, the autonomy of the self, moral conscience, and the ethics of love. These values promote a teleological or evolutionary vision of the future and faith in human reason's capacity to achieve social progress. As William Connolly (1999) astutely remarked, this specific brand of secularized universalism has passed itself off as the embodiment of secularism, thus achieving absolute moral authority and the social status of a dominant norm.

The extent to which this normative consensus has been shaken is best demonstrated by Habermas himself who, in his conversations with then Cardinal Ratzinger and in his Lodz lecture of April 2005, gave clear indications that he has fallen into postsecular anxiety. Habermas offers a significant example of the kind of cognitive and moral panic that has seized the humanistic community under the pressure of the clash of civilizations and the current political economy of fear on the one hand and melancholia on the other. Part of this panic is the result of contemporary biotechnological advances. Seldom has the future of human "nature" been the subject of such concern and in-depth discussions by elderly white men as in our globalized times. Habermas coined the term "postsecular societies" to signal the urgency of a critical reconsideration of the function of scientific beliefs and belief-systems in the world today. The mainstream reaction to our biotechnological progress has been a return to Kantian moral universalism. This is extremely influential in feminist theory, notably through the work of Martha Nussbaum (1999, 2006) and Seyla Benhabib (2002).

I wish to take some critical distance from these positions, both conceptually and politically. I will outline the former case in the next section. My political argument rests on a rejection of the mournful discourse about the crisis of humanist values—which paradoxically reverses into a triumphant celebration of humanism. Feminism is not prone to panic attacks, as we are used to living in states of permanent emergency and backlash. What is a crisis for the majority is a great historical opportunity for the marginal. This is politics of locations, not relativism (Braidotti, 2002, 2006).

The system of feminist civic values rests on a social constructivist notion of faith as the hope for the construction of alternative social horizons, new norms, and values. Ultimately, it is a belief in the perfectibility of Wo/Man, albeit it in a very grounded, accountable mode that privileges, as Haraway (1988) put it, partial perspectives. To call this position secular is slightly self-congratulatory, though not entirely inaccurate, in that it is an immanent, not transcendental theory, which posits generous bonds of cosmopolitanism, solidarity, and community across locations and generations. I shall return to this in my conclusion.

Faith in social progress and the self-correcting powers of democratic governance is the key idea. Faith itself, however, is the operative concept here. We are confronting today what I would call a postsecular realization that all beliefs are acts of faith, regardless of their propositional content, even or especially when they invoke the superiority of reason, science, and technology. All such systems contain a hard core of spiritual hope; as Lacan put it, if you believe in grammar, you believe in God.

There is a psychoanalytic aspect to this, the awareness of the importance of the emotional, affective, unconscious, and visceral elements of our otherwise rational and discursive belief system (Connolly, 1999). Today, however, psychoanalytic theories are sidelined in social and political philosophy, in favor of a neomaterialist reappraisal of political passions. Contemporary political ontology is Spinozist rather than Freudian-Hegelian. The emphasis falls on positivity and the critique of the negative. The Freudian theory of libido harnesses the drives back onto a system that equates desire with a dialectical structure of recognition and sameness. This inscribes alterity as a limit or negation at the core of the desiring subject. Desire is deployed along an entropic curve for Freud and equated with lack in Lacan. My argument is that today we are in a position to delink them. Contemporary desire is nomadic, not libidinal; relational, not specular; connective, not dialectical; affirmative, not melancholic. Contemporary desiring subjects are relatively disengaged from a linguistically mediated system of signification. Desire is directed outwards, in flows of multiple relations: Deleuzian rhizomes (1976); Guattari's molecular politics (1984); Negri's multitudes (2004); feminist critiques of scattered hegemonies by Grewal and Kaplan (1994); of diasporic belongings by Avtar Brah (1996); Haraway's cyborgs (1985)—they are all figurations of multilayered relationality. They express the empowering force of transformative processes of becoming: biopower in the sense of vital politics.

The political economy of desire I defend does not condition the emergence of the subject on negation but on creative affirmation, not on "Loss" but on vital generative forces. Nomadic feminist thought imagines a subject whose existence, ethics, and politics are not indexed on negativity and hence on the horizon of alterity and melancholia. Nomadic subjectivity looks for the ways in which otherness prompts, mobilizes, and allows for the affirmation of what is not contained in the present conditions. It is the virtual or incorporeal politics of becoming: the quest for new creative alternatives, the politics of "Life," as in "zoe" itself. This is the third aspect of the postsecular turn, which I want to explore in-depth.

TRANSFORMATIVE OR AFFIRMATIVE ETHICS

The starting point of my case for affirmative ethics is the assumption that the proper object of such enquiry is not the subject's universalist or individualist core, "His" moral intentionality or rational consciousness (the gender is not coincidental), as much as the effects of truth and power that his/her actions are likely to have upon others in the world. This insight is drawn from poststructuralist thought, which prioritizes the ethical relation, rather than the moral essence of the subject. The emphasis on the relation expresses a pragmatic approach, which defines ethics as the practice that cultivates affirmative modes of relation, active forces, and values. The ethical good is that which acts as empowering modes of becoming, whereas morality is the implementation of established protocols and sets of rules (Ansell-Pearson, 1999; Deleuze, 1968).

What this means practically is that the conditions for politics and ethical agency are not dependent on the current state of the terrain; they are not oppositional and thus not tied to the present by negation—but are instead affirmative and geared to creating possible futures. Ethical relations create possible worlds by mobilizing resources that have been left untapped, including our desires and imagination. They are the driving forces that concretize in actual material relations. They constitute a network, web, or rhizome of interconnection with others. This vision of ethics, inspired by Deleuze's reading of Spinoza, does not restrict the ethical instance within the limits of human otherness, but also opens it up to interrelations with nonhuman, posthuman, and inhuman forces.

This emphasis on nonhuman ethical relations can also be described as an eco-philosophy, in that it emphasizes one's reliance on the environment in the broadest sense of the term. Considering the extent of our technological development, emphasis on the ecology of belonging is not to be mistaken for biological determinism. It rather posits a nature-culture continuum (Haraway, 1997) within which subjects construct multiple relations. I also refer to this ethics in terms of social sustainability (Braidotti, 2006), although I cannot pursue this argument further here. According to this ethical approach, the practice or the pragmatics of ethical relations are essential. We need to create the conditions for the emergence of affirmative relations, by cultivating relational ethics of becoming.

Contrary to the Hegelian tradition—which is strong in psychoanalysis as in deconstruction—alterity is not a structural limit but rather the condition of expression of positive (i.e., nonreactive alternatives). The other is a threshold of transformative encounters. The "difference" expressed by subjects especially positioned as "other-than," that is to say always already different from, has a potential for transformative or creative becoming. This "difference" is not an essential given, but a project and a process that is ethically coded.

IMPLICATIONS FOR POSTSECULAR FEMINIST ETHICS

My position in favor of complexity promotes consequently a triple shift. First, it continues to emphasize the radical ethics of transformation in opposition to the moral protocols of Kantian universalism. Second, it shifts the focus from unitary rationality-driven consciousness to a process of ontology, that is to say a vision of subjectivity propelled by affects and relations. Third, it disengages the emergence of the subject from the logic of negation and attaches subjectivity to affirmative otherness—reciprocity as creation, not as the re-cognition of Sameness. In the rest of this section, I will concentrate on this third aspect: affirmation, or the critique of the negative. This will lead me to discuss affirmation as the politics of life itself, as "zoe," or generative force.

Let me start with an example. Otherness in our culture has historically functioned as the site of deprecation or negativity. Difference is postulated on a hierarchical scale that opposes it to the vision of "Subjectivity" as "Sameness." The subject is expected to be the same as a number of assumed values. In our culture, these values are framed with reference to humanist ideals, which equate the subject with rationality, consciousness, and moral and cognitive universalism. This vision of the "knowing subject"—or the "Man" of humanism—posits itself as much by what it includes within the circle of his entitlements, as in what it excludes. Otherness is excluded by definition. This makes the others into structural or constitutive elements of the subject: the other functions as a negatively framed fraction of the same. The others play an important—albeit specular—role in the definition of the norm, the norm-al, the norm-ative view of the subject.

These others are: the sexualized other, also known as women, gays, and transsex; the ethnic, native, or racialized others; and the natural, animal, and environmental others. They constitute the interconnected facets of structural otherness, which are constructed as excluded. To say that the structural others reemerge with a vengeance in postmodernity amounts to making otherness not into the site of negation, but rather into polyvalent sites of affirmation.

For example, it is a historical fact that the great emancipatory movements of postmodernity are driven and fuelled by the emergent "others": the women's and gay rights movement; the antiracism and decolonization movements; the antinuclear and proenvironment movements, animal rights included; are the voices of the structural "Others" of modernity. They also mark the crisis of the former "center" or dominant subject. In the language of philosophical nomadology, they express both the crisis of the majority and the patterns of becoming of the minorities.

A postsecular ethics for a nonunitary subject based on "Life" as "zoe" proposes an enlarged sense of interconnection between self and others, including the nonhuman or "earth" others. This practice of relating to others requires and is enhanced by the rejection of self-centered individualism. It implies a new way of combining self-interests with the well being of an enlarged sense of community, which includes one's territorial or inhuman (i.e., environmental) interconnections. It is an eco-philosophy of multiple belongings for subjects constituted in and by multiplicity, which stands in open disagreement with dominant Kantian morality and its feminist components.

This also affects the question of universal values. An ethics of affirmation is capable of a universalistic reach, though it is critical of moral universalism. It expresses a grounded, partial form of accountability, based on a strong sense of collectivity, relationality, and hence community building. There is a simple sense in which, as I argued earlier, contemporary biogenetic capitalism generates a global form of mutual interdependence of all living organisms, including, but not only humans. This sort of unity tends to be of the negative kind, as a shared form of vulnerability. Biotechnological advances like the Human Genome project, for instance, unify all human species in the urgency to oppose commercially owned and profit-minded technologies. Franklin, Lury, and Stacey refer to this situation as "pan humanity" (2000, p. 26), that is to say a global sense of interconnection between the human and the nonhuman environment in the face of common threats. Again, notice the force of the negative here, but affirmation, as usual, is just around the corner.

The positive elements are twofold. First, the global recontextualization induced by the market economy also produces a sense of interconnection. Second, the renewed sense of interconnection produces the need for an ethics. The fact that "we" are in *this* together results in a renewed claim to community and belonging by singular subjects, who have taken critical distance form individualism. Far from falling into moral relativism, this results in a proliferation of locally situated micro-universalist claims.

One evident and illuminating example of this is the brand of situated cosmopolitan neohumanism that has emerged as a powerful ethical claim in the work of postcolonial and race theorists, as well as in feminist ones. Examples are: Paul Gilroy's planetary cosmopolitanism (2000); Avtar Brah's diasporic ethics (1996); Edouard Glissant's politics of relations (1997); Ernesto Laclau's micro-universal claims (1995); Homi Bhabha's "subaltern secularism" (1994); and Vandana Shiva's antiglobal neohumanism (1997) as well as the rising wave of interest in African humanism or Ubuntu, from Patricia Hill Collins (1991) to Drucilla Cornell (2004). American black feminist theory has been postsecular for a long time, as bell hooks (1990) and Cornell West (1994) *demonstrate*.

Edward Said (1978) was among the first to alert critical theorists in the West to the need to develop a reasoned account of Enlightenment-based secular humanism, which would take into consideration the colonial experience, its violent abuses and structural injustice, as well as its aftermath existence. French poststructuralist philosophers also argued that in the aftermath of colonialism, Auschwitz, Hiroshima, and the Gulag—to mention but a few of the horrors of modern history—we Europeans need to develop a critique of Europe's illusion of grandeur in positing ourselves as the moral guardian of the world and motor of human evolution. This line is pursued in philosophy by Deleuze's rejection of the transcendental vision of the subject (1968); Irigaray's decentering of phallologocentrism (1974); Foucault's critique of humanism (1975); and Derrida's deconstruction of Eurocentrism (1997).

The antihumanism of social and cultural critics within a Western poststructuralist perspective can therefore be read alongside the cosmopolitan neohumanism of contemporary race, postcolonial, or non-Western critics. Both these positions, all other differences notwithstanding, produce inclusive alternatives to humanist individualism. Without wishing to flatten out structural differences, nor drawing easy analogies between them, I want to practice the politics of location and hence try to synchronize their efforts and tune their respective political aims and passions. It is an example of an encounter with otherness as a generative or affirmative force. Biocentered, egalitarian posthumanism on the one hand and non-Western neohumanism on the other transpose hybridity, nomadism, diasporas, and creolization processes into means of regrounding claims to connections and alliances among different constituencies. This allows them to. . .

. . . STEP TOWARD AN ETHICS OF AFFIRMATION

About Pain and Vulnerability

The ethics of affirmation, with its emphasis on "Life" as a generative force, may seem counterintuitive at first. Yet, the urge that prompts this approach is anything but abstract. It is born of the awareness that in-depth transformations are at best demanding and at worst painful. My political generation, that of the baby-boomers, has had to come to terms with this harsh reality, which put a check on the intense and often fatal impatience that characterizes those who yearn for change. We may all be human, but some are definitely more mortal than others. We lost so many of our specimen to dead-end experimentations of the existential, political, sexual, narcotic, or technological kind and to the inertia of the *status quo*—also known as the "Stepford wives' syndrome!"

This is not a complaint, nor is it meant as a deterrent against change. I consider melancholic states and the rhetoric of the lament as integral to the logic of advanced capitalism and hence as a dominant ideology. Many leading intellectuals specialize in and profit from this genre. Our conservative political context, moreover, has placed undue emphasis on the risks involved in change, playing *ad nauseam* the refrain about the death of transformative processes. Nothing could be further removed from my project. I simply want to issue a cautionary note: Processes of change and transformation are so important and ever so vital and necessary, that they have to be handled with care. We have to take the pain of change into account, not as an obstacle to, but as a major incentive for, an ethics of transformations.

Let us us talk about pain for a moment. In our culture it is associated with suffering by force of habit and tradition and accordingly is given negative connotations. Suppose we look a bit more critically into this associative link, however; negative affects, such as suffering, envy, and anger tell us that our subjectivity consists of affectivity, interrelationality, and forces. The core of the subject is affect and the capacity for interrelations to affect and to be affected. Let us agree to depsychologize this discussion from this moment on, not in order to deny the pain, but rather to find ways of working through it.

If we assume the affective core of subjectivity, for instance with Spinoza's theory of *conatus* or active desire for empowerment, then the aim of ethics becomes the expression of the active or productive nature of desire. It then follows that affirmative politics is not about an oppositional strategy; it is not another discourse about storming the Bastille of phallocentrism or undoing the winter palace of gender. Politics becomes multiple micropolitical practices of daily activism or interventions in and on the world we inhabit for ourselves and for future generations. If this is the aim, then what happens to that traditional association between pain and suffering? More specifically, how do we assess the pain linked to political processes of change and transformation?

We need to delink pain from suffering and rethink its role in constituting ethical relations. Transformative ethics involves a radical repositioning on the part of the knowing subject, which is neither simple, self-evident, nor free of pain. No process of consciousness-raising ever is. In feminist theory over the last 30 years we have explored this issue from the initial slogan "the personal is the political," through the politics of location (Rich, 1987) to the multiple situated perspectives of today. Feminist theory is double-edged and involves both critique and creativity. In poststructuralist feminism, this has also been discussed in terms of disidentifying ourselves from familiar and hence comforting values and identities (Braidotti, 1994; De Lauretis, 1986).

Disidentification involves the loss of cherished habits of thought and representation, which can produce fear, sense of insecurity, and nostalgia. Change is certainly a painful process. If it were not, more people might actually be tempted to try it out. This does not, however, equate it with suffering and hence acquire necessarily negative connotations. To believe this would be a politically conservative position. The point in stressing the difficulties and pain involved in the quest for transformative ethics and politics is to raise an awareness of both the complexities involved and the paradoxes that lie in store.

Changes that affect a person's sense of identity are especially delicate. Given that identifications constitute an inner scaffolding that supports such identity, shifting our imaginary identifications is not as simple as casting away a used garment. Psychoanalysis taught us that imaginary relocations are complex and as time-consuming as shedding an old skin. Moreover, changes of this qualitative kind happen more easily at the molecular or subjective level, and their translation into a public discourse and shared social experiences is a complex and risk-ridden affair. Spinozist feminist political thinkers like Genevieve Lloyd and Moira Gatens (1999) argue that such socially embedded and historically grounded changes are the result of "collective imaginings"—a shared desire for certain transformations to be actualized.

Let me give you a series of concrete examples of how disidentifications from dominant models of subject-formation can be productive and creative events. First of all, feminist theory is based on a radical disengagement from the dominant institutions and representations of femininity and masculinity, designed to enter the process of becoming-minoritarian or of transforming gender. In so doing, feminism combines critique with creation of alternative ways of embodying and experiencing our sexualized selves. In spite of massive media battering and the marketing of political conservatism, there is no credible evidence among European women of a nostalgic desire to return to traditional gender and sex roles.

Second, in race discourse, the awareness of the persistence of racial discrimination and of white privilege has led to serious disruptions of our accepted views of what constitutes a subject. This has resulted on the one hand in the critical reappraisal of blackness (Gilroy, 200; Hill Collins, 1991) and on the other in radical relocations of whiteness (Griffin & Braidotti, 2002; Ware, 1992). Finally, I would like to refer to Edgar Morin's account of how he relinquished Marxist cosmopolitanism to embrace a more "humble" perspective as a European (1987). This process includes both positive and negative affects: Disappointment with the unfulfilled promises of Marxism is matched by compassion for the uneasy, struggling, and marginal position of postwar Europe, squashed between the United States and the Union of Soviet Socialist Republics. This produces a renewed sense of care and accountability that leads Morin to embrace a postnationalistic redefinition of Europe as the site of mediation and transformation of it own history (Balibar, 2002).

Beneficial or positive aspects balance the negative aspects of the process. The benefits are epistemological but extend beyond this; they include a more adequate cartography of our real-life conditions and hence less pathos-ridden accounts. Becoming free of the topos that equates pain with suffering and links in-depth change to the latter results in a more adequate level of self-knowledge. It enhances the lucidity of our assessments and therefore clears the grounds for more adequate and sustainable relations. This means that the emphasis commonly placed on the force of the negative is out of balance and needs to be reconsidered.

ON AFFIRMATION

In order to understand the kind of transmutation of values I am defending here, it is important to depsychologize this discussion about pain and approach it instead in more conceptual terms. We can then see how common and familiar this concept actually is. The distinction between good and evil is replaced by that between affirmation and negation, or positive and negative affects.

What is positive in the ethics of affirmation is the belief that negative affects can be transformed. This implies a dynamic view of all affects, even those that freeze us in pain, horror, or mourning. The slightly depersonalizing effect of the negative or traumatic event involves a loss of ego-indexes perception, which allows for energetic forms of reaction. Clinical psychological research on trauma testifies to this, but I cannot pursue this angle here. Diasporic subjects of all kinds express the same insight. Multilocality is the affirmative translation of this negative sense of loss. Following Glissant (1990), the becoming-nomadic marks the process of positive transformation of the pain of loss into the active production of multiple forms of belonging and complex allegiances. Every event contains within it the potential for being overcome and overtaken—its negative charge can be transposed. The moment of the actualization is also the moment of its neutralization. The ethical subject is the one with the ability to grasp the freedom to depersonalize the event and transform its negative charge.

Affirmative ethics puts the motion back into e-motion and the active back into activism, introducing movement, process, becoming. This shift makes all the difference to the patterns of repetition of negative emotions.

What is unfavorable about negative affects is not a normative value judgment but rather the effect of arrest, blockage, and rigidification, which comes as the result of a blow, a shock, an act of violence, betrayal, a trauma, or just intense boredom. Negative passions do not merely destroy the self, but also harm its capacity to relate to others, both human and nonhuman, and thus to grow in and through others. Such affects diminish our capacity to express the high levels of interdependence, the vital reliance on others that is the key to both a nonunitary vision of the subject and to affirmative ethics. Again, the vitalist notion of "Life" as "zoe" is important here because it stresses that the "Life" I inhabit is not mine; it does not bear my name—it is a generative force of becoming, of individuation, and differentiation.

What is negated by negative passions is the power of life itself, as the dynamic force, its vital flows of connections and becoming. This is why they should neither be encouraged nor should we be rewarded for lingering around them too long. Negative passions are black holes.

This is an antithesis of the Kantian moral imperative to avoid pain, or to view it as the obstacle to moral behavior. Postsecular affirmative ethics is not about the avoidance of pain, but rather about transcending the resignation and passivity that ensue from being hurt, lost, and dispossessed. One has to become ethical, as opposed to applying moral rules and protocols as a form of self-protection.

Taking pain into account is the starting point, the aim of the process; however, there also exists the quest for ways of overcoming the effects of passivity, the paralysis brought about by pain. The internal disarray, fracture, and pain are also the conditions of possibility for ethical transformation. The qualitative leap through and across pain is the gesture that actualizes affirmative ways of becoming. This is a gesture, which constructs hope as a social project.

It is those who have already cracked up a bit, those who have suffered pain and injury, who are better placed to take the lead in the process of ethical transformation. Their "better quality" consists not in the fact of having been wounded, but of having gone through the pain. Because they are already on the other side of some existential divide, they are anomalous in some positive way. They are a site of value transposition. Marxist epistemology and postcolonial and feminist standpoint theory have always acknowledged the privileged knowing position of those in the "margins."

The figure of Nelson Mandela—a contemporary secular saint—comes to mind, as does the Truth and Reconciliation Commission, a world-historical phenomenon in postapartheid South Africa. This is a case of repetition that engenders difference and does not install the eternal return of revenge and negative affects, a massive exercise in transformation of negativity into something more sustainable, more life enhancing. Endurance is the Spinozist code word for this process. Endurance has a spatial side to do with the space of the body as an enfleshed field of actualization of passions or forces. It evolves affectivity and joy, as in the capacity for being affected by these forces, to the point of pain or extreme pleasure. Endurance indicates the struggle to sustain the pain without being annihilated by it.

Endurance also has a temporal dimension, duration in time. This is linked to memory: Intense pain, a wrong, a betrayal, a wound are hard to forget. The traumatic impact of painful events fixes them in a rigid, eternal present tense, out of which it is difficult to emerge. This is the eternal return of that which precisely cannot be endured and, as such, returns exactly in the mode of the unwanted, the untimely, the unassimilated or inappropriate/d. They are also, however, paradoxically difficult to remember, insofar as to do so entails retrieval and repetition of the pain itself.

Psychoanalysis, of course, has been here before (Laplanche, 1976). The notion of the return of the repressed is the key to the logic of unconscious remembrance, but it is a secret and somewhat invisible key, which condenses space into the spasm of the symptom and time into a short-circuit that mines the very thinkability of the present. Kristeva's notion of the abject (1980) expresses clearly the temporality involved in psychoanalysis—by stressing the structural function played by the negative, by the incomprehensible, the unthinkable, the other of understandable knowledge.

Deleuze calls this alterity "Chaos" and, as I indicated earlier, he defines it positively as the virtual formation of all possible form. Lacan, however, and Derrida with him I would argue, defines "Chaos" epistemologically as that which precedes form, structure, language. This makes for two radically divergent conceptions of time, and—more importantly for me today—of negativity. What which is incomprehensible for Lacan—following Hegel—is the virtual for Deleuze, following Spinoza, Bergson, and Leibniz. This produces a number of significant shifts: from negative to affirmative affects; from entropic to generative desire; from incomprehensible to virtual events to be actualized; from constitutive outsides to a geometry of affects that require mutual synchronization; from a melancholy and split to an open-ended web-like subject; and from the epistemological to the ontological turn in poststructuralist philosophy.

Nietzsche also has been here before, of course. The eternal return in Nietzsche is the repetition, not in the compulsive mode of neurosis nor in the negative erasure that marks the traumatic event. It is the eternal return of and as positivity (Ansell-Pearson, 1999). In a nomadic Deleuzian-Nietzschean perspective, ethics is essentially about transformation of negative into positive passions (i.e., moving beyond the pain). This does not mean denying the pain, but rather activating it, working it through. Again, the positivity here is not supposed to indicate a facile optimism or a careless dismissal of human suffering. It involves compassionate witnessing of the pain of others, as Zygmunt Bauman (1993) and Susan Sontag (2003) point out—in the mode of empathic copresence.

THE QUESTION OF LIMITS

I end this section with the suggestion that one of the reasons why the negative associations linked to pain, especially in relation to political processes of change, is ideologically laden, in that it fits in with the logic of claims and compensations, which is central to advanced capitalism. This is a form of institutionalized management of the negative, something that also has become quite common in gender and antiracism politics.

Consequently, two more problematic aspects need to be raised. The first is that our culture tends to glorify pain by equating it with suffering, thus promoting an ideology of compensation. Contemporary culture has encouraged and rewarded a public morality based on the twin principles of claims and compensation, as if legal and financial settlements could constitute the answer to the injury suffered, the pain endured, and the long-lasting effects of the injustice. Cases that exemplify this trend are remuneration for the Shoah in the sense of restitution of stolen property, artworks, and bank deposits; similar demands have been made by the descendants of slaves forcefully removed from Africa North America (Gilroy, 2000) and more recently for damages caused by Soviet communism, notably the confiscation of properties across eastern Europe, both from Jews and others. A great deal of contemporary mainstream feminism has also moved in this direction. This fact makes affirmative ethics of transformation into a struggle against the mainstream. It also makes it appear more counterintuitive than it actually is.

The second problem is the force of habit. Starting from the assumption that a subject is a sedimentation of established habits, these can be seen as patterns of repetitions that consolidate modes of relation and forces of interaction. Habits are the structure within which nonunitary or complex subjects get reterritorialized, albeit temporarily. One of the established habits in our culture is to frame "pain" within a discourse and social practice of suffering, which requires rightful compensation.

Equally strong is the urge to understand and empathize with pain. People go to great lengths in order to ease it completely. Great distress follows from not knowing or not being able to articulate the source of one's suffering, or from knowing it all too well, all the time. The yearning for solace, closure, and justice is understandable and worthy of respect.

This ethical dilemma was already posed by J. F. Lyotard (1983) and, much earlier, by Primo Levi about the survivors of Nazi concentration camps; the kind of vulnerability we humans experience in face of events on the scale of small or high horror is something for which no adequate compensation is even thinkable. It is just incommensurable: a hurt, or wound, beyond repair. This means that the notion of justice in the sense of a logic of rights and reparation is not applicable. For the poststructuralist Lyotard, ethics consists in accepting the impossibility of adequate compensation—and living with the open wound.

This is the road to an ethics of affirmation, which respects the pain but suspends the quest for both claims and compensation and resists the logic of retribution of rights. This is achieved through a sort of depersonalization of the event, which is the ultimate ethical challenge. The displacement of the "zoe"—indexed reaction reveals the fundamental meaninglessness of the hurt, the injustice, or injury one has suffered. "Why me?" is the refrain most commonly heard in situations of extreme distress. This expresses rage as well as anguish at one's ill fate. The answer is plain: actually, for no reason at all. Examples of this are the banality of evil in large-scale genocides like the Holocaust (Arendt, 1963), the randomness of surviving them. There is something intrinsically senseless about the pain, hurt, or injustice: Lives are lost or saved for all and no reason at all. Why did some go to work in the World Trade Center on 9/11 while others missed the train? Why did Frida Kahlo take that tram, which crashed so that she was impaled by a metal rod, and not the next one?—for no reason at all. Reason has nothing to do with it. That is precisely the point. We need to delink pain from the quest for meaning and move beyond, to the next stage. That is the transformation of negative into positive passions.

This is not fatalism, and even less resignation, but rather Nietzschean ethics of overturning the negative. Let us call it *amor fati;* we have to be worthy of what happens to us and rework it within an ethics of relation. Of course, repugnant and unbearable events do happen. Ethics consists, however, in reworking these events in the direction of positive relations. This is not carelessness or lack of compassion, but rather a form of lucidity, which acknowledges the meaninglessness of pain and the futility of compensation. It also reasserts that the ethical instance is not that of retaliation or compensation, but rather rests on active transformation of the negative.

This requires a double shift. First, the affect itself moves from the frozen or reactive effect of pain to proactive affirmation of its generative potential. Second, the line of questioning also changes from the quest for the origin or source to a process of elaboration of the questions that express and enhance a subject's capacity to achieve freedom through the understanding of its limits.

What is an adequate ethical question? It is one that is capable of sustaining the subject in his/her quest for more interrelations with others (i.e., more "Life," motion, change, and transformation). It provides the subject with a frame for interaction and change, growth and movement. It affirms life as difference-at-work. An ethical question had to be adequate in relation to how much a body can take. How much can an embodied entity tolerate in the mode of interrelations and connections (i.e., how much freedom of action can we endure)? Affirmative ethics assumes, following Nietzsche, that humanity does not stem out of freedom but rather that freedom is extracted out of the awareness of limitations. Postsecular ethics is about freedom from the burden of negativity, freedom through the understanding of our bondage.

THE QUESTION OF OTHERNESS AS
TRANSFORMATIVE ETHICS

The relationship to "others" is set in a different frame of reference, which redefines the question of limits. These are corporeal and materially grounded conditions; this means that they cannot be reduced to linguistic forms of mediation or representation. By moving away from the human emphasis on speech and actions to allow for events that do not yet have governing conditions, I want to defend the vital politics of life as posthuman becoming. This postsecular ethics expresses a mode of engagement that does not tie conditions of possibility to negation but rather to creation, not the dialectics of "Lack" and recognition of sameness, but the affirmation of otherness as a horizon of creative becoming. It is crucial to keep in mind the vital politics of life itself, which means external nonhuman relations as a point of reference. The "others" in question here are nonanthropomorphic and include planetary forces. This runs against the humanistic tradition of making the anthropocentric "Other" into the privileged site and inescapable horizon of otherness.

This is a point of major difference between nomadic philosophy and a number of Continental philosophers, like Jessica Benjamin (1988) in her radicalization of Irigaray's notion of "horizontal transcendence"; Lyotard in the "differed" (1983) and his notion of the "unatoned"; and Butler (2004a) in her emphasis on "precarious life." To pursue my dialogue with Judith Butler on this point (Braidotti, 2002; Butler, 2004b), given that we express different branches of the poststructuralist tradition, let me expand this to a discussion of the role of the other's face in our respective philosophies. On the one hand you can approach otherness as the expression of a limit—albeit a negotiable one—which calls for an always already compromised set of negotiations. This is the function of the other's face in Levinas' (1999) and, by extension, Derrida's ethics. On the other hand, you can look, as I stated earlier, for the ways in which it prompts, mobilizes, and allows for flows of affirmation of values and forces, which are not yet sustained by the current conditions. That is affirmative ethics.

I should add for the sake of scholarly accuracy that Levinas' case is complex, as there are significant resonances between his notion of passivity and Deleuze's affirmation. Levinas' brand of immanence, however, differs considerably from Deleuze's life-oriented philosophy of becoming. Levinas—

like Irigaray—inscribes the totality of the "Self's" reliance on the other as a structural necessity that transcends the "I" but remains internal to it. Deleuze's immanence, on the other hand, firmly locates the affirmation in the exteriority, the cruel, messy outside-ness of "Life" itself. Creative chaos is not chaotic—it is the virtual formation of *all* possible forms (Deleuze,1969). Life is not an a priori that gets individuated in single instances, but is immanent to and thus coincides with its multiple material actualizations. It is the site of birth and emergence of the new—life itself. I refer to this generative force as "zoe," which is the opposite therefore of Agamben's "bare life"—in that it is a creative force that constructs possible futures.

Moral reasoning locates the constitution of subjectivity in the interrelation to others, which is a form of exposure, availability, and vulnerability. This recognition entails the necessity of containing the other, the suffering, and the enjoyment of others.

I want to argue instead that an embodied and connecting containment as a moral category can also emerge from the radical redefinition of the same–other relation by the vital politics of life itself, as external and nonhuman forces: cells, as Franklin (2000) argues; viruses and bacteria, as Luciana Parisi (2004) points out; and earth others, as Bryld and Lykke have been arguing for a long time (1999). This posthuman ethics assumes as the point of reference not the individual, but the relation. This means openness to others, in the positive sense of affecting and being affected by others, through couples and mutually dependent corealities. Containment of the other occurs through interrelational affectivity. This displaces the grounds on which Kantian negotiations of limits can take place. The imperative not to do onto others what you would not want done to you is not rejected as much as enlarged. In affirmative ethics, the harm you do to others is immediately reflected in the harm you do to yourself, in terms of loss of *potentia*, positivity, capacity to relate, and hence freedom.

Biocentered egalitarianism breaks the expectation of mutual reciprocity, which is central not only to liberal individualism, but also to poststructuralist ethics of otherness. Accepting the impossibility of mutual recognition and replacing it with one of mutual specification and codependence is what is at stake in postsecular affirmative ethics. The ethical process of transforming negative into positive passions introduces time and motion into the frozen enclosure of seething pain. It is a postsecularist gesture of affirmation of hope, in the sense of creating the conditions for endurance and hence a sustainable future.

THE CASE OF INTERGENERATIONAL JUSTICE

The last aspect of the postsecular ethics of affirmation I spell out is generational time-lines—in the sense of the construction of social horizons of hope (i.e., sustainable futures).

Modernity, as an ideology of progress, postulated boundless faith in the future as the ultimate destination of the human. Zygmunt Bauman quotes one of my favorite writers, Diderot, who stated that modern man is in love with posterity. Postmodernity, however, is death-bound and sets as its horizon the globalization process in terms of technological and economic interdependence. Capitalism has no built-in teleological purpose, historical logic, or structure, but is rather a self-imploding system, which would not stop at anything in order to fulfill its aim: profit. This inherently self-destructive system feeds on and thus destroys the very conditions of its survival; it is omnivorous and what it ultimately eats is the future itself.

Being nothing more than this all-consuming entropic energy, capitalism lacks the ability to create anything new: It can merely promote the recycling of spent hopes, repackaged in the rhetorical frame of the "next generation of gadgets." Affirmative ethics expresses the desire to endure in time and thus clashes with the deadly spin of the present.

The future today is no longer the self-projection of the modernist subject: Eve and the New Jerusalem. It is a basic and rather humble act of faith in the possibility of endurance, as duration or continuity, which honors our obligation to the generations to come. It involves the virtual unfolding of the affirmative aspect of what we managed to actualize here and now. Virtual futures grow out of sustainable presents and vice versa. This is how qualitative transformations can be actualized and transmitted along the genetic/time line. Transformative postsecular ethics affirmatively takes on the future, as the shared collective imagining that goes on becoming, to effect multiple modes of interaction with heterogeneous others. Futurity is made of this. Nonlinear evolution is an ethics that moves away from the paradigm of reciprocity, the logic of recognition and installs a rhizomic relation of mutual affirmation.

By targeting those who come after us as the rightful ethical interlocutors and assessors of our own actions, we are taking seriously the implications of our own situated position. This form of intergenerational justice is crucial. This point about intergenerational fairness need not, however, be expressed or conceptualized in the social imaginary as an Oedipal narrative. To be concerned about the future need not result in linearity (i.e., in restating the unity of space and time as the horizon of subjectivity). On the contrary, nonlinear genealogical models of intergenerational decency are a way of displacing the Oedipal hierarchy.

They involve a becoming-minoritarian of not only the elderly, senior, and parental figures, but also the de-Oedipalization of the bond of the young to those who preceded them. It calls for new ways of addressing and solving intergenerational conflicts—other than envy and rivalry, joining forces across the generational divide by working together towards sustainable futures and practising an ethics of nonreciprocity in the pursuit of affirmation.

An example: The older feminists may feel the cruel pinch of aging, but some of the young ones suffer from 1970s envy. The middle-aged survivors of the second wave may feel like war veterans, or survivors, but some of generation Y, as Iris v.d. Tuin taught me, call themselves "born again baby boomers!" So who's envying whom?

We are in *this* together, indeed. Those who go through life under the sign of the desire for change need accelerations that jolt them out of set habits; political thinkers of the postsecular era need to be visionary, prophetic, and upbeat—insofar as they are passionately committed to writing the prehistory of the future (i.e., to introduce change in the present, so as to affect multiple modes of belonging through complex and heterogeneous relations). This is the horizon of sustainable futures.

Hope is a sort of "dreaming forward"; it is an anticipatory virtue that permeates our lives and activates them. It is a powerful motivating force grounded in our collective imaginings, indeed. They express very grounded concerns for the multitude of "anybody" (*homo tantum*) who composes the human community, lest our greed and selfishness destroy or diminish it for generations to come. Given that posterity per definition can never pay us back, this gesture is perfectly gratuitous.

Against the general lethargy, the rhetoric of selfish genes, and possessive individualism on the one hand, and the dominant ideology of the melancholic lament on the other, hope rests with an affirmative ethics of sustainable futures. There is a deep and careless generosity, the ethics of nonprofit at an ontological level.

Why should one pursue this project? For no reason at all. Reason has nothing to do with this. Let us just do it for the hell of it and love of the world.

REFERENCES

Agamben, G. (1998). *Homo sacer: Sovereign power and bare life*. Stanford: University Press.

Ansell Pearson, K. (1999). *Germinal life: The difference and repetition of Deleuze*. London and New York: Routledge.

Arendt, H. (1963). *Eichmann in Jerusalem: A report on the banality of evil*. New York: Viking.

Badinter, E. (2003). *Fausse route*. Paris: Odile Jacob.

Balibar, E. (2002). *Politics and the other scene*. London: Verso.

Bauman, Z. (1993). *Postmodern ethics*. Oxford: Blackwell.

Benhabib, S. (2002). *The claims of culture: Equality and diversity in the global era*. Princeton: Princeton University Press.

Benjamin, J. (1988). *The bonds of love: Psychoanalysis, feminism and the problem of domination*. New York: Pantheon.

Bhabha, H. (2004). *The location of culture*. London and New York: Routledge.

Brah, A. (1996). *Cartographies of diaspora: Contesting identities*. New York and London: Routledge.

Braidotti, R. (1994). *Nomadic subjects: Embodiment and sexual difference in contemporary feminist theory*. New York: Columbia University Press.

———. (2002). *Metamorphoses: Towards a materialist theory of becoming*. Cambridge, UK, and Malden: Polity Press/Blackwell Publishers.

———. (2006). *Transpositions: On nomadic ethics*. Cambridge: Polity Press.

Bryld, M., & Lykke, N. (1999). *Cosmodolphins:. Feminist cultural studies of technologies, animals and the sacred*. London: Zed Books.

Butler, J. (2004a). *Precarious life*. London; Verso.

———. (2004b). *Undoing gender*. London and New York: Routledge.

Connolly, W. (1999). *Why am I not a secularist?* Minneapolis: University of Minnesota Press.

Cornell, D. (2002). *The Ubuntu project with Stellenbosch University*. Retrieved February 1, 2007, from www.fehe.org/index.php?id=281

Dawkins, R. (1976). *The selfish gene*. Oxford: Oxford University Press.

De Lauretis, T. (1986). *Alice doesn't*. Bloomington: Indiana University Press.

Deleuze, G. (1968). *Spinoza et le problem de l'expression*. Paris: Minuit. English translation (1990). *Expressionism in philosophy: Spinoza*. New York: Zone Books.

———. (1969). *Logique du sens*. Paris: Minuit. English translation: *The logic of sense* (M. Lester & C. Stivale, Trans.). New York: Columbia University Press.

Deleuze, G., & Guattari, F. (1976). *Rhizome*. Paris: Minuit.

Derrida, J. (2001). *The work of mourning*. Chicago: The University of Chicago Press.

———. (2002). *Acts of religion*. London and New York: Routledge.

Fallaci, O. (2002). *The rage and the pride*. New York: Rizzoli International.

Foster, H. (1996). *The return of the real*. Cambridge: MIT Press.

Franklin, S., Lury, C., & Stacey, J. (2000). *Global nature, global culture*. London: Sage.

Fukuyama, F. (1989). *The end of history?* Washington DC: United States Institute of Peace.

———. (2002). *Our posthuman future. Consequences of the bio-technological revolution*. London: Profile Books.

Gatens, M., & Lloyd, G. (1999). *Collective imaginings: Spinoza, past and present*. London and New York: Routledge.

Gilroy, P. (2000). *Between camps. Race, identity and nationalism at the end of the colour line*. London: Allen Lane.

———. (2004). *After empire. Melancholia or convivial Culture?* London and New York: Routledge.

Glissant, E. (1990). *Poetique de la relation* [Poetics of relation]. Paris: Gallimard.

———. (1997). *Poetics of relation* (B. Wing & A. Arbor, Trans.) University of Michigan Press.

Grewal, I. & Kaplan, C. (Eds.) (1994). *Scattered hegemonies: Postmodernity and transnational feminist practices*. Minneapolis: University of Minnesota Press.

Griffin, G., & Braidotti, R. (2002). *Thinking differently: A reader in European women's studies*. London: Zed Books.

Guattari, F. (1984). *Molecular revolution: Psychiatry and politics*. New York: Penguin.

Haraway, D. (1985). A manifesto for cyborgs: Science, technology, and socialist feminism in the 1980s. *Socialist Review, 5, 2*.

———. (1988). Situated knowledges: The science question in feminism as a site of Discourse on the privilege of partial perspective. *Feminist Studies, 14(3)*, 575–599.

———. (1997). *Modest witness@ second millennium. Female man meets oncomouse*. London and New York: Routledge.

Hill Collins, P. (1991). *Black feminist thought: Knowledge, consciousness and the politics of empowerment*. New York and London: Routledge.

hooks, b. (1990). Postmodern blackness. In *Yearning: Race, gender and cultural politics*. Toronto: Between the Lines.

Huntington, S. (1996). *The clash of civilizations and the remaking of world order*. New York: Simon & Schuster.

Irigaray, L. (1974). *Speculum: De l'autre femme*. Paris: Minuit.

Kristeva, J. (1980). *Pouvoirs de l'horreur*. Paris: Seuil, English translation: 1982 *Powers of horror*, translation by L.S. Roudiez. New York: Colombia University Press.

Lacan, J. (1981). *The four fundamental concepts of psycho-analysis*. New York: Norton.

Laclau, E. (1995). Subjects of politics, politics of the subject. *Differences*, 7(1),146–164.

Laplanche, J. (1976). *Life and death in psychoanalysis*. Baltimore and London: Johns Hopkins University Press.

Levinas, E. (1999). *Alterity & transcendence*. London: The Athlone Press.

Lyotard, J. F. (1983). *Le Différend*. Paris: Editions de Minuit.

Morin, E. (1987). *Penser l'Europe*. Paris: Gallimard.

Negri, A., & Hardt, M. (2004). *Multitude: War and democarcy in the age of empire*. New York: Penguin Press.

Norton, A. (2004). *Leo Strauss and the politics of American empire*. New Haven: Yale University Press.

Nussbaum, M. (1999). *Cultivating humanity*. Cambridge: Harvard University Press.

———. (2006). *Frontiers of justice. Disability, nationality, species membership*. Cambridge: Harvard University Press.

Parisi, L. (2004). *Abstract sex: Philosophy, bio-technology and the mutation of desire*. London: Continuum.

Rich, A. (1987). *Blood, bread and poetry*. London: Virago Press.

Said, E. (1978). *Orientalism*. London: Penguin Books.

Schmitt, C. (1996). *The concept of the political*. Chicago: Chicago University Press.

Scott, J. (1996). *Only paradoxes to offer: French feminists and the rights of man*. Cambridge, MA: Harvard University Press.

Seltzer, M. (1999). Wound culture: Trauma in the pathological public sphere. *October* 80 3–26.

Shiva, V. (1997). *Biopiracy. The plunder of nature and knowledge*. Boston: South End Press.

Sontag, S. (2003). *Regarding the pain of others*. New York: Picador.

Ware, V. (1992). *Beyond the pale: White women, racism and history*. London: Verso.

West, C. (1994). *Prophetic thought in postmodern times*. Monroe, ME: Common Courage Press.

3 Return of Men's Narratives and the Vicious Circle of Gender Play

Marek Wojtaszek

Thinking is not a cognitive means for us; it is to categorize events, order them, facilitate their use: thus we think of thinking today— tomorrow we might think differently.

Friedrich Nietzsche

It is not difference which presupposes opposition but opposition which presupposes difference, and far from resolving difference by tracing it back to a foundation, opposition betrays and distorts it.

Gilles Deleuze

. . . The proper task of men who intend to deconstruct phallic premises should be to speak as singular men, not as representatives of Mankind, and develop new way of thinking masculinity.

Rosi Braidotti

RETURN OF GENDERED NARRATIVES

At the twilight of postmodernism, one can observe far from unprecedented and unanticipated rebirth and activization of divergent social groups and movements, globally conceived of as "minorities," cartographically pushed to the margins of society (materialism) and ideologically interred under the monument of dominant culture (idealism): Maghrebian immigrants in France, lesbians and homosexuals in Poland, immigrants in the United States, and urban violence, to name just a few. This return of the repressed, social ideological forces appears to coincide with the resurgence of powerful conservative doctrines (neoconservatism, essentialism, new spiritualism) and theories as a reaction to the former. These universalizing and regulatory, thus unifying and oppressive, narratives are best depicted by Jean François Lyotard in his work *The Postmodern Condition: A Report on Knowledge.* He defines what he calls "meta-narratives" as systems that endeavor to explain cultural phenomena in terms of a single overarching principle, the quest for ultimate truth and order in human experience (Lyotard, 1993, p. 72). Significantly, both Lyotard and other postmodern authors (e.g., Henry

Giroux, Jacques Derrida) refer to postmodernism as a general "incredulity toward meta-narratives" (Lyotard), or utter distrust in "universalizing categories or general abstractions that deny the specificity and particularity of everyday life, that generalize out of existence the particular and the local, that smother difference under the banner of universalizing categories" (Giroux, 1993, p. 463). Interestingly enough, however, it is difficult to concede that they put their sole existence in question, which by implication makes one consider them as substantial explanations of the world and processes one participates in. Deleuze, in his critical diagnosis, makes a point rather disdainfully, "We always have the beliefs, feelings, and thoughts that we deserve given our way of being or our style of life" (1983, p. 1). Stated otherwise, the way we think and experience the world around us, and us within it, does not reflect, but rather, is expressive of the way we are and vice versa. As Moira Gatens puts it succinctly in her Spinozian reading of Deleuze, "One's power of being does not affect but is *expressed* through one's power of thinking," which consequently leads her to evince that "one's power of thinking is inseparable from one's power of being" (1996, pp. 168, 165). Admittedly, the aforementioned oppositional phenomena can well be read as the "returns," the former of the repressed and the latter as a wave of rationalizing meta-narratives. These two tend to occur simultaneously, one always being considered as a reaction to the other.

GENDER CONUNDRUM

These social processes posited dialectically, when investigated from the point of view of their most prominent contributors, remain far from ungendered. It is largely men who have fostered and elaborated such a dualistic manner of thinking about the human condition and development. Philosophy and psychoanalysis have perennially been dominated by men and their modes of reasoning; it was they who largely animated the development of Western thought (i.e., specifically *masculine* mode of thought). It is of vital importance not to remain oblivious of the fact that those men have never been representatives of all humanity, although imagined and thought of as such, produced, allegedly, impersonal, and impartial knowledge of the self and the world. This is best evidenced by the overwhelming presence of metaphysics, or as Jacques Derrida concretized it, "metaphysics of presence" in the history of Western thought. It is metaphysics, as a dominant school of Western ontology, that—as its very name implies (meta-*physis*)—is to be held responsible for erasure of any physicality of the body (embodied, thus always embedded existence[1]) from the theoretical field of philosophy, from the very activity of thinking, thus rendering it to appear disinterested and *naturally* neutral. All that is left is pure reason and thought beyond *mat(t)er*-iality, beyond corporeality. This divorce from bodily, worldly condition in fact emerges as a *conditio sine qua non* of epistemology, as a very condition of thinking (Plato). It is men who become the founding fathers of Western rationalism, its main acolytes and followers. Within this rational and disembodied framework, women get bounded to their physical beings, which is supposedly justified and ensured by life-generating powers of their bodies (essentialistic, biologistic discourses). Thereby, men associate and identify themselves with the mind while women become enslaved to their bodies, bodies *naturally* conceived of as volatile and untamable, thus perfectly embodying difference. Women's fragmentation of the self has become their basic historical condition; as Braidotti rightly states, "Women have been poststructuralist since the beginning of time" (1996, p. 122). They are construed as the constitutive, if unacknowledged, *other*, "a ghostly body of metaphysics" (Colebrook, 2002) that helps erect the masculine hierarchical order. This dualistic framework juxtaposing one (man) against its other (woman), or rather, expelling the *other*, pressing it down for self-constitution (Butler, 1999, p. 25), has laid groundwork for the negative dualistic ontology, which proves highly restrictive and oppressive in that it is predicated upon the original exclusion. The *other* is produced by and maintained within this framework as its phantom member without which the entire system becomes destabilized and eventually collapses. The *other* is thereby *made* dependent on, and simultaneously reflective of, the one with the moral undertones inscribed into such logic of being that justifies its inferior status.

Thus, constituted logic of sameness (identity) could be erected only upon complete denial and expulsion of pure difference, difference freed from negativistic grips, affirmative and generative. It is sameness that is secondary to, and indeed repressive of, difference, and not conversely; it is, therefore, a reduction, a simplification. "Beneath the platitude of the negative lies the world of disparateness," Deleuze asseverates (1994, p. 266). This "absolute difference," the forgotten essence of Western thought,[2] no longer has anything to do with the negative conception of difference (binarity, contradiction), which exists within the metaphysically established and historically rejuvenated framework. What is noteworthy here is that an application of the category "gender" to social phenomena, necessarily juxtaposing one against the other, is always already charged with systemic valuation, subsequently, confirms and *nolens volens* reproduces psychically (imaginary) and socially (symbolic) oppressive situations. Thinking in this way, one perpetuates intrinsic dualism, dualism that can only be effectuated under, and in fact be presupposed by, the negative ontology productive of dissymmetrical power relations between genders. Therefore, one still remains in the confines of the logic of two, the classical model of thinking predicated upon notions of "identity" and "contradiction," the Aristotelian logic of "either–or," which the presence and popularity of the notion of "gender" at the opening of the 21st century clearly reasserts.

Men are not disembodied carriers of knowledge potential; they are above all enfleshed beings embedded in the context of everyday existence as much as women are. What Braidotti underscores, women's profoundly different relation to their bodies from men's—biocultural, or a sociosymbolic one (1996)—appears to me adequate as far as the ideological (symbolic) level, or rather, metaphysical problem of sexual difference is concerned. The problem, however, lies elsewhere. Men are not—neither are women—allowed to live and think about their bodies truly distinctly, beyond the crude logic of sameness and recognition. Men's bodies are equally different likewise within and without when stripped of the illusion of identity, which always already presupposes negative ontology and thinking in terms of two. Constituting the paramount group within the social field, once faced with the return of repressed social forces, men immediately have to pulverize all difference it uncovers to reassert their being, hence dominance of metaphysics in Western philosophical enquiry. Terrified, they immediately situate themselves—according to the underlying dualistic logic—in opposition to a systemically generated "threat." Whence the violent attitudes and reactions toward feminist and other minority movements and whatever does not fit into the dominant mode of thought or dare question its legitimacy. Every return of the repressed elements has structurally to be met with a reaction of ideology, which by definition is founded upon psychic expulsion, legal exclusion, and subordination (Colebrook, 2002, p. 92). I would argue that it is neither the social nor even the psychological context, nor even both together, that suffices to explicate this violent reaction. Rather, it is at the level of thought itself where the problem of violence is situated.

Feminist women's attempts to reconstruct subjectivity and create representations—hitherto submerged under phallogocentrism—tend to theorize the feminine from the standpoint of specificity of (the) female morphology. For example, Luce Irigaray's endeavor, however socially and politically important, can become at some point also restrictive and even exclusionary. Underscoring the radical sexual difference, Irigaray monumentalizes it, viewing it as a threshold for any further differences, thus inevitably prioritizing it. This, in her account, is crucial for the *feminine*[3] subject to be able to emerge as *positively* different from the dominating male counterpart. Exploring feminine subjectivity, particularly from the viewpoint of her specific sexuality, Irigaray depicts a feminine subject as a virtual multiplicity, pure difference (1999, pp. 82–90). This radically distinct feminine subjectivity can be reclaimed—at least in theory—via opposition from the dominant transcendental masculine subject, constructed as a unitary and *in*-dividual being. Although she is presented as pure difference, her subjectivity is still posited in theoretical contradistinction to the masculine identity. In other words, at the level of thought men, and consequently male bodies, are denied the right to feel, experience, and most importantly, think pure difference. She refuses the masculine subject any other conception of difference than the one she is struggling with, that is, the hierarchical. One can have the impression of a simple inversion, thus reinscription of the hitherto existing dualistic model. Inasmuch as Irigaray strips the category "woman" of its imposed masculine representation, and insofar as she retrieves her corporeal multiplicity, she posits this condition as radically and necessarily different from the other sex, that is, male. She appears unwilling to grant men the right to experience difference ontologically, to become multiplicity. Consequently, the risk of upholding the dualistic mode of thought, one dialectically located against the multiple, man opposite the (new affirmative) feminine seems inevitable.

What Irigaray argues about feminine subjectivity well resonates, I believe, with what Deleuze accomplishes in his critique of the representational, Platonic–Hegelian ideational framework. They both release generative real difference from the logical as well as ideological constraints. Whereas Deleuze speaks of a univocity of being, therefore multiple differences that are *being,* Irigaray assigns to the sexual difference a unique status, a primary one that has to be recognized before any other dissimilarities come into being. This is the point where Irigaray's and Deleuze's roads depart, leaving the former's argument, however politically innovative, affirmative, and socially indispensable, still within the Hegellian logic of the two, the two that for Deleuze become the greatest enemy.

Dualism is what prevents thought. Dualism always wants to deny the essence of thought, namely, that thought is a process. . . . There is only one form of thought; it is the same thing: One can only think in a monistic or pluralistic manner. The only enemy is two. Monism and pluralism: It is the same thing (Deleuze, 1973).

Contradiction then becomes accused of being a misreading and misconceiving of foundational generative difference, a falsity that destroys the substantial nature of being and fails to grasp the concreteness and specificity of real being.[4]

ALL FOR MULTIPLICITY, MULTIPLICITY FOR ALL

So long as humans continue to adhere to a negativistic framework of thinking, the pursuant dualism will not allow authentic appreciation of difference. Metaphysics will continually recreate itself, endorsing and legitimating the ontological *status quo* of being (self) and its not-being (the *other*). Under such circumstances, anything encountered is always already submerged unto a preexisting form in accordance with the logic of sameness and otherness (recognition). Capitalistic production and creation of novel differences (deterritorialization) can lead only to taking advantage of their market potential (disempowering them) and leaving them within the same old system of thought (reterritorialization). Therefore, emphatically, it is men who need to emancipate themselves as well, or even, first and foremost. Otherwise, what the last three decades aptly demonstrate, even with enormous political and social effort made by feminists and other minority groups, is that dominant paternalistic ideologies (meta-narratives) will still prevail recreating and reinstating themselves. Metaphysics of being and therefore everything it supports, as Nietzsche already discerned, has this astonishing capacity of resiliency, which his own case brilliantly proves. Nietzschean groundbreaking critique of the ossified representational system, exerting power to keep all its members in their place, displays untimely innovation; itself, being construed as the dialectical enemy (itself being an opposition to dialectical opposition[5]), gets repressed, subjugated and channeled into the ideological mainstream, thus deprived of its liberating potency, which both Martin Heidegger's and Max Horkheimer and Theodor Adorno's readings of Nietzsche astutely prove.[6] This once again demonstrates the great immunity of the masters' power and its tangibility, pliability, and adaptability to new conditions. So long as the dominant negativity holds one in check, hardly can one envisage any real change.

Change originates in our embrained body, no longer thought of as a phenomenological holistic entity, endowed with a supreme reason, a molar, essentialistic reality, no longer as primary to social change. Rather, the two—the body (bodies) and the social—go hand in hand. The body, instead of being seen as entering social contexts, by initiating change emerges as a multiplicity, *par excellence*. It is to be viewed as coforming contexts, establishing divergent relations, being always a lived multiplicity of the multiplicity of factors on the road to change (incorporeal materialism[7]). Deleuze and Guattari remind us of what apparently we have consigned to oblivion, "That our criticism of these abstract models is not that they are too abstract but, on the contrary, that they are not abstract enough," that they do not reach the abstract machine connecting the body to "a whole micropolitics of the social field" (2004, p. 8). Abstraction is no different here from a superior form of empiricism[8] and has nothing to do with a commonsensical understanding of idealism. It is a radically complex figuration, an envisioning embrace of other worlds that the ideology of androcentrism has deliberately omitted. It exceeds and overcomes the traditional domain of the human, inaugurating a novel mode of thought beyond recognition, which both men and women have yet to learn. This emerges as beyond the simple cognitive and epistemological dualism of "immaculate" perception (empiricism) and "pure" reason (rationalism).[9] The immanence of thought and life has to be regained for us to be able to experience life in all its complexity and to effectively account for it, that is, to produce passionate and sexual knowledge capable of generating ethics of *difference*.

In light of the preceding, humanistic concept of "gender" as a category predicated upon the logic of identity, assuming prior subject or discursively constructing it, explicitly points to the two genders—be they hierarchical or positively different—in fact, exhibits its entanglement in the dualistic framework and ipso facto contributes to the maintenance of dominant masculine ideology.[10] It proves insufficient to account for all the differences that bodies and worlds simultaneously produce. Braidotti stands her point very lucidly, adequately grasping the gist of the matter, "The problem is that we already live this way, but we cannot represent it to ourselves in a creative manner" (2000). Prior, though, to proposing a novel manner of thinking, being, and difference, one should pose a simple question—why do this? Why renounce transcendence (negativity) and all its corollaries, the notion of identity, gender, and traditional logic? Why sacrifice the—however dubious or questionable—pleasure of stability, which the system seems to guarantee for the no less cruel apprehension of difference and monstrous creation it entails? It is my contention that without theories and politics that render difference and change genuine and material, that take into account their ontological status, life triggers death, domination becomes ineluctable, and any social change is nothing but an illusion. In other words, both men and women have always changed over time; the problem is not, as psychoanalysis would recommend, to work on activation of someone's desire for only then can one putatively change, but to make this transformation figurative enough to us, thus helping us to commence thinking affirmatively-differently, which will liberate us from the constraints of the negative. As Deleuze boldly appeals, "Difference must leave its cave and cease to be a monster" (1994, p. 29).

LIBERATION BEYOND GENDER: DELEUZE AND IMMANENCE

However politically justifiable they may seem, all the social movements that have grown at the margins and are depicted in the foregoing as returns of the repressed, which ground both their self-legitimatization and self-understanding in the concept of "identity," still remain, as the text attempts to emphasize, enchained to the bidirectional representational logic. In so doing, they offer but an illusion of real change. In fact, envisaging themselves marginalized, they unwittingly confirm the existence of an oppressive center. They reinscribe the status quo allowing it to be captured by the male-stream ideology, which so gladly welcomes change, immediately incorporating it, rendering it subordinate, making oppression become even more insidious. In Deleuze and Guattari's account, this power of reterritorialization of any potentially rebellious elements or factors by the advanced capitalistic and patriarchal regime testifies to its enormous flexibility and pliability and posits great, yet well-masked, peril to any return of the repressed groups and members of society. Hence, there is the necessity of going beyond the representational logic that makes of both men and women the victims of ideology, and of liberation of pure and unrepressed energy (desire) in a schizophrenic fashion, which translates into—in lieu of negation—a multiplication and proliferation of different differences. Going beyond representation essentially entails leaving all transcendent legacies behind (i.e., "negativity of power," notion of "subjectivity"). Epistemologically, this amounts to moving both beyond the reductionism of social constructivism which, to a large extent, remains reliant upon already constituted social categories such as "gender," "sex," or "race," and simultaneously beyond any sort or brand of essentialism. The former runs the risk of essentializing "construction" whereas the latter, thanks to its astonishing resiliency, poses great danger of recollapsing into the logic of the negative. It, therefore, means going beyond "gender," going beyond "femininity" and "masculinity," for these preclude, affirmatively, that is nondualistically, thinking difference. Pluralization of the previous categories also proves politically insufficient, precisely in that different masculinities or femininities presuppose prior dualistic positioning; pluralities can only derive from, and be a multiplication of, the original, in Deleuze's language, *molar* two. For genuine critique to happen, one must not commit the Kantian error, which Deleuze exposes as that which compromised totality and success of Kant's critical project. Deleuze evinces, "It begins by believing in what it criticizes" (1983, p. 90). It barely comes as a surprise that if one commences by simply depicting what one encounters in the social, empirical, or even in men or women—ideologically or historically—without first submitting the very logic we utilize to critique, one must by implication fall into the same trap. Advised of Nietzsche's successful avoidance of Kantian error in his critique of the *value* of value,[11] one must descend into the molecular prepersonal level[12] and renounce identity-based categories if one wants to fight social-material inequalities. Only difference disengaged from the negativistic framework can provide us a novel, affirmative, and creative figuration of men and women, indeed, of life and thought. Deleuze and Guattari, in their collaborative two-volume work *Capitalism and Schizophrenia*, propose such a novel manner of thinking, being, and difference.

Back in the 1960s, when everyone on the waves of the cultural-sexual revolution was immersed in reading Marx and Reich, Deleuze turned to Spinoza and Nietzsche, not out of will to contest but very purposefully. He chose the ones who went the farthest in rejecting any transcendence, thus releasing the greatest potential for thought. Realizing how rapidly freed desire can be captured and reterritorialized, Deleuze knows it cannot be left all by itself. A decisive action needed to be immediately undertaken to help it accomplish a total critique and thus bring a complete social liberation. In so doing, he rejected the category of "identity" as a core set of attributes, unvarying across time and space, such as a "natural" sex drive or gender-linked propensity to be aggressive or care. In light of this, essence, which is the end product of the logic of sameness, exhibits nothing more than the sedimentation of repeated habits; put differently, the repetition of familiar gestures is socially encouraged over experimentation and risk. Thus, ontological dispersion, equivocity, polymorphousness, and difference have been encapsulated in a pessimistic and totalizing conception of being. This highly restrictive and oppressive notion, by grounding itself in the transcendental, religious, or metaphysical, finds justification only in the void of mysticism, or that of democracy, with the aid of their apparatuses of capture and phallic oppression. It is high time the creative potential of thought and being were liberated from the confines of the pervasive, idealizing, and Oedipalizing machinery of philosophy and society. This machinery, which views the world as mere appearance, institutes an indisputable subordination to transcendentally established values and morals and therefore precludes thinking beings in all their difference and multiplicity. Thinking, then, still depends on representational reactive forces that abduct thought. Deleuze flatly states that so long as thought remains an instrument of dualistic representation, we are not yet thinking (1983). Thinking difference within the representational framework of thought proves ineffective by virtue of its subordination to the dialectical twist, which fuels the resiliency of metaphysics. As Michael Hardt remarks,

> Hegelianism is probably the most difficult of adversaries because it possesses such an extraordinary capacity to recuperate opposition. The dialectical negation is always directed toward the miracle of resurrection. (1993, p. XI)

Hegel himself astutely says, "It is a negation which supersedes in such a way as to preserve and maintain what is superseded, and consequently survives its own supersession" (1977, §188).[13] Hence, here is the importance of Nietzsche and his philosophy for Deleuze's project of going beyond, "overcoming" the reactive and restrictive structures. To postulate liberating difference, or rather difference as liberation, is pointless in this dialectical bind; it will always appear not feasible, untranslatable into praxis. Difference thus construed tends to be liberating seemingly only for the benefit of malevolent and dreadful subaltern forces, unleashed orgiastic sexuality, a threat to order, bringing chaos and anomy (return of the repressed).

If one thinks of entire Western "dogma of transcendence,"[14] as Deleuze and Guattari suggest, as a simple reduction or inability to account for life-multiplicity, then the whole metaphysical (masculine) endeavor emerges only as an attempt, one amidst many, which failed. It signals the debacle of a certain conception of the human subject, a figuration that might have been applicable and adequate at best to a fraction of the population—mostly men—who were opulent and powerful enough and also had sufficient leisure to theorize themselves as autonomous beings exercising their ostensibly free will through agency and choice. It is a flight from the anthropo/ (andro)centric, anthropomorphic discourses that constitute the doctrinal groundwork of the phallogocentric regime. All there is, and always has been, is productive difference; yet no longer assigned to being or subject (transcendence), thus trapped within the negative. On the contrary, difference—being affirmation of creative power—encompasses everything, an immanence of difference, difference-immanence, difference that is being. This allows Deleuze and Guattari firmly to state, "There is no ideology, and never has been" (2004b, p. 5), in that such an understanding of power assumes its intrinsically negative (reactive) status. This vehement rejection of the negative is crucial for the project of an immanent critique, one which prevents one from committing "Kantian error." Therefore, one can only speak of men and women as living multiplicities encountering—becoming—other multiplicities, continually interacting, forming relations with them, perceptibly or abstractly (imperceptibly), affecting and being affected.

CONCLUSIONS

This highly complicated and complex system of thought emerges as one capable of accounting for the phenomenon of life, life no longer held in service of thought, its object of investigation, but life as a subject of enquiry, life as thought, a true immanence. "Gender," then, stands for an ideological concept, deriving from the system of social-material oppression, a category that might be substituted for men and women theorized as open systems, as multiplicities. Difference can no longer be dialectical, ruthlessly reduced to two: two beings with two oppositional clusters of bodily features and accoutrements, ways of thinking, social behaviors attributed to them on whatever basis, be it ontological, biological, social, or psychological. For Deleuze and Guattari, the human subject becomes dispersed in a multitude of active and affective molecules and particles, intensities. Therefore, the notion of "human sciences," as Braidotti pointedly remarks, for the authors of *A Thousand Plateaus* is nonsensical (1991, p. 127). Following this line of thought, study of this subject is a question of dispersing a molar/moral system (identity) into a myriad of varied forces, which continually traverse and affect it, itself being but a more consolidated body of these forces, and not a separate and unitary entity. It assumes a joyous determinism, a Nietzschean *amor fati* that brings liberation and freedom through multiplication; in the language of Deleuze and Guattari, "Social production is never anything other than desiring production, and *vice versa*" (2004a, p. 413). Civilization therefore does not rest, as Freud wanted us to believe, upon the repression of the libidinal economy of our bodies, but on the contrary, it is the very production thereof (2004a, p. 387).

Read with Deleuze's Nietzsche, all these contemporary returns of the socially, thus also individually, repressed phenomena display a creative potential of forces within the field of social desire. Every profound movement in society originates from escape, *"line of flight,"* and not from antagonisms or contradictions between some rigid or ossified structures. The clash, or better clashes, can no longer be conceived of in a dialectical, Oedipalizing fashion, and remain stuck in the representational state system, which, disturbed by creative movements within the social field, desperately seeks self-legitimization. In so doing, it contributes hugely to enclosing ontological dispersion in the logic of sameness and submission, castrating and forcing it to obey the rules of the dominant masculine mode of thought. The politics of difference as envisaged by Deleuze and Guattari not only provides a toolbox for making war on the state ideology endorsed by philosophical systems, but above all succeeds in recognizing and appreciating the singularity of being, each being in all their multiplicity, all their difference.

To commence thinking truly differently, both men and women need a change of logic that necessarily entails, I argue, change of ontology. Both have to proceed intertwined to produce a veritable ontology of change. This has already emerged as an ethical-political task for which we should think of ways to implement.

NOTES

1. I borrow this expression from Rosi Braidotti.
2. "Essence is difference." This is the central idea of Deleuze's *Difference and repetition* (New York: Columbia University Press, 1994). It is already anticipated in an important passage of his *Proust and signs* (London: Continuum, 2000, pp. 48–49)
3. I follow Luce Irigaray in her understanding and application of the adjective "feminine." In her account, it does not refer to the dominant (masculine) conception of femininity; rather, it is an implementation of Irigaray's strategic essentialism (mimesis) to retrieve the senses and values of the words male discourse has appropriated. By "feminine," she means *authentically* feminine, no longer the *other* of the same (male), but the genuine *other* of the "Other," denoting pure difference.
4. Deleuze, G., (1983). *Nietzsche and philosophy*. New York: Columbia University Press, p. 189. Deleuze follows Nietzsche in his understanding of being as becoming; the being of becoming is returning.
5. Deleuze, G., (1983). *Nietzsche and philosophy* New York: Columbia University Press, pp. 156–157.
6. Heidegger, M. (1998). *Nietzsche*. Warszawa: Wydawnictwo Naukowe PAN; Horkheimer, M., & Adorno, T. W., (1994). *Dialektyka o wiecenia* (M. Łukasiewicz, Trans.).Warszawa: Wydawnictwo Naukowe PAN.
7. I borrow this conceptual formulation from Brian Massumi's reading of Gilles Deleuze's philosophy; Massumi, B. (2002). *The parables of the virtual: Movement, affect, sensation.* Durham & London: Duke University Press, p. 5. Originally, it derives from the work of Michel Foucault.
8. Hence, this is Deleuze's critique of Kant's transcendental method and reconceptualization of his theory of sensibility in terms of "transcendental empiricism". In lieu of assuming an accord of the faculties, ensured by the identity of the transcendental subject, which makes recognition a dominant image of thought, Deleuze allows their difference and proposes a higher form of empiricism that goes beyond common sense (objects of recognition). Transcendental sensibility can only be sensed (theory of encounters/signs) with no detour through a subject. See Deleuze, G. (1984). *Kant's critical philosophy: The doctrine of the faculties.* London: Athlone Press & Minneapolis: University of Minnesota Press.
9. Here, I am in concord with Moira Gatens, who discovers in Deleuze's philosophical endeavor the possibility of going beyond a crude distinction

between metaphysical oppositions, that of materialism and idealism. "Historical materialist approaches mistake the material for a definitive cause of thought or consciousness, while political voluntarism mistakes consciousness for a causal site of material change." See Gatens, M. (1996). Through a Spinozist lens: Ethology, difference, power. In *Deleuze. a critical reader* (P. Patton, Ed., pp. 162–187. Oxford: Blackwell Publishers.

10. Poststructuralist attacks leveled against the humanistic identitarian logic, exposing the subject as a mere "fiction added to the deed" (Nietzsche) and— predominantly out of Foucauldian inspiration—proposing a constructionist view of power and subjectivity, in my view, do not go far enough. I endorse Massumi's appeal to return to nature, its radically vitalist reconceptualization as productive of the real (hence in Massumi's terms, "productivism precedes construction"): "*Ideas about cultural or social construction have dead-ended because they have insisted on bracketing the nature of the process. If you elide nature, you miss the becoming of culture, its emergence (not to mention the history of matter"*; Massumi, B. (2002). *The parables of the virtual:. Movement, affect, sensation*. Durham & London: Duke University Press, p. 12.

11. In Deleuze's view, it is Friedrich Nietzsche and his genealogical method that sought to radicalize and extend Kantian critique. Nietzsche's objection was directed to its partial success. On Nietzsche's account, Kant did not accomplish, as he intended, total critique in that he failed to pursue the critique to the point at which it would become a genuine critique of values. As Deleuze asseverates, it is Nietzsche who departs by first submitting the very origin (value) of value to scrutiny.

12. This is precisely what Deleuze's "transcendental empiricism" accounts for.

13. This quotation comes from Hegel, G. W. F. (1977). *Phenomenology of spirit*. Oxford: Oxford University Press.

14. Deleuze follows Michel Foucault's description of the Western tradition of thought as a "subjection to transcendence." See Foucault, M., (1972). *The archeology of knowledge and the discourse on language*. New York: Pantheon, p. 203; and Deleuze, G., & Guattari, F. (2004b). *A thousand plateaus. Capitalism and schizophrenia*. London: Continuum, p. 20.

REFERENCES

Appadurai, A. (1994). Disjuncture and difference in the global cultural economy. In P. Williams & L. Chrisman (Eds.), *Colonial discourse and post-colonial theory*. New York: Columbia University Press.

Braidotti, R. (1996). *Patterns of dissonance*. Cambridge: Polity Press.

———. (2002). *Metamorphoses: Towards a materialist theory of becoming*. Cambridge: Polity Press.

Colebrook, C. (2000). Incorporeality: The ghostly body of metaphysics. *Body and Society*, 6(2), 25–44.

———. (2002). *Gilles Deleuze*. London and New York: Routledge.

Deleuze, G. (1983). *Nietzsche and philosophy*. New York: Columbia University Press.

———. (1984). *Kant's critical philosophy: The doctrine of the faculties*. London: Athlone Press and Minneapolis: University of Minnesota Press.

———. (1994). *Difference and repetition*. New York: Columbia University Press.

———. (2001). Dualism, monism and multiplicities (desire-pleasure-jouissance). Seminar of March 26, 1973, Online Journal of Philosophy *Contretemps*, 2(05) 95. Retrieved August 4, 2006, from http://www.usyd.edu.au/contretemps/2may2001/deleuze.pdf

Deleuze, G., & Guattari, F. (2004a). *Anti-Oedipus*. London & New York: Continuum.

———. (2004b). *A thousand plateaus*. London & New York: Continuum.

Fukuyama, F. (2002). *Our posthuman future*. London: Profile Books.

Gatens, M. (1996). Through a Spinozist lens: Ethology, difference, power. In P. Patton (Ed.), *Deleuze: A critical reader* (pp. 162–187). Oxford: Blackwell.

Giroux, H. (1993). Postmodernism as border pedagogy: Redefining the boundaries of race and ethnicity. In Natoli & Hutcheon (Eds.), *A postmodern reader*. Albany, NY: SUNY Press.

Hardt, M. (1993). *Gilles Deleuze: An apprenticeship in philosophy*. Minnesota: University of Minnesota Press.

Irigaray, L. (1999). When our lips speak together. In J. Prince & M. Shildrick (Eds.), *Feminist theory and the body: A reader* (pp. 82–90). New York: Routledge.

Lyotard, J. F. (1984). *The postmodern condition: A report on knowledge*. Manchester: Manchester University Press.

Massumi, B.(2002). *The parables of the virtual. Movement, affect, sensation*. Durham and London: Duke University Press.

Part II

Negotiating Citizenship

Gender, Sexuality, Politics

4 (Trans)Forming Gender
Social Change and Transgender Citizenship

Sally Hines

INTRODUCTION

This chapter aims to contribute to recent sociological debates about gendered identity constructions and formations, and gendered and sexual citizenship, by exploring citizenship debates within the context of the gender transformations of trans women and men. "Transgender" is an umbrella term, which includes transgender, transsexual, bigendered, and intersex people, transvestites, cross-dressers, and drag kings and queens. "Transsexual" refers to people who change their anatomical sex through hormones and/or surgery. In this study, the terms "trans" and "transgender" apply to individuals who have changed their bodies through the use of hormones and/or surgery as well as those who have not.

First, I map the ways in which transgender has emerged as a subject of increasing social and cultural interest in recent years. This section initially charts the "cultural turn" to transgender and moves on to address how shifting attitudes toward transgender people are evident through recent legislative changes in the United Kingdom brought by the *Gender Recognition Act* (GRA; 2005). Representing the civil recognition of gender transition, the GRA marks an important change in attitudes toward trans people, enabling the change of birth certificates and granting the right to marry. I suggest that these social, cultural, and legislative developments reflect the ways in which gender diversity is acquiring visibility in contemporary United Kingdom society. The chapter will question, however, a linear reading, which positions these moves as evidence that gender diverse people *as a whole* are experiencing greater levels of social inclusion.

The second part of the chapter develops this argument by examining transgender citizenship. This section first addresses conceptual understandings of citizenship, and moves on to explore how issues pertinent to transgender citizenship are "medicalized," "claimed," and "transgressed." The study argues that transgender citizenship is both an uneven and contested terrain. I suggest that while some new forms of (trans) femininities and masculinities are benefiting from recent policy developments, other experiences and practices of gender transformation remain marginalized.

METHODOLOGY

Substantively, this chapter draws on up-to-date empirical research to examine how issues central to recent policy developments are understood and experienced by trans men and women in the United Kingdom. Inversion was completed at the University of Leeds between 2000 and 2004 as part of the ESRC research project "Care, Values and the Future of Welfare" (CAVA). The aims of the inquiry were to examine individual and collective transgender practices of identity and intimacy. Data was generated through two-stage in-depth interviews with 30 trans men (13) and women (17) in the United Kingdom over a 9-month period in 2002. Participants were at different stages of transition, and the sample included people who use hormone therapy and/or a range of surgical modifications as well as those who reject such interventions. Whereas some subjects chose to use their own names, others adopted pseudonyms. Interviews took between 1 and 2 hours, mostly in participants' homes.

Interviews were used to explore the social world of participants (Blaikie, 2000). Rather than approaching the interview method as a means to a "fixed" text, which reveals "true" meaning, I followed Plummer (1995) in viewing narratives as socially constructed and socio-historically specific. I was influenced by Hollway and Jefferson's (2000) "narrative approach," which moves beyond a "question and answer" interview style and allows the interviewer to respond flexibly to the narrator. One of the central characteristics is that questions are open-ended so that "stories" may be told. In the course of the research, I asked people about some of the most intimate aspects of their lives, including sexuality, bodily changes, and surgery, as well as close relationships, which, for some, touched on difficult experiences with friends, families, partners, and children. Ethical considerations were thus paramount throughout the investigation. I followed Hollway and Jefferson's criteria for social researchers in which "the ethical principles of honesty, sympathy and respect would be central" (2000, p. 102). I was aware that the particularly sensitive nature of dealing with transgender issues required that I remain "extra aware" of such considerations. Transphobia leads to violence, hostility, and the loss of jobs, homes, and custody of children. Although all participants were open about their identities to some extent (if they had not been, they would not have agreed to be involved in the research), this differed in degrees. On the ethics of researching transgender, I was influenced by Griggs (1998) and Cromwell (1999) who stress the importance of avoiding misrepresentation; in addition, Hale (1997) offers guidelines to a nontransgender person carrying out work on this topic.

As a nontransgender researcher, I had anticipated difficulty in gaining access to subjects. This, however, was not the case, and I was unable to interview all who volunteered. The large response led me to wonder and ask, why the willingness to participate. The most common reason concerned the social awareness of transgender issues and experiences. Their representation—especially in popular media and journalism—was associated with misconceptions of "who" these individuals "were" and, in turn, with discrimination on both a social (i.e., hostility on the street) and a political (i.e., lack of legal recognition of gender of choice) level. Involvement in the research was linked to dynamics of social and political change, as participants cited cases of "speaking out" and trying to "put the record straight." Here we can see an understanding of knowledge as a vehicle for social change. This connects with Plummer's (1995) discussion of storytelling as a political process and illustrates how it may be used by previously disenfranchised communities to assert their growing strength. In this way, it is significant that the timing of the research coincided with initial legislative proposals representing the civil recognition of transgender people. Plummer's model for understanding the social construction of storytelling incorporates the "cultural and historical level," which denotes the specific historical moment in which a narrative is told and heard. Plummer notes that "many stories are in silence—dormant, awaiting their historical moment" (1995, p. 35). Perhaps the large response to this project, then, can be seen as an indication that the "historical moment" has arrived for some transgender individuals.

My position as a nontransgender researcher will have affected the outcome of the research, although it is not possible to know to what extent. Common experiences between researcher and participants have been seen to affect positively the levels of trust in an interview, and thus significantly to impact the emerging data (Dunne, 1997; Oakley, 2000). A transgender investigator may have benefited from an "insider" position to build confidence with potential subjects. This could have given her/him access to people who might not have replied to my requests for participants, which clearly stated my position as a nontransgender person. A transgender researcher might also have had "inside" knowledge, which could have led her/him to ask different questions. Two personal contacts were invaluable in providing a "way in," on occasions when I directly contacted particular interviewees, thus acting as a starting point for the development of trust in these instances. Weeks, Heaphy, and Donovan, (2001) importantly caution against overemphasizing areas of commonality between respondents and researchers, and follow Edwards (1993) and Song and Parker (1995) in addressing how other differences are always at play. Yet, I recognize that the inquiry can only be a partial study and that my nontransgender status (as it affected the research design as well as the research process itself) is built into that partiality.

THE TURN TO TRANSGENDER

The Cultural Turn

In recent years, transgender has emerged as a subject of increasing social and cultural interest. Popular representations of it are apparent in drama, sitcom, and reality television, whereas the "trans confessional" is a chat show staple. Tabloid journalists and magazine feature writers increasingly search for trans people for "real life" stories, and television documentary and broadsheet journalism has focused upon the experiences of both female and male trans people. Transgender characters have had central roles in several mainstream films, and on-stage cross-dressing performers such as Eddie Izzard, Lilly Savage, and RuPaul draw large audiences. Although I do not wish to overprioritize the political significance of such cultural representations—and indeed many barely move beyond stereotypes—yet they can indicate how minority gender and sexual identities are able to shift to some degree beyond their marginalized status. In 2004, for example, artist Grayson Perry won the Turner Prize for his multimedia artwork, which explores his transvestite persona, Claire. In the same year, the most wide-reaching cultural representation of transgender arose from the reality television show *Big Brother 5*, whose housemate and winner was 27-year-old trans woman Nadia Almada. In and out of the *Big Brother* house, Almada received extensive television and newspaper coverage, leading *Observer* columnist Barbara Ellen to comment, "The triumph of a Portuguese transgender woman in the nation's greatest unofficial popularity contest threw up important questions about Britain today. Are attitudes shifting? Is there a greater tolerance and broadmindedness, at least among the nation's youth?"(2004).

For Christine Burns of transgender political lobbying group and educational organization *Press for Change* (PfC), Almada has emerged as an unlikely role model, "I never in my wildest dreams imagined that after all these years it would be a big-breasted golden-hearted Portuguese nicotine junkie who really turned people's ideas about us upside down" (2004). Similarly, Lynne Jones, MP and Chair of the *Parliamentary Forum on Transsexualism*, says, "The Big Brother result indicates people haven't got the kind of prejudices that would in the past have prevented them voting for a transsexual housemate. They're just voting for her as a woman in her own right. The fact of her being transsexual is not important" (2004). Both Burns and Jones optimistically suggest a cultural sea-change in attitudes toward transgender people. Against the backdrop of the *Gender Recognition Act* (GRA), then, it might be tempting to deduce that citizenship rights for trans men and women have now been gained.

The Legislative Turn

Before the *Gender Recognition Act* (2005), Britain was one out of four European countries that failed legally to recognize the acquired gender of transsexual people (Whittle, 2000, p. 44). In enabling trans people to change their birth certificates and to marry, the GRA marks a dramatic shift in socio-legal attitudes. Read alongside the cultural milieu, the GRA suggests that gender diversity is acquiring visibility in contemporary society.

This has been welcomed by transgender organizations and individuals as a marker of increased tolerance. PfC was instrumental in setting up the cross-party *Parliamentary Forum on Transsexualism* and, for a decade, worked closely with government on drafting and amending the bill. For PfC, the GRA is highly significant; "The Gender Recognition Act is a crucial step towards ending 33 years of social exclusion for trans people in the U.K." (www.pfc.org.uk homepage). Indeed, for many trans people, the GRA is momentous, as the following quotation from a letter posted on PfC's website testifies, "This morning I received an envelope containing a document, which I have been longing for over a length of time bordering forty years. To say that I am happy is the understatement of the century. . ." (www.pfc.org.uk).

Although I do not wish to diminish the significance of the GRA, unpacking current debates about transgender citizenship calls for caution against a perceived trajectory of progress in relation to (trans) gender transformation and social change. Normative binary understandings of gender that underpin the legislation mean that some trans people are excluded from these new citizenship rights, while others remain unrecognized. Moreover, debates around the desirability of assimilation suggest that understandings and experiences of social citizenship are complexly situated.

CONCEPTUALIZING CITIZENSHIP

The concept of citizenship gained academic capital during the 1980s and 1990s and was articulated as a means through which to stress the importance of political activity (Phillips, 1993). It has been broadly defined as the collection of rights and responsibilities that establish political membership and enable access to benefits and resources (Turner & Hamilton, 1994). Although dominant Western notions of citizenship have traditionally followed a liberal model in which individual rights are stressed alongside minimum state intervention and market freedom (Marshall, 1950), it is a contested concept, which is culturally and historically specific. While neo-conservatives argue that the balance between rights and duties is weighted too heavily in favor of the former, radical critics have variously pointed to how the rights of dominant social groups are protected at the expense of marginal ones (Turner & Hamilton, 1994).

Such perspectives stress the need to broaden the concept of "citizenship" to take greater account of minority groups' social position. Work on citizenship and ethnicity (Back & Solomos, 2000; Lewis, 1998), for example, has illustrated how traditional models of the former have failed to acknowledge ethnicity and nationality. Meanwhile, feminist study on the same topic has drawn attention to the ways in which women's interests have been neglected by a traditional model of citizenship, which focused upon the "private" (paid labor) rather than the "personal" (domestic), thus marginalizing women's interests in the latter—for example, in unpaid caring work (Lister, 1997). Feminist scholars have challenged traditional assumptions of the citizen as male (Bussemaker & Voet, 1998; Daly & Cowen, 2000; Lister, 1997; Pateman, 1989; Walby, 1994). Lister (1997) draws attention to the ambiguities of citizenship for feminism—on the one hand, citizenship offers the possibility of universal rights, which are central to feminist goals, yet on the other, women historically have been excluded from such debates, and inequalities remain. As Monro argues,

> Inequalities persist despite support for formal equality in many countries, partly because mainstream notions of citizenship continue to be based on implicit assumptions that citizenship means the same thing for women and men, masking differences in their interests. Current notions of citizenship still hide gender inequality. (2005, p. 150)

Writers within sexuality studies (Bell & Binnie, 2000; Cooper, 1995; Evans, 1993; Plummer, 1995; Richardson, 1998, 2000; Seidman, 1996; Weeks, 1995, 1998; Weeks et al., 2004) have also addressed how traditional models of citizenship mask difference, in this instance to marginalize the experiences and discriminate against the rights of those who variously live outside the hetero norm. Thus, traditional notions of citizenship imply heterosexuality so that the domain of citizenship itself is heterosexualized (Richardson, 1998). The concept of "sexual citizenship" has been developed to draw attention to sexuality, which has been excluded from the "public" notion of citizenship. In the first discussion of this idea, Evans (1993) maps the relationship between sexuality, morality, and the capitalist market. He argues that the process of "consumer citizenship" enables capitalism to detach morality from legality. In order for the state to reap benefits from the economic power held by some sexual minority groups, for example, middle-class gay men, legal rights are granted at the expense of political. For Evans, "consumer citizenship" has led to the commodification of sexuality, which loses its political edge through the branding of sexual identity as "lifestyle." While the "male homosexual citizen" holds economic rights, he remains an "immoral" citizen. Moreover, sexual minorities who hold few obvious material assets, for example, bisexuals and transvestites, are marginalized and granted neither economical nor political citizenship (Evans, 1993).

For Richardson (2000a), the notion of sexual citizenship articulates sexual alongside wider rights and their impact on sexuality in recognition of sexual minorities. Weeks (1998), meanwhile, contextualizes the same concept in relation to broader social shifts, identifying the prerequisite of sexual citizenship as respect for diversity and consideration of minority groups claims. He positively suggests that these requirements are in sight, pointing to the democratization of sexual relationships, an increased reflexivity about sexuality, and the emergence of new sexual subjectivities in contemporary society. Others, however, are less optimistic. Richardson argues that the granting of lesbian and gay rights leads to the privatization and circumscription of these sexual identities, "lesbians and gay men are granted the right to be tolerated as long as they stay within the boundaries of that tolerance. . ." (1989, p. 90). Since notions of citizenship are heterosexualized, such boundaries of tolerance depend on rights based claims (such as the right to marry), which fit with this particular model of the "good citizen." For this reason, Stychin points to the perils of articulating homosexual rights through the concept of citizenship, ". . . lesbians and gays seeking rights may embrace an ideal of 'respectability,' a construction that then perpetuates a division between 'good gays' and (disreputable) 'bad queers'" (Stychin, 1998, 2000). It is the latter who are excluded from notions of citizenship. Similarly, Bell and Binnie (2000) posit that sexual citizenship implies a set of "rights based" claims, for example, that of lesbians and gay men to marry and to serve in the military, which, in turn, entails a set of duties, notably assimilation. This constructs a binary between the "good homosexual" (the assimilator) and the "bad homosexual" (the dissident), with the former being granted citizenship. "The effect of this maneuver on activist strategies can be to surrender some 'rights' for the sake of others. This means that agitating under the banner of sexual citizenship is always going to involve potential compromise" (Bell, 2004, p. 204). Bell and Binnie propose "queering" citizenship to acknowledge and celebrate the ways in which nonnormative sexual practices and arrangements (e.g., nonmonogamy) challenge the institution of heterosexuality and traditional conceptualizations of citizenship.

A further way in which the relationship between sexuality and citizenship has been considered is through the notion of "intimate citizenship" (Plummer, 1995; Weeks, 1998; Weeks et al., 2001), which offers a framework for discussing rights and responsibilities emerging from the diversification of intimate life. Plummer (1995) defines "intimate citizenship" as the rights concerning people's choices about their bodies, emotions, relationships, and desires, and proposes adding "intimate citizenship" to the traditional models of political, social, and civil rights. For Weeks, intimate citizenship concerns "those matters which relate to our most intimate desires, pleasures and ways of being in the world" (1998, p. 121).

Work on feminist, sexual, and intimate citizenship has addressed how traditional definitions and requirements of citizenship have neglected the complex features of gender and sexuality (Richardson, 2000a). Broadening the notion of citizenship in this way enables the recognition of difference and problematizes the public/private dichotomy. Yet, this research largely assumes a gender binary, which acknowledges only male and female categories. Significantly, Monro (2003, 2005) has brought to light the ways in which existing models of citizenship function within such a gender binary system. This model of citizenship has discriminated against gender diverse people in terms of the "public" (employment and welfare rights) and "private" (the rights of self-identification regarding gender of choice and partnership recognition). The GRA is important in enabling such processes of self-identification. Additionally, employment and welfare rights for trans people increasingly occupy a place on the public agenda. Such moves represent a dramatic shift in conceptual understandings of "gender" as distinct from "sex" (Butler, 1994), and indicate how feminist scholarship has entered the mainstream public and political agenda. Rather than biological "sex" being the fixed marker of identity, "gender" recognizes that identity is more fluidly experienced and articulated. However, while the structural framework of the gender binary model of citizenship has flexed to concede that a person may change her/his gender, the male/female poles of the edifice remain firmly intact. The effects of this bear down not only on the rights afforded to gender-different people but also on a more profound level, which impacts self-identification. As I explore next, a gender binary model of citizenship continues to marginalize both the experiences and subjectivities of those who cannot or will not be defined as "man" or "woman," and, as such, is unable to account for the full spectrum of gender diversity.

MEDICALIZING TRANSGENDER

Medical and psychological studies have constructed particular ways of thinking about gender diversity, which continue to inform social, cultural, and legal understandings of transgender. The theoretical shifts that accompanied the increasing acceptance of reconstructive surgery from the late 1950s onwards strengthened the role of the medical practitioner. Benjamin's *Transsexual Phenomenon* (1966), Stoller's *Sex Reassignment* (1968), and Green and Money's *Transsexualism and Sex Reassignment* (1969) introduced the notion of "gender" into discourses of transsexuality, and "gender" came to be recognized independently of "sex." As Ekins and King explain, "If gender is immutable, even though psychologically produced, and if harmony between sex and gender is a precondition of psychic comfort and social acceptability, it 'makes sense' to achieve harmony by altering the body" (1996, p. 94). Thus it was believed that surgery enabled the "true" self to emerge and most practitioners aligned with this narrative. From the early 1970s, the concept of "gender dysphoria" was developed in medical writing. It suggests that those seeking hormone therapy or surgery have been born, and so are living in the "wrong" body.

By the late 1970s, surgical procedures had become the orthodox method of "treatment" for gender dysphoria (Cromwell, 1999). Contemporary medical perspectives continue along a biologically based line, as the 1996 report for the United Kingdom *Parliamentary Forum on Transsexualism* illustrates. "The weight of current scientific evidence suggests a biologically based, multifactoral aetiology for transsexualism" (Transsexualism: The Current Medical Viewpoint, 1996). Although later medical insights represent a more complex understanding of transgender practices than were offered within founding medical perspectives, there remain serious problems in the correlation of transgender and biological or psychological pathology. The epistemological power of medical discourse has thus worked to structure specific aetiologies of transgenderism. Significantly, the concept of "gender dysphoria" remains a key classificatory term within medical discourse and practice. The GRA marks a major shift in sociolegal understandings of "gender" as distinct from "sex" and, importantly, gender reassignment surgery is not a requirement to gender recognition. Yet, the Act is shaped by a medical perspective of transgender, which privileges a connective relationship between gender identity and body parts and presentation. PfC's advice on seeking gender recognition under the GRA states,

> If you can demonstrate reasonable evidence that you have undergone "surgical treatment" for the purpose of modifying sexual characteristics (i.e., surgery to alter the shape and function of genitals) then this is by far the easiest way to apply. . . . The alternative way in which the law allows an application to be accepted by the panel is if you can provide evidence of having being diagnosed with "gender dysphoria." (www. PfC.org.uk)

From its inception in the 1970s, then, the concept of "gender dysphoria" has guided understandings of, and practices toward, transgender. Therefore, it is not surprising that its central tenet—dissonance between sex (the body) and gender identity (the mind)—figures large in many trans narratives. Research participant Bernadette reflected this in reply to my question, "what are the most important changes transition has brought?"

> Before I transitioned, I had become terrified of mirrors. I couldn't look at myself. I was absolutely horrified looking at myself and this was completely resolved. . . . These are the things which have changed, and made me feel what I am. They are the external manifestations that balance. (Bernadette, age 71)

Corresponding with the concept of "gender dysphoria," Bernadette positions her pretransition body as the "wrong" vehicle in which her essential self was trapped. Surgical "correction" is subsequently related as the means through which her authentic gender is released. In her discussion of MtF autobiography, Stone shows how accounts of the wrong body lie at the heart of many personal accounts of transition.

> They go from being unambiguous men, albeit unhappy men, to unambiguous women. There is no territory between. Further, each constructs a specific narrative moment when their personal sexual identification

changes from male to female. This moment is the moment of neocol-
porraphy—that is, of gender reassignment or "sex change surgery."
(Stone, 1991, p. 286)

Such an account is oppositional to a poststructuralist framework and to
queer theory, in which all gender and sexual identities are denaturalized
and notions of authenticity deconstructed. Much debate within transgender studies has been concerned with addressing the contradictions between
a deconstructionist analysis of transgender and the representation of a fixed
identity within many transgender autobiographies. Thus a key question for
Prosser (1998) is how to theorize sex, gender, and identity in the light of
continued transsexual demand for reconstructive surgery. He suggests that
the "wrong body" narrative reflects a genuine transsexual emotion, which
he discusses as the desire for an embodied "home."

My contention is that transsexuals continue to deploy the image of
wrong embodiment because *being trapped in the wrong body is simply
what transsexuality feels like.* If the goal of transsexual transition is to
align the feeling of gendered embodiment with the material body, body
image—which we might be tempted to align with the imaginary—clearly
already has a material force for transsexuals. The image of being trapped
in the wrong body conveys this force. It suggests how body image is radically split off from the material body in the first place, how body image can
feel sufficiently substantial as to persuade the transsexual to alter his or her
body to conform to it. The image of wrong embodiment describes most
effectively the experience of pretransition (dis)embodiment: the feeling of
a sexed body dysphoria profoundly and subjectively experienced (Prosser,
1998, p. 69, my emphasis).

Yet, it has been widely acknowledged that, in order to gain access to hormone therapy or surgical procedures, trans people frequently reproduce the
officially sanctioned aetiology of transsexualism, that of gender dysphoria
(Bolin, 1998; Cromwell, 1999; Green, 1987; Hausman, 1995; Stone, 1991).
Indeed, in the 1970s, Stoller acknowledged this process, remarking, "Those
of us faced with the task of diagnosing transsexualism have an additional
burden these days, for most patients requesting 'sex change' are in complete
command of the literature and know the answers before the questions are
asked" (1975, p. 248). Subsequently, medical professionals have suggested
that trans people may "distort their autobiographies (and) tend to be less
than honest about their personal histories" (Lothstein, quoted in Cromwell,
1999, p. 124). As Stone remarks, "This raises several sticky questions, the
chief two being: Who is telling the story for whom, and how do the storytell-
ers differentiate between the story they tell and the story they hear?" (1991,
p. 291). Thus, the "wrong body" narrative may be seen to be medically constructed and internalized as a means to an end, "The idea has been imposed
upon transpeople by those who control access to medical technologies and
have controlled discourses about transpeople. Some individuals may believe

or come to believe that they are in the wrong body or at least use language that imparts the same meaning. . ." (Cromwell, 1999, p. 104). In the following quotation from our interview, Gabrielle illustrates how this process may work,

> G: If you see a doctor for an hour once every three months and they go "how are you?" and you go "I'm fine". And they go "any issues?" you go "no". 'Cos you want what they've got to give you and so you quickly learn the script as people call it, for what you should say and not say. And I think people buy into that, people do say these things that the doctors need to hear to tick off on the form to make you eligible.
>
> S: And what are those things?
>
> G: "I'm a woman trapped in a man's body" or "A man trapped in a woman's body".
>
> "I've known always", you know, those sort of things, the things that people say. (Gabrielle, age 45)

Gabrielle's narrative connects with Shapiro's argument that "One cannot take at face value transsexuals' own accounts of a fixed and unchanging (albeit sex-crossed) gender identity, given the immense pressure on them to produce the kinds of life histories that will get them what they want from the medical-psychiatric establishment" (quoted in Nataf, 1995, p. 19). The extent to which trans people continue to research diagnostic guidelines is illustrated in the Harry Benjamin *Standards of Care*, which formulate the "professional consensus about the psychiatric, psychological, medical, and surgical management of gender identity disorders" (Benjamin, 2001). The document details the means by which trans people may find "new gender adaptations" stating that "both genders may learn about 'transgender phenomena from studying these Standards of Care, relevant lay and professional literatures about legal rights pertaining to work, relationships, and public cross-dressing" (The Harry Benjamin International Gender Dysphoria Association's Standards of Care for Gender Identity Disorders, Version Six, 2001).

Questions about the impact of a medical model on trans subjectivities brings to mind Foucault's writing on the body, which is constructed through power, "The body is directly involved in a political field; power relations have an immediate hold upon it; they invest it, mark it, train it, torture it, force it to carry out tasks, to perform ceremonies, to emit signs" (Foucault, 1977, p. 25). Thus, subjects are produced *through* discourses of the body. Complicity with a medical model of transgender both supports and paradoxically challenges Foucault's notion of the "docile body," which is a "direct locus of control" produced by external power. Therefore the "wrong body" hypothesis can be seen as a discourse that produces its subject, the self-conscious repetition of this narrative can be read as an agency driven process whereby transpeople employ knowledge as power. Foucault's later work is more relevant to this interplay between structure and agency. In discussing "techniques of the self" (1985), he creates a space for agency by examining the relationship between external power and subjectivity. From this point, the notion of the "wrong body" can be conceptualized as a rehearsed narrative, which is consciously repeated as a means to an end. Yet such narratives are not only characteristic of transsexual stories, as Shapiro acknowledges,

> To take the problem one step further, the project of autobiographical reconstruction in which transsexuals are engaged, although more focused and motivated from the one that all of us peruse, is not entirely different in kind. We must all repress information that creates problems for culturally canonical narratives of identity and the self, and consistency in gender attribution is very much a part of this. (quoted in Nataf 1995, p. 19)

Stone argues that the "wrong body" narrative has led to the invisibility of transsexualism as an identity in itself, "The highest purpose of the transsexual is to erase him/her, to fade into the 'normal' as soon as possible. . . . What is gained is acceptability in society. What is lost is the ability to authentically represent the complexities and ambiguities of lived experience. . ." (1991, p. 295). She proposes that analyses of transgender move away from this paradigm in order to negotiate "the troubling and productive multiple permeabilities of boundary and subject positions that intertextuality implies" (Stone, 1991, p. 297). Halberstam also problematizes the "wrong body" diagnosis,

> Who, we might ask, can afford to dream of a right body? Who believes that such a body exists? Many bodies are gender strange to some degree or another, and it is time to complicate on the one hand the transsexual models that assign gender deviance only to transsexual bodies and gender normativity to all other bodies, and on the other hand the hetero-normative models that see transsexuality as the solution to gender deviance and homosexuality as a pathological perversion. (1998, pp. 154–155)

Halberstam argues that Prosser's analysis depends upon a strict demarcation of gender, "It relies on a belief in the two territories of male and female, divided by a flesh border and crossed between surgery and endocrinology" (Halberstam, 1998, p. 164). Prosser's focus may thus be critiqued for implying that all transsexual narratives are alike and, moreover, for denying instances of gender dysphoria within other subject positions (trans and nontrans). His emphasis may also work against the interests of transpeople by further pathologizing their "condition" through reinstating the duel categories of "wrong" (trans) and "right" (nontrans) bodies. For many participants in my research, the "wrong body" narrative was deeply unsatisfactory, and trans identification was discussed as a more complex and nuanced process. I asked Rebecca how she felt about the "wrong body" metaphor,

> It's [transition] been a progression. It's never been fixed from the outset and I've never had those overwhelming feelings of being in the wrong body. There's always been fluidity in my feelings. (Rebecca, age 55)

In the following quotation Amanda presents an explicit critique of the "wrong body" and, like Rebecca, suggests that gender transition is more complex than this metaphor indicates,

> The way in which some people talk about being born in the wrong body is such a cliché and to come back to components, we all have a male and a female component. . . . So "wrong body" that's a plumbing job. That's nothing to do with the core person I am, what makes me a person. (Amanda, age 45)

For these participants, gender identity formation is a nuanced process, which does not necessarily signify movement across a gender binary. In the following quotation Del, attempts to work through these complexities,

> . . . the wrong body stuff does bother me. I think a lot of it is that our culture is wrong, and if our culture was more accepting of gender diversity, would we need to? You know, if men could wear make up and dresses, and for women if there was no glass ceiling, would it be necessary?. . . . (Del, age 44)

Thus, while the narrative of the "wrong body" within discourses of "gender dysphoria" is repeated to gain surgical reconstruction, the demand for it may be seen as an outcome of the social and cultural investment in a gender binary system. This is particularly significant since the medical model of transgender, which influences access to the new framework of rights, remains tied to a gender binary model.

While Prosser returns to Descartes' mind/body split, Merleau-Ponty's (1962) work offers an alternative framework through which to explore these issues of embodiment. In challenging this duality, Merleau-Ponty theorizes the intersections between the material body and the phenomenological realm to explore how the former is consciously experienced. The "corporeal schema" indicates how the embodied agent is positioned between the subjective and the social world. For Merleau-Ponty, embodiment is not necessarily a conscious state, but may be experienced as an "inner sense," which influences our bodily actions and responses. The intersections of the

subjective, material, and social were apparent in this research when participants discussed surgery as a way of reconciling self and social identity. For
example, in answer to my question "how important was surgery for you?"
Dave says,

> Surgery was very important. Because even without hormones, the way
> I presented myself and the way I dressed, people would see me as male.
> But because of my chest I had to bind myself up everyday and, apart from
> the discomfort, I just felt they shouldn't be there. . . . (Dave, age 26)

In articulating the complex relationship between embodiment and gender identification, these narratives resonate with Freud's (1923) notion of
"bodily ego," whereby the sense of "self" develops through our sense of
the body. Grosz (1994) conceptualizes this as a "psychical map," through
which the formation of "self" involves a psychical image of our body. Yet
while the understandings and experiences of surgery of several participants
in this research suggest that the material body "matters," as Nataf argues,
"The achieved anatomy is a way of relieving the confusion and anxiety, and
the body is a point of reference, not a nature" (1997, p. 45). Although the
significance placed upon a congruent relationship between gender identity
and bodily appearance is reflected by some participants, the desire for surgery is rarely a straightforward manifestation of "gender dysphoria." The
only participant to articulate without hesitation the "wrong body" experience was Cheryl, who, in answer to my question, "how do you describe
your gender identity?" replied "female trapped in a male body" (Cheryl,
age 45). Significantly, Cheryl had sought medical advice from her general
practitioner only 4 months before our interview and was still waiting for
her first appointment with a psychiatrist. Epstein's (1995) application of a
Foucauldian analysis is useful for understanding the influence of a medical model upon transsubjectivities. Through surveillance, the "patient" is
viewed as a special type of person and individual experience is lost as the
person emerges as a "medical type" (Epstein, 1995, p. 26). Thus, personal
accounts are written into medical discourse, which converts "unclear subjectivity into an interpretable text, which takes precedence over the frag-
ments of human experience" (Epstein, 1995, p. 29). Power is transferred
from the "speaking subject" to the "expert" (Sharpe, 2002, p. 25) to sustain a "regime of truth" (Foucault, 1980). In this way, medical case studies
do not simply "record," but work to "produce" knowledge. As well as constructing transsubjectivities, this process regulates claims to citizenship.

CLAIMING CITIZENSHIP

Nadia's role in *Big Brother 5* highlights the tensions apparent in the question of transgender citizenship. She found a place in the *Big Brother* house

following her openness about gender transition during auditions for the show. Yet, although program makers, the media, and *Big Brother* audiences knew about her recent transition, Nadia did not speak of it to her housemates. She was clearly aware that the public would be interested in her gender experience, explicitly coming out as a trans woman in her audition video. Yet, in the *Big Brother* diary room and in subsequent media interviews, she spoke of her decision not to tell her housemates in terms of being accepted as a woman,

> I wanted to enjoy it, embrace the world. I didn't want to sit around and have deep conversations or anything like that. . . . I don't want to tick a box and say I'm transgender. I don't understand why people want to categorise themselves like that. . . . Rather than consider themselves transgender they [trans women] should just let their personalities shine. We are women. I am a woman. If you want to get into that, you're going to be stuck most of the time talking about what you've been through, and that is the last thing I want. (Nadia Almada, quoted in *The Observer*, 2004)

Some participants in this research also articulated individual rather than transgender identities. In answer to my question "is the term transgender relevant to you?", Tony, for example, says,

> I've never thought of myself as transgender. I'm just a bloke who's gone through one or two shit things but that's all I've ever been. (Tony, age 39)

Narratives of moving beyond a transgender identity are characteristic of "claims to citizenship." Weeks et al. (2001) suggest that recent social movements, particularly feminism and the lesbian and gay movement, are characterized first by moments of transgression and second by claims to citizenship. Transgression is defined as ". . . the constant invention and reinvention of new senses of the self, and new challenges to the inherited institutions and traditions that hitherto had excluded these new subjects" (Weeks et al., p. 91). The moment of transgression is followed by the claim to citizenship, ". . . the claim to equal protection of the law, to equal rights in employment, parenting, social status, access to welfare provision, and partnership rights and same sex marriage" (Weeks et al., 2001, p. 91). The moment of citizenship mirrors the goals of many transgender organizations and, importantly, was the lynchpin of the GRA.

Legislative changes brought by the GRA, however, show the complexities of "claiming citizenship" for some trans people. For married people, the legislation is problematic as marriages have to be annulled before a change of birth certificate is permitted. Bernadette transitioned from male-to-female 15 years ago and remains married to her wife of 40 plus years.

The GRA means that Bernadette now has to choose between legal recognition as female, and her long-standing marriage. One option for Bernadette and her wife is to divorce and then register as a same-sex civil partnership. However, since neither Bernadette nor her wife considers themselves to be in a lesbian relationship, this is a problematic choice. PfC lobbied unsuccessfully to overturn this requirement of the GRA. Claire McNab, Vice-President of PfC, summarises the outcome,

> We were left with the consequences of the government's coldly symmetrical logic: that marriage was for opposite-sex couples, and civil partnerships for same-sex couples, with no exception even for the hundred or so couples about to move from one category to the other. A harsh logic, requiring people to change their legal relationship just for logical neatness. . . . (McNab, 2004)

As I have suggested elsewhere (Hines, 2006), transgender practices of intimacy indicate that partnering and parenting relationships are amenable to complex shifts in gendered meaning and expression. Such transformations show how intimate relationships, more broadly, are subject to on-going contest, negotiation, and innovation.

Whereas these intimate narratives speak of socio-historical changes in the diversification of meanings and experiences of gender, they are muted by legislation, which denies the storyteller the recognition and rights of citizenship. Weeks et al. (2001, p. 91) state that, ". . . without the claim to full citizenship, difference can never be fully validated." Yet, although the GRA aims to enable trans people to claim citizenship, it reinforces inequality for those who are married. Such a paradox supports Williams' claim that ". . . moves to recognize diversity may sometimes expose or reinforce inequality" (2004, p. 82). Moreover, if a "moment of citizenship" is conceived out of the desire for inclusion, we must also bring a more radical voice into the frame.

TRANSGRESSING CITIZENSHIP

What are downplayed in discussions about claims to citizenship are the factions of social movements that place more import on the moment of transgression than that of citizenship. From this perspective, the wisdom of soliciting validation is questioned. Such a position preserves the celebration of difference, and questions the merits of normativity and assimilationism. Radical gender and sexual movements such as *Queer Nation* and *Transsexual Menace* act as a cautionary reminder of the dangers of a whole-hearted liberal approach to citizenship claims. Hence, those who remain "different" are frequently constructed as "difficult" and become further marginalized. In discussing a moment of citizenship, it must not be forgotten that most recent social movements divide on the desirability of citizenship as a political goal, with many arguing that such a route inevitably leads to the subjugation of difference and transgression. This debate is apparent within transgender communities on the question of "passing." While some trans people see it as a prerequisite of social acceptance and inclusion, others argue against assimilating into an incomprehensible binary gender system (Bornstein, 1994; Feinberg, 1992, 1999; Stone, 1991). Research participant, Rebecca, for example, identifies as neither male nor female but as "bigendered." For Rebecca, rejecting the surgical route of transition has enabled increased gender fluidity,

> I suppose my story has changed and matured as time has gone, and my view of my gender has appeared differently to me at different times. In terms of my place in society now in many ways I feel that I have the best of both worlds. . . . I see that as a benefit because I don't live in fear of being acknowledged as either male or female or having both characteristics should I say. (Rebecca, age 55)

For Del, it is also important to articulate gender fluidity,

> I don't think it's linear. I think it's more like if you have [Del draws diagram]. Here we have our source and that's whoever we are and it shoots out in a more kind of radial way, so it's more like a kind of color chart and you can pick all the different colors. I think that some people are very asexual for example. They don't have a lot of sexuality and others are very sexual, and it's the same way with gender in a way. I am very gendered. I have a lot of gender and that expresses itself in a lot of different ways, whereas other people don't. They stay at one point but with me I'm kind of moving around. . . . There's lots of different levels so there's not just one way in which I describe my identity. I've called myself a gender terrorist; I've called myself intersex by design, an intentional mutation, FtM, but not transsexual, and FtM is more about how people perceive me. I call myself a hermaphrodyke sometimes. I've been a lesbian or a dyke, I've been a queer dyke. Queer is probably the term I feel best describes me. I could call myself a queer trannie boy. Everything is qualified in one way or another [laugh]. (Del, age 44)

The law now allows for movement *across* the binary of male/female, but the spectrums *in-between* male and female, such as transgendered, intersexed, bigendered, and androgynous, remain outside current frameworks of citizenship. Furthermore, although current law concedes that gender identity may change across the life-span, it remains spatially fixed. Rather than seeing gender transition as an end-point, however, many participants discussed how their understandings and experiences of gender shifted through transition. In answer to my question "how would you describe your gender identity now?" Karen says,

I think I've probably learnt that I'm not really that different from before. I can still be quite aggressive. I still have a competitive side. Initially I went way over to the feminine side and became really girlie,
which isn't me. But now I've got a bit of male and a bit of female in me
which has been interesting for me and I've settled down to where I am.
(Karen, age 31)

The narratives of participants in this research suggest that whereas identity is embodied, rather than being rigid, the relationship between gender
identity and the physical body shifts and evolves through transition. Thus,
my research findings support Nataf's comment that, "The form gender
identity and role finally take can be more or less fixed or fluid, depending upon the individual" (1997, p. 20). Yet, an understanding of gender as
intertextual and precarious is at odds with current concepts of citizenship.
Monro (2005) has discussed the pitfalls of constructing a model, which
that pits the "nice trans person" against the "less nice trans people." In
this way, people who rebuff the gender binary by refusing neatly to dovetail gender presentation and gender identity (e.g., bigendered trans people,
butch trans lesbians, camp trans men, cross-dressers, and drag kings and
queens) continue to be excluded from the rights and recognition of citizenship. In rejecting the surgical route, then, transgender people fall outside
the domain of the "deserving citizen" (Richardson, 1998).

Weeks et al. point out that debate concerning recognition within lesbian
and gay communities is ". . . one based on boundary-defenders who argue for
a social movement based on a collective identity, and boundary-strippers who
argue for the deconstruction of identity and binary categories. . ." (2001, p.
192). Although similar themes are apparent about recognition and assimilation within transgender communities, the tensions around a transgender politics of identity are more complex in that the "boundary strippers" of gender
may simultaneously act as "boundary defenders" in arguing for the importance of a transgender (rather than transsexual) identity that denotes gender
difference. There are, then, conceptual problems as well as civil inequalities
in recent moves to grant trans people citizenship. Based upon a gender binary
model, the GRA is unable to recognize the diversity of new (trans) masculinities and femininities as they are variously constructed and experienced.
Hence, rather than broadening the realm of citizenship in relation to gender
diversity, the Act works to reinforce a normative gender model.

CONCLUSION

This chapter has examined issues of transgender citizenship in relation to
recent social, cultural, and legislative developments. Representing the civil
recognition of gender transition, the GRA marks an important change in
attitudes toward trans people and aims to end social exclusion. Here, it has

been argued, however, that legislative understandings of transgender remain tied to a medical perspective. Although the "claims to citizenship" of some trans people—those who have undergone surgery or who articulate "gender dysphoria"—may be facilitated through the new framework of rights, the enduring influence of a medical model upon social and legal understandings of transgender mean that those who "transgress"—married trans people who choose not to divorce and those who construct identities outside the gender binary—remain on the margins of citizenship, residing as "noncitizens." My findings support Richardson's (2004) argument that social change sought through the notion of "citizenship" tends to emphasize "sameness" rather than equality of "difference." Thus, the current framework of transgender citizenship still fails to account for gender diversity.

Research findings suggest that while some participants articulate individualism and are reluctant to position themselves as members of a collective transgender culture, others present distinct transgender identity positions, which are consciously created in opposition to traditional ways of thinking about gender. These latter gender identity practices offer a challenge to political goals of assimilation, signposting a radical politics of gender transformation in which "difference" is positioned as a site of importance and celebration in its own right.

The complexities of trans identity positions and identity politics mean that transgender citizenship is an uneven and contested terrain. As Bell and Binnie argue in their discussion of sexual citizenship, ". . . to disidentify—to remain as non-citizens—will maintain systems of exclusion and discrimination that brings real material harm to many people" (2000, p. 146). The GRA must be welcomed for its aim to remedy exclusionary systems for trans people. The task now is to deconstruct critically the gender binary in order to account fully for contemporary gender transformations.

REFERENCES

Bell, D. (2004). Sexual citizenship. In J. Eadie (Ed.), *Sexuality: The essential glossary*. New York and London: Arnold.
Bell, D., & Binnie, J. (2000). *The sexual citizen: Queer politics and beyond*. Cambridge: Polity Press.
Benjamin, H. (1966). *The transsexual phenomenon*. New York: Julian Press.
Blaikie, N. (2000). *Designing social research*. Cambridge: Polity Press.
Bolin, A. (1998). *In search of Eve: Transsexual rites of passage*. South Hadley: Bergin & Garvey.
Bornstein, K. (1994). *Gender outlaws: On men, women and the rest of us*. London: Routledge.
Burns, C. (2004). Retrieved September 2005, from www.bigbrother.digitalspky.co.uk, accessed
Bussmaker, J., & Voet, R.(1998). Citizenship and gender: Theoretical approaches and historical legacies. *Critical Social Policy, 18*(3), 278–307.
Butler, J. (1994). *Gender trouble: Feminism and the subversion of identity*. London: Routledge.

Cooper, D. (1995). *Power struggle: Feminism, sexuality and the state.* Buckingham: Open University Press.

Cromwell, J. (1999). *Transmen and FTMs: Identities, bodies, genders and sexualities.* Chicago: University of Illinois Press.

Crossley, N. (1995). Merleau-Ponty, the elusive body and carnal sociology. *Body and Society, 2*(2).

Daly, G., & Cowen, H. (2000). Redefining the local citizen. In L. McKie & N. Watson (Eds.) *Organising bodies.* London: Macmillan.

Dunne, G. (1997). *Lesbian lifestyles: Women's work and the politics of sexuality.* London: Macmillan.

Edwards, R. (1993). An education in interviewing: Placing the researcher and the research. In C. M. Renzetti & R. M. Lee (Eds.), *Researching sensitive topics.* London: Sage.

Ekins, R., & King, D. (1996). *Blending genders: Social aspects of cross-dressing and sex-changing.* London: Routledge.

Ellen, B. (2004). The more people criticised, the stronger I became. *The Observer,* August 22, 2004.

Epstein, J. (1995). *Altered conditions: Disease, medicine and storytelling.* London: Routledge.

Epstein, J., & Straub, K. (1991). *Body guards: The cultural politics of gender ambiguity.* New York and London: Routledge.

Evans, D. (1993). *Sexual citizenship: The material construction of sexualities.* London: Routledge.

Feinberg, L. (1992). *Transgender liberation: A movement whose time has come.* New York: World View Forum.

Foucault, M. (1977). *Discipline and punish: The birth of the prison.* Harmondsworth: Penguin.

———. (1980). *Power/knowledge: Selected interviews and other writings 1972–1977.* New York: Pantheon.

Freud, S. (1923). The ego and the id. In J. Strachey et al. (Ed. & Trans.), *The standard edition of the complete psychological works of Sigmund Freud (1953–1965).* London: Hogarth Press.

Green, R. (1969). *Transsexualism and sex reassignment.* Baltimore: Johns Hopkins University Press.

———. (1987). Definition and synopsis of aetiology of adult gender identity, Retrieved July 2006, from www.gires.org.uk/Text_Assets/Etiology_Definition

Griggs, C. (1998). *S/He: Changing sex and changing clothes.* Oxford: Berg.

Grosz, E. (1994). *Volatile bodies: Towards a corporal feminism.* Bloomington and Indianapolis: Indiana University Press.

Halberstam, J. (1998). *Female masculinity.* Durham: Duke University Press.

Hale, J. (1997). Suggested rules for non-transsexuals writing about transsexuals, transsexuality, transsexualism, or trans. Retrieved September 2006, from www.sandystone.com/hale.rules.html

Harry Benjamin International Gender Dysphoria Association. (2001). *Standards of care for gender identity disorders.* Retrieved from *www.pfc.org.uk/medical/soc2001.htm* Hausman, B. (1995). *Changing sex: Transsexualism, technology, and the idea of gender.* London: Duke University Press.

Hines, S. (2006). Intimate transitions: Transgender practices of partnering and parenting. *Sociology, 40*(2).

Hollway, W., & Jefferson, T. (2000). *Doing qualitative research differently: Free association, narrative and the interview method.* London: Sage.

Jones, L. (2004). *The Observer,* August 8, 2004.

Lister, R. (1997). *Citizenship: Feminist perspectives.* London: Macmillan.

Marshall, T. (1950). *Citizenship and social class and other essays.* Cambridge: Cambridge University Press.

McNab, C. (2004). Married trans people and civil partnerships: Where next? Retrieved September 2006, from www.pfc.org.uk/pfclists/news-arc/2004q3/msg00044.htm Merleau-Ponty, M. (1962). *The phenomenology of perception.* London: RKP.

Monro, S. (2003). Transgender politics in the UK. *Critical Social Policy, 23*(4), 433–452.

———. (2005). *Gender politics: Citizenship, activism and sexual diversity.* London: Pluto.

Nataf, Z. (1995). *Lesbians talk transgender.* London: Scarlett Press.

Oakley, A. (2000). *Experiments in knowing: Gender and method in the social sciences.* New York: The New Press.

Pateman, C. (1989). *The disorder of women: Disorder, feminism and political theory.* Cambridge: Polity Press.

Phillips, A. (1993). *Democracy and difference.* Cambridge: Polity Press.

Plummer, K. (1995). *Telling sexual stories: Power, change and social worlds.* London: Routledge.

Prosser, J. (1998). *Second skins: The body narratives of transsexuality.* New York: Columbia University Press.

Richardson, D. (1994). Locating sexualities: From here to normality. *Sexualities, 7*(4).

———. (1998). Sexuality and citizenship. *Sociology, 32,*83–100.

———. (2000a). Constructing sexual citizenship. Theorizing sexual rights. *Critical Social Policy, 20*(1).

———. (2000b). Claiming citizenship? Sexuality, citizenship and lesbian/feminist theory. *Sexualities, 3*(2).

Shapiro, J. (1991). Transsexualism: Reflections on the persistence of gender and the mutability of sex. In J. Epstein & K. Straub (Eds.), *Body guards: The cultural politics of gender ambiguity.*

Sharpe, A. N. (2002). *Transgender jurisprudence: Dysphoric bodies of law.* London: Cavendish.

Song, M., & Parker, D. (1995). Commonality, difference and the dynamics of disclosure in in-depth interviewing. *Sociology, 29*(2).

Stoller, R. (1968). Passing and the continuum of gender identity. In J. Marmor (Ed.), *Sexual inversion: The multiple roots of homosexuality.* New York: Basic Books.

———. (1975). The transsexual experiment. *Sex and Gender (Vol. 11).* London: Hogarth Press.

Stone, S. (1991). The empire strikes back: A posttransexual manifesto. In J. Epstein & K. Straub Eds.), *Body guards: The cultural politics of gender ambiguity.* London: Routledge.

Stychin, C. (1998). *A nation by rights: National cultures, sexual identity politics and the discourse of rights.* Philadelphia: Temple University Press.

Turner, B., & Hamilton, P. (Eds.). (1994). *Citizenship: Critical concepts.* London: Routledge.

Walby, S. (1994). Is citizenship gendered? *Sociology, 28*(2), 379–3795.

Weeks, J. (1995). *Invented moralities: Sexual values in an age of uncertainty.* Cambridge: Polity Press.

———. (1998). The sexual citizen. *Theory, Culture and Society, 15,* 35–52.

Weeks, J., Heaphy, B., & Donovan, C. (2001). *Same sex intimacies: Families of choice and other life experiments.* London: Routledge.

Wieringa, S., & Blackwood, E., (Eds.). (1999). *Cultures, identities, sexualities.* New York: Columbia University Press.

Williams, F. (2004). *Rethinking families.* London: Calouste Gulbenkian Foundation.

5 Blood, Water, and the Politics of Biology

Examining the Primacy of Biological Kinship in Family Policy and (Step) Family Discourse

Karin Lenke

INTRODUCTION

What is thicker—blood or water? Why do we even compare the two and what does this mean for families that form affinities based on water (social ties)—not blood (biological ties)? The seemingly casual expression "blood is thicker than water" is part of a network of discourses, which together make up what I have chosen to call the politics of biology, discourses that grant legal and cultural priority to biological ties in kinship networks.

In late modernity, the family is under pressure. Some scholars argue that this social unit in its traditional form is dissolving. Tendencies such as larger numbers of divorces and reconstituted families, the inclusion of gay and lesbian families in law and social policy (in some Western countries), and the transition from being a closed social unit to a network of relations (Bäck-Wiklund & Johansson, 2003) support this idea. A dynamic multitude of living arrangements call for recognition as families, and they all differ from the heterosexual, biological, first marriage, nuclear arrangement in one or more ways.

In this study, I take as a departing point the politics of biology to map how the primacy of biological kinship is reproduced and challenged in Swedish late modernity. This term is meant to include different types of cultural, social, political, and legal patterns of thought, which naturalize and privilege biological ties. I examine ways that biological/nonbiological differentiation is articulated in family law and policy in Sweden and in the narratives of four young adults from reconstituted families. These individuals share the experience of growing up with one or more social parent. Relationships between adults who are social (but not the biological) parents and their children can take on many forms. Not only reconstituted but also adoptive and queer families fall under this category. I choose to look at reconstituted families, stepfamilies, because they occupy a hybrid position, being both culturally accepted but also legally and politically undefined.

They are both socially "normal" and at the same time a possible threat to "the real family," a site for forming affinities based on water, not blood. Unless we believe that there is something cosmic, innately pure, and true in biological kinship ties, unattainable in nonbiological ones, we have to look at these distinctions through how they originate in language, how they are socially constructed, as being more than social.

PURPOSE AND RESEARCH QUESTIONS

The politics of biology are, of course, an offspring of biological determinism, conservative discourses that have been used as "powerful political tools to legitimate social inequalities and power differentials along the lines of gender, race, sexual preference, age, class, nation, culture, etc." (Lykke, 2000, p. 1). Biological determinism, as well as biological essentialism, has been the target of feminist social constructivist critique in efforts to deconstruct, challenge, and oppose power relations that feed upon such thinking (Lykke, 2000). The politics of biology could then be almost any political discourse based on biological essentialism, for example, patriarchy—built upon the (perceived) biological difference between men and women. In this chapter, however, the politics of biology will stand for discourses that grant legal and cultural priority to biological ties in kinship networks.

The purpose of this chapter is to examine the ways that politics of biology are constituted, expressed, and challenged in late modern Sweden. To achieve this, I look for discourses in which a differentiation between biological and nonbiological kinship ties is articulated. During the research process, two different locations appeared as privileged sites for this purpose: family policy in Sweden and in the narratives of my four young adult who grew up with one or more social parents. The research question that has been a guideline throughout the project is: How are the politics of biology expressed, constituted, and challenged in late modern Sweden?

WHAT IS A BIOLOGICAL PARENT ANYWAY?

How are we to analyze parenting as biological and/or social in an age when new reproductive technologies challenge the very foundation of parenting as we know it, and what is the use of writing out terms like biological mother or half-brother or step dad if the whole purpose of this study is to deconstruct the binary between biological and social ties in kinship relations, which make such concepts as half-brother significant? For a lack of suitable vocabulary, I will use the term "biological" in reference to a parent–child relationship to distinguish it from a nonbiological tie where relevant. In this text, social parent is preferred over stepparent; however, since a social parent is often also a biological one, this expression cannot always be used as a substitute for the more problematic word stepparent. Stepfamily, stepmother, and stepfather are used to denote family ties commonly articulated as step-ties. The term "reconstituted family" will also be used, but I choose not to let it replace stepfamily altogether. "Reconstituted" implies that there has been a previous deconstitution or divorce, something that is not always true for stepfamilies.

THE INTERVIEWS

For this study, I conducted four in-depth interviews with young adults brought up by one or more social parents/stepparents. The interviews, in Swedish, were semistructured, covering a set of predefined themes: family relations, familiar social norms, and attitudes toward their families by outsiders.

The participants found via inquiries of people in my own social network comprised volunteers, two women and two men, all "ethnic whites" from middle-class and lower middle-class backgrounds, ages 22 to 30 years. The homogeneity of the sample means that experiences of other family backgrounds have not been explored. However, I have no intention to generalize or to draw conclusions about other young adults with similar pasts. Instead, the narratives of my interviewees fulfill the purpose of illuminating the complex position of stepfamilies, simultaneously socially accepted and "normal" yet possibly transgressing boundaries regarding hegemonic notions of belonging and kinship. Names and some other personal information have been changed to preserve anonymity.

Theoretical Frameworks

This project is inspired by recent developments in British welfare research which by rethinking the concept of "the social" have illuminated how social policy shapes and is shaped by social solidarities and the formation of nation (Fink, Lewis, & Clarke, 2001; Lewis, Gewirtz, & Clarke, 2000). This research is coupled with theories that seek to understand the role that the family plays in relation to the nation, presented in the next section, and which also aims to explore the ways that heterosexuality can be analyzed in relation to the welfare state. The following part deals with theoretizations of stepfamilies and nonbiological parenthood in general, and serves to introduce analytical concepts that have been developed to analyze constructions of family and parenthood.

NATION, FAMILY, AND BIOLOGY

Social policies are not merely the product and effect of their implementation, they are also an integral part of the formation of nation, constituting who belongs to it and does not. They are part of discursive practices, which shape and regulate normality, reproducing or altering normative assumptions of gender, sexuality, class, "race," and so on, through the way that welfare subjects are constituted in political regimes. Furthermore, powerful regimes of normative discipline, such policies constitute both the practices aimed at these subjects as well as the subjects themselves in a welfare state (Watson, 2000, p. 73f); they constitute social solidarities and the forming of an imagined national "we." Social policies must therefore be thought of in relation to how they interact and intersect with power relations of gender, class, "race," and (hetero)sexuality and, in turn, how these intersections relate to national boundaries and belonging.

Anne McClintock, among others, has shown how metaphors of the nation are not only constructed in relation to gender but also to "race" in discourses such as speaking of a colony as "a family of black children ruled over by a white father" (1995, p. 358). The family, as a metaphor for the nation, is firmly rooted in the cultural imaginary: mother as nation, brothers as fellow citizens, sons as soldiers, fathers as founders of the countries, and so on. The vocabulary used to talk about national solidarities is often the language of the intimate family sphere translated into patriotic calls for unity and loyalty, explicit or more subtle. These discourses have been mapped by postcolonial and feminist scholars. There are specific historical contexts within which these metaphors are employed, but I would argue that they all stem from an assumption that there is only a small step between thinking about the family as a person's most important community, to thinking that it is the nation.

In "It's All in the Family," Patricia Hill Collins tells an intersectional tale on two levels, paralleling the narrative of the family with that of the nation. As she puts it, "The nation state is grounded in an idea that as a national family, people share some sort of biological oneness" (2000, p. 169). In other words, the family as well as the nation is based on notions of biological kinship. I borrow the words of Jacqui M. Alexander to stress the way that heterosexuality enters the equation: The nation has always been conceived in heterosexuality, since biology and reproduction are at the heart of its impulse (Alexander, 1997, p. 84). To be able to think about heterosexuality and the way that political systems benefit from heteronormativity, it is necessary to examine the role that such a phenomenon plays in the mode of production. Marxist feminists[1] make the claim that normative reproduction of gender is essential to the mode of production, not only because it reproduces heterosexuality, but also the family itself. In theorizing the intersections between class and gender, they have also rearticulated the links between production and reproduction, between naturalization of wage labor as capitalist exploitation of workers and that of the heterosexual nuclear family as a site of oppression of women (Butler, 1998, p. 40). In Marxist feminism, the family is treated analytically as a part of the mode of production, one that not only enables capitalism to benefit from women's unpaid reproductive labor, but also embodies the very essence of the reproduction of heterosexuality. Not only is the family tied to the economic through normative heterosexuality, as Butler asserts, but it is also based on notions of biological sameness, and this primacy of biological kinship, entrenched as it may be with racism and heterosexism, must also be treated as a part of the political economy. Ultimately, capitalism depends on families for the reproduction of human beings themselves (Butler, 1998).

THEORIZING STEPFAMILIES

Stepfamilies connect to normality in complex ways. On one hand, they may be viewed as incomplete, less functional, and lacking in relation to nuclear families; this is a perspective purported both by social scientific research and popular discourse (Malia, 2005). On the other hand, they are considered "culturally normal" (Ritala-Koskinen, 1994). The formation of a stepfamily can actually reinstate normality; a reconstituted family can thus be a normalizing factor, which provides the social units members with a fresh new start or a second chance to achieve what was not accomplished in the previous relationship that ended in a divorce (Ritala-Koskinen, 1994). The way that stepfamilies are positioned in relation to normality, however, can only be examined through their location in social hierarchies of class, sexuality, gender, ethnicity, and "race." White, middle-class stepfamilies are likely to be situated in a social context where their status is not to their disadvantage. Gay stepfamilies or those with members marginalized through racialization, however, are more likely to face discriminatory practices. Janet M. Wright, in a study on lesbian stepfamilies, notes,

> [h]eterosexual supremacy serves to make the lesbian stepmother invisible to the outside world, which communicates that invisibility to the children, the biological mother, and the stepmother. She is unnamed— and therefore erased. Surely the job of lesbian stepmother is not for the faint of heart. (1998, p. 116).

A study on male gay stepfamilies (Crosbie-Burnett & Helmbrecht, 1993) recognizes another type of difference between them and straight stepfamilies, based on the observation that a homosexual (step) father is caught between two mutually exclusive worlds; he belongs both to a gay male subculture where having children means deviation, and to the role of fatherhood, with the status, identity, and tradition that comes with it, all of which are coded heterosexual (Crosbie-Burnett & Helmbrecht, 1993, p. 257). Sandell (1998), in a study on lesbian parenthood, argues that such lesbian couples who start families with gay men form what the author calls "the perfect (divorced) family," modeled after a heterosexual norm, which prescribes both biological parents to share responsibility. These families accommodate to the politics of biology by choosing to prioritize biological parenthood over social parenthood—lesbian couples can often choose not to include any (active) father in the child's life. But since, in these families, both biological parents and their respective partners take on parental identities and duties, this accommodation to the politics of biology also functions to create a confusion in terms: the occurrence of three/four-parent families, or in Sandell's words: "the perfect (divorced) family." This concept, apart from denoting a specific gay/lesbian family practice, also serves as a link between queer families and stepfamilies, stressing a similarity in the way that both are constituted in relation to a heterosexual, biological, first-marriage family.

The ways in which queer families deviate from normality, I would argue, could analytically be divided into three different, yet overlapping sets of norm aberration. The first one is homosexuality itself, entrenched as it is with perversity and abnormality (see, e.g., Bryld, 2000). The second one is gender and the subversion of parenthood present in family formations that break up the heterosexual nuclear norm (see, e.g., Dalton & Bielby, 2000). The subversion of gender regimes, however, obviously has different meanings for gay fathers and lesbian mothers. The third one, I would argue, lies in the conscious subversion of biology (i.e., breaking the bloodline). What does it mean to create and sustain relationships between adults and children based on something other than the sharing of common biological origins? It is in this last respect that queer families and stepfamilies are both constituted against the heterosexual biological family.

Cultural beliefs affect families. They "exert a strong influence on the ways in which family members perceive themselves and expect to be regarded by others, which in turn may affect family conduct and functioning" (Malia, 2005, p. 298). The stepfamily is not a marginalized position by definition. However, in the cultural imaginary that shapes the way these social unit and their members are allowed to create identities and come into being as subjects, the traditional, heterosexual, first-marriage family with biological children is still the norm, in relation to which other families are constituted. Jaqueline Stevens (2005) points out how the notion of a "real family" "renders some families and ties authentic and others as copies that, as such, perform the superiority of the original." Drawing on Judith Butler's theoretization of the performativity of sex/gender (see, e.g., Butler, 1999), Stevens argues that the "real family" is created by the existence of other families, and that this distinction is performed, much like Butler argues that gender is performed. In Stevens' case, the adoptive family serves as an illustration of that. Through a legal order that distinguishes between adoptive and genetic families, Stevens argues, the law functions formally to ratify a "natural" family, seen to be prepolitical. But, as Stevens points out, "Families have never existed without a political society providing rules for what counts as a family" (2005, p. 77). Thinking of the family as a performative act can be used as a tool to understand the distinctions made between unmarked families (i.e., heterosexual, nuclear, biological, first marriage-families, and those that need prefixes such as adoptive, same-sex or step).

There is an on-going discussion in legal theory as to whether and how to accommodate new expanded families into the legal system (Holtzman, 2006; Malia, 2005). Proponents of a more inclusive family legislation argue that it is children's rights, not just their interest, to establish and maintain ties to their "de facto parents," be they biological or nonbiological. A more encompassing vision of the family is called for, and the term exclusive parenthood has been used to denote the legal and cultural priority to biological ties (Malia, 2005). Scholarship devoted to exploring the implications of exclusive parenthood (i.e., that a child can never have more than two legal parents) is well developed in the United States. Although the same restrictions to parenthood are present in Swedish family law, this issue has not been addressed extensively. An integral part of exclusive parenthood is the view of children as "natural property," an assumption that is present in law and tradition throughout Western culture. Farrell Smith asserts that,

> [a] biologistic paradigm coupled with a property-based view of parental rights has historically tended toward the stigmatization and unequal status and worth of orphaned, foster and adopted children. (2005, p. 112)

With a property-based view of the relationships that parents have to their children, biological kinship continues to be privileged over social ties that can form between adults and children, ones of love and affection, which do not carry any rights or obligations in a parent–child relationship. Why then, might it be important to incorporate "new" family constellations into family law? Chesire Calhoun writes about having access to familial status and argues that it means,

> [h]aving the cultural authority to challenge existing familial norms, to redefine what constitutes a family, and to demand that the preferred definition of the family be reflected in cultural and legal practices. (2000, p. 156).

This means that laws and policies should reflect the multitude of living arrangements among families in late modernity. However, as I discuss in the following sections, legislation in Sweden favors biological ties and enforces exclusive parenthood through family law that limits a child's legal parents to two.

Social Policy and Politics of Biology

Discourses that grant legal and cultural priority to biological ties in kinship networks are what I have chosen to call politics of biology. These politics are played out against their natural backdrop, the family, and the main protagonists, children. Pinkney writes about children as "imagined and symbolic subjects," which are often used as "a legitimizing image or representation for social policies" (2000, p. 113). In this chapter, I look at the ways children's needs are constituted in Swedish family policy by examining how parenthood is constructed and gendered through the biological/social binary.

Social and Legal Constructions of Parenthood

According to Statistics Sweden[2], 25% of Swedish 17-year-olds (2003) are children of parents who have separated. This number rapidly increased in the latter half of the 20th century (www.scb.se). Many of these children form affinities outside the boundaries of their biological family. Their parents may enter into relationships with men or women who become social parents of their partner's children. The ties between children and adults that are immediately recognized by law, however, are only the biological ones. However, as noted by Stevens, "Custodial relations for children based on anything but pregnancy are all rooted in legal and social conventions, not biology" (2005, p. 68).

In 2002, the Swedish parliament passed a law that allowed for same-sex couples to adopt children legally. Assisted donor insemination for lesbians had to wait until another commission had investigated the implications such a procedure would have on legal parenthood (i.e., what status to grant the donor and the lesbian mother, who is not the birth-mom of the child; Ds, 2004, p. 19) The resulting law, passed in 2005, was designed so that the nonbiological partner is (also) presumed to be the mother of a child born by assisted insemination in the Swedish health care system.

Children conceived through donor insemination have the option to learn the identity of their donor upon reaching age 18. (The same opportunity is available to those born by donor sperm or egg into heterosexual families.) This way young people may discover their origins, and couples unable to procreate, straight or gay, can become parents. The system of donor-identity-release, however, must be put in context and not treated as an absolute solution to the "problem" of such children. In other countries, where donors cannot be traced, more emphasis is put on the privacy of the donor than a child's right to know. This is one of the ways in which the politics of biology are written into Swedish family law, a legislative system shaped by biological kinship as a norm (Singer, 2002).

In Sweden, the two-parent restriction can be understood through the concept of exclusive parenthood. Exclusivity in parenthood, however, is not only restricted to notions of biology, but also to patterns of thought allowing for the idea that adults control and "own" children, who belong exclusive by to the (biological) parents. The construction of parenthood as a relationship to a child in which the sharing of DNA automatically gives biological parents immediate access to their children is problematic in many ways. Maria Eriksson's work grasps the normative implications of efforts in social policy to link children (and mothers) with their biological fathers/ex-partners, even potentially violent men (2003). Farrell Smith opposes, rightly in my view, such normative implications inherent in much of social policy and states that "[n]either society nor the state should valorize the biological tie as paradigmatic, normal, primary, and most desired" (2005, p. 113). To this I would add that privileging biological parenthood over social parenthood is coded in heterosexual normativity, since reproduction is primarily understood to be by definition heterosexual, although this link is being challenged by the development of new reproductive technologies.

Gendering Parenthood

By making assumptions about biological kinship in social policy explicit, the politics of biology can be located in many of the ways that the family is regulated and constituted. The widespread belief that it is "in the best interest of a child" to be parented by, or at least know the identity of, their biological parents is heavily invested with cultural and historical framings of what counts as a family, who is recognized as a parent, and the rights and obligations of those seen as mothers and fathers. Different norms apply to women's and men's parenting responsibilities. As legal or biological parents, the latter can still choose how much responsibility to take on, whereas the former do not have that option; they are seen as primary carers with an nonnegotiable responsibility, as shown by, for example, Bekkengen (2002).

What constitutes the parental responsibilities of stepmothers and stepfathers has not been addressed extensively. Larsson Sjöberg (2003), who studies stepfamilies in Sweden, which she refers to as "linked family systems," asserts that stepfathers can be described as nonfathers by principle. Their role in the family may be that of a parent, performing such duties, but the biological father's role is accentuated to the extent that the stepfather literally steps back. She sees connections between this tendency, at the level of individual families and that of family policy discourse, which has had its focus on biological fathers. Social research as well the growing literature on fatherhood and masculinities has been preoccupied with biological fatherhood in relation to postdivorce families, but stopping there instead of including reconstituted families (Larsson Sjöberg, 2003). Stepfamilies and social parenthood remain an underresearched field in relation to family policy and gender regimes.

Neither stepfathers nor stepmothers have received an abundance of scholarly attention. Biological fathers, however, are included in the growing field of Critical Studies on Men and Masculinities (Hearn, 2002). Looking at the history of the coding of fatherhood in the Swedish welfare state, Bergman and Hobson note that in the way fathers' responsibilities are constituted there has been a shift "from cash to care," from providing financial security to being an active parent, a dad. The rights of children born out of wedlock were the main scope of a 1917 law that entitled each child to two parents. At that time, establishing paternity depended solely on whether it could be presumed that the alleged father and mother had had sexual contact during the time of conception. The primary objective of the law was to find a father for the child, not necessarily the actual father. It was not until the 1930s that discussions about the importance of biological origins surfaced. With the rise of eugenics and social engineering, notions of "biological inheritance" entered into discussions about establishing paternity (Bergman & Hobson, 2002).

This history of the politics of biology must be taken into account when examining the ways social policy, law, discourse, and practice are shaped by the ideological framing of the primacy of biological kinship. For parenthood, this practice has a specifically gendered dimension. During the existence of the welfare state, men's parenthood has been controlled and regulated for different reasons depending on varied social conditions and practices. In 1917, the child's right to financial support and a man's obligation to provide it, along with normative hopes for a decrease in the number children born out of wedlock, were the main reasons articulated in the effect to identify biological fathers. Since then, a shift "from cash to care" has occurred in the coding of what the main role is that the father should play in the lives of his children, but as Bergman and Hobson note,

> [e]ven with the changing legal definitions of parenting, marriage and cohabitation, the rising divorce rates, and the emergence of reconstituted families, biological fatherhood remains crucial to the Swedish coding of men as fathers. (2002, p. 97)

Family policy has held a firm grip on the significance of biological fatherhood, albeit filling it with different meanings in different periods (Klinth, 2002). But the political implications of the coding of fatherhood cannot be understood when separated from the way that parenthood is conceived as heterosexual and conditioned by heteronormativity. Access to parental status is regulated by family law, which, only as recently as 2002, allowed for both individual composing same-sex couples to achieve equal parental status. Still, heterosexual biological parenthood is the starting point for politics and legislation (Eriksson, 2003). The emphasis placed on joint custody after divorce, "obligatory joint custody" (Bergman & Hobson, 2002), Eriksson argues, can be seen as a (re) construction of primarily biological parenthood, rather than social or psychological (2003, p. 74). Swedish family law constitutes parenthood through biological kinship ties, rather than what a parent can provide for a child, such as love and care.

Everyday Negotiations

A fundamental problem in family discourse is the lack of language to express familial relations beyond the nuclear vocabulary. Mother, father, sister, brother seem to be words that require no further explanation. Linguistic creativity has introduced terms such as plastic (plast-), pretend (låtsas-), and bonus as prefixes to moms and dads who need to be distinguished from the unmarked, "real" parents of their children. In family policy and public discourse, the categories "mother" and "father" are thought to be fixed and permanent. By examining the meanings that challenge the fixity of these words, however, tensions and cracks in the nature of parenthood become visible. New reproductive technologies question the very essence of biological father and motherhood. Lesbian parents are suggested axiomatically and directly to dispute normative assumptions about the traditional family model (Dalton & Bielby, 2000) that legally and socially is based on biological reproduction. Still, gay couples with children demand to be recognized as families, to be incorporated into family discourse.

The language used to talk about families is constituted through differences between unmarked ties, and their marked others; a father is thought to be biological unless he has a prefix, which marks him as an adoptive, step-, or bonus father. The language available to articulate kinship links is at the same time very exclusionary—the difference between "real" and nonbiological parents, siblings, and children is reproduced in social policy and family discourses and inscribed into the legal foundation of the welfare state. It is also a language, however, in which meanings are shifted and played with. Feminists and women of color have used the notion of sisterhood as a basis for solidarity among females, a use of the word that transgresses the biological/social boundary. Members of families with adopted children constantly face questions such as, "is she your own or did you adopt her?" (Smith, 2005, p. 112), thereby placing adoptive parents and their children in family borderlands. Are they really a family or are they not?

In this chapter, I have chosen to look at the stepfamily as a location where hegemonic notions of family are being renegotiated and rearticulated. I have argued that in social policy, stepfamilies are made invisible due to the primacy given to biological kinship. In the interviews with young adults who had grown up with one or more social parent, I asked what words that they used to talk about their families. One interviewee, Roger, 22, responded that when he was younger, he used mom and dad for all of his parents,

> *So you would say "mom" about your father's wife?*
> Yes, exactly, mostly to simplify, but . . .
> *But . . . mm.*
> But it is also somehow what I feel.
> *Have you used the word step mom and step dad?*
> Well, I think when I joke about it that yes, other than that, never.

Not even to simplify?
No, I think it sounds so terrible, it makes you feel like "I got beaten as
a child by my "step" something."
What else do you think about that word, what are your associations?
Well, I associate it to not liking the person. . . . I do have friends who
immediately call their new parents "stepmom" and so on. I think
it feels a little disturbing, it sounds sad.

To Roger there is no immediate identification with the term "step," so he
has different strategies to deal with his experience of having, as he says,
four parents. He refers to everyone as mom or dad, but calls them, in direct
communication, by their first name, even though his "biological" mother
finds it a little bit sad, "I think she wants to be called mom," he says.

Another solution comes from Fredrik, 30, who at first counts two parents in his family his first (biological) mother and father. Later on in the
interview, however, he says that his mother's husband has taken on parental responsibilities and is a very important figure in his life. This person,
about whom Fredrik jokes as his "pretend" dad, is otherwise referred to
only by his first name, Björn. When asked whether he has used the term
"stepdad" or "bonus dad," Fredrik explains that since he has always been
in touch with his biological father, Björn has wanted to stay "Björn" and
for Fredrik's dad to stay "dad." Fredrik counts six brothers and sisters, who
from the outside would be a mixture of full, half, and stepsiblings, but he
does not want to make these distinctions. He also has other siblings not
included in his definition of his own family, which is based on social bonds.
The same is true for Moa, 22, who says,

Usually when I am asked the question ["how many brothers and sisters
do you have?"], I say that I have six, on both sides, but the ones
that I meet, who are my family, are on my mother's side, my full
sister and my two half siblings on my mother's side. And my sister's family there, or both my sisters.
And these? [pointing at chart drawn of family]
And Emma, absolutely.

The last addition to the account of the number of siblings is Emma, daugh-
ter of Moa's social father. She at first is not included in the more formal answer to the question, when Moa counts the six siblings to whom
she is related by blood. Then it occurs to Moa, however, when she goes
into detail, that siblings can also be those "who are in my family," meaning the ones she meets and spends time with; consequently, some of her
blood-related siblings are no longer included, whereas Emma is. This is
an example of the sliding of terms, which occurs when experiences of
who belongs to one's family do not correspond with formal definitions.
Another woman, Alex, 26, says, "I really, really sometimes just want to

say that I have four parents," but people have presumed that her parents consist of two gay couples. She fears that because, she herself identifies as gay, and that when people find out that her parents are just "normal, remarried heterosexuals," they will think she is trying to brag or come across as more exotic than she is. She continues,

> But I don't feel like it's exotic, well sometimes I guess I do, because I do feel very close to all my parents, that's one thing, I would never say "both my parents," there were never just the two of them. I say "all my parents" and people sometimes react because of that. Anyway, I think that nuclear families are what's really exotic, I have always been fascinated with them. . . . I guess there has been a sort of envy as well. It always seems so special to me to have a mom a dad, and just one of each, living under the same roof.

Alex is frustrated with the suspicion toward how she defines her family. Her definitions are too strange, she assumes. Alex wants to include all her parents in the category of parent, but finds that the outside world may not always be willing to accept that. Fredrik tells a story from his own life, which humorously displays how the category parent is filled with meaning and that more than two can create confusion,

> Like my younger brother, he was at some fair with both my mom and Björn, and my dad and his wife were there, so he told his friends [after the mother and her husband showed up] "here are my parents," and then my dad came and he said "and here are my parents" [laughter].

The story does not tell how the brother's friends reacted. The humor for Fredrik is how one set of parents can come and go, and then a completely new one can appear, without any explanation as to why both are called "parents." The story is symptomatic of a family discourse that only allows for two parents at one time. In adoption, a fundamental principle has been for the biological parents to give up the child and any future claims on it (Haslanger & Witt, 2005). In this way, the adoptive family can reestablish exclusive parenthood, which for stepfamilies, remains intact through social policies that perpetuate "a stable family unit, an imagined community of father, mother and child," even after a divorce (Bergman & Hobson, 2002, p. 103). The stepfamily discursively remains a nonfamily, as long as only biological parenthood is articulated as parenthood.

Social bonds may form and even replace ties to a biological parent. This is Moa's experience; she says, "I am happy that my parents did not continue trying, because there was really no point. But, I don't know, I don't know if I had wanted to grow up with my father at all!" Moa, like the other interviewees, makes a statement about being content with the divorce of their parents. I talk to Roger about having to say "I had a happy childhood, even though my parents got divorced," and his reaction is that,

> It can be some subconscious thing that I feel [I have to do] because there's maybe not a lot of people who had a great upbringing who go "I really had a great childhood—I promise!"

Alex, whose parents got divorced before she was born, identifies the same need to defy the stereotype of "children from broken families."[3] She says she realized as an adult that,

> like a parrot, I had always repeated, "I am happy that my parent's got divorced," and I am, but that doesn't mean that my childhood was nothing but blue skies. But I don't blame the divorce for that. But I know I have said too many times that I had a wonderful childhood, especially when I was younger, I think it's some sort of defence.

This disidentification with being a "child from a broken home," which all my interviewees share, can be used as a strategy to resist pity and victimization. Moa cannot identify as a "child from a broken home" either; she says,

> It sounds tragic and categorical and, I mean, of course it has shaped my childhood and all. But it is not just the divorce, it gets really awkward if you, I don't know. No, I don't like it. [It's] almost like a victim category . . . .

Children of divorcees, just like those of subordinate groups whose parental abilities are questioned and scrutinized (e.g., children of queer and/or racialized parents) can grow up to be defenders of their respective family. The statement, "I had a happy childhood even though my parents got divorced," carries a potential threat to hegemonic family models. "I am happy that my parents got divorced" is also one that questions a fundamental principle of this traditional social unit. This is happening of course at the same time when divorces have ceased to be stigmatizing and reconstituted families are socially accepted by large segments of the population. This statement, however, also allocates the experience of the unhappy child from a broken home and places it somewhere else.

Is it possible to trace analogies between the ways I perceive children, who have been parented by those other than their biological parents, and the cyborg figuration (Haraway, 1991)? I would not want to claim that the relationship works at any level, but rather that the cyborg, as a transgressive figuration, could contribute to an understanding of other hybrids, such as children of social parents. Unlike the cyborg, these children are not new to our cultural imaginary. They have always been here, brought up not in nuclear families, but in a wide array of family settings, legitimate or not, in a number of historical contexts. The family in late modernity is constituted in interplay between "traditional" accounts of the family and practices that deviate from it. Like the cyborg, children of stepfamilies cannot "dream of community on the model of the organic family" (Haraway, 1991, p. 151). Like the cyborg, they are also illegitimate young people in a world where human beings are better off within the realms of a nuclear heterosexual family, never disrupted by circumstances other than the tragic death of one of its members. All other discrepancies from the model family are punished, if not so violently for kids of merely divorced parents, as for those belonging to groups, which in more radical ways deviate from normality. This might also be a clue, however; children of the merely divorced may be carriers of all sorts of privileges, yet they exist in a borderland between the normal and the monstrous. They inhabit a subject position that is necessarily treacherous and in contrast to offspring in nuclear families; they are forced to build, or at least consider building, coalitions which contest kinship based on biology. In this they are active in (un)makings of the social/biological binary, a separation that plays into gender and heterosexuality as well as in the formation of national belonging.

I now turn to Patricia Hill Collins, who helps me conclude, "Instead of engaging in endless criticism, reclaiming the language of family for democratic ends and transforming the very conception of family itself might provide a more useful approach" (2000, p. 172). Dalton and Bielby (2000) see the challenge for the creation of a more encompassing vision of the family as that of avoiding the reproduction of a language, which keeps pointing out the persons who theoretically can give birth and naming them "mothers" as opposed to those who theoretically cannot give birth and calling them "fathers." The authors also suggest that a better, less biologically essentialized language would be ungendered, one that focuses on parents' behavior rather than their roles in biological reproduction. Such a language may also be one that challenges the division between biological and social parenting, a separation that has normalizing, regulatory, even violent effects on the lives of women, children, and men.

CONCLUDING REMARKS

Families that form affinities based on social rather than biological ties come in many forms. Prefixes such as adoptive, step, or queer demonstrate that the unmarked family is constituted as an original against which others are understood. Sometimes these families copy the idea of the "real" family, through, for instance, forming "the perfect (divorced) family,", a practice in which a lesbian couple starts a family with gay men (Sandell, 1998). In Swedish family policy, the nuclear version remains as an "imagined community," even after a divorce, due to "obligatory joint custody" (Bergman & Hobson, 2002), a practice that can be interpreted as a (re)construction of parenthood as primarily biological, rather than social or psychological (Eriksson, 2003). Insemination by donor egg or sperm in Sweden follows a so-called donor-identity release system, in which the child, at the age of 18, has the right to know the identity of the donor. This is yet another example of the primacy granted biological kinship. Social ties, however, are not protected by law. Stepfamilies are social units where affinities based on social rather than biological ties may occur. Due to the fact that a child can only have two legal parents, links between children and their social parents remain unprotected and unrecognized. I trace this lack of representation to the politics of biology.

Nevertheless, the politics of biology are also contested in families where members negotiate the meanings of family and kinship in everyday practices. Children of stepparents may have close bonds to their social parents, unrecognized by the legal system and unrepresented in family discourse, built on essentialized biologized language. In the interviews I have conducted with four young adults brought up in stepfamilies, I trace hesitation and resistance toward being confined to recognizing only two people as parents. My interviewees also express discontent with being categorized as "children from broken homes." These narratives exemplify the hybrid position of these subjects, being both socially accepted and a possible threat to hegemonic family discourse, shaped by the politics of biology. Their narratives show that they are carriers of experiences that challenge meanings of family and parent–child relationships.

I conclude that parenthood in Swedish family law is constituted through the politics of biology. The politics of biology consists of discourses, which grant legal and cultural priority to biological kinship ties. They are fueled by biological determinism and heteronormativity, but challenged by the dynamic multitude of living arrangements represented by late modern families. The language used to speak about families is under pressure from members of those social units that do not contain one of the basic principles for what is in the idea of a "real" family, namely the bloodline that is passed on from generation to generation. To be able to think of the family not in terms of biology but in coalitions of affinity, the language employed regarding kinship structures must be remodeled. The role that the family plays in the political economy must also be addressed with a feminist, intersectional perspective sensitive to the many dimensions of the politics of biology.

NOTES

1. I use the term Marxist feminism for clarity. For a discussion on distinctions between Marxist, socialist, and materialist feminism, see Whelehan (2005).
2. A government authority for official statistics and other government statistics.
3. In Swedish: *skilsmässobarn*.

REFERENCES

Alexander, J. M. (1997). Erotic autonomy as a politics of decolonization: An anatomy of feminist and state practice in the Bahamas tourist economy. In J. M. Alexander & C. T. Mohanty (Eds.), *Feminist genealogies, colonial legacies, democratic futures* (pp. 63–100). New York: Routledge.

Bäck-Wiklund, M. (2003). Familj och modernitet. In M. Bäck-Wiklund & T. Johansson (Eds.), *Nätverksfamiljen* (pp. 17–39). Stockholm: Natur och Kultur.

Bäck-Wiklund, M., & Johansson, T. (2003). *Nätverksfamiljen.* Stockholm: Natur och Kultur.

Bekkengen, L. (2002). *Man får välja - om föräldraskap och föräldraledighet i arbetsliv och familjeliv.* Disssertation Karlstad Universitet: Liber.

Bergman, H., & Hobson, B. (2002). Compulsory fatherhood: The coding of fatherhood in the Swedish welfare state. In B. Hobson (Ed.), *Making men into fathers: Men, masculinities and the Social politics of fatherhood* (pp. 92–124). Cambridge: University Press.

Bryld, M. (2001). The infertility clinic and the birth of the lesbian: The political debate on Assisted Reproduction in Denmark. *European Journal of Women's Studies, 8*(3) 299–313.

Butler, J. (1998). Merely cultural. *New Left Review,* 1/227, 33–44.

———. (1999). *Gender trouble.* New York and London: Routledge.

Calhoun, C. (2000). *Feminism, the family, and the politics of the closet: Lesbian and gay displacement.* Oxford: Oxford University Press.

Crosbie Burnett, M., & Helmbrecht, L. (1993). A descriptive empirical study of gay male stepfamilies. *Family Relations, 42*(3), 256–262.

Dalton, S. E., & Bielby, D. D. (2000). That's our kind of constellation: Lesbian mothers negotiate institutionalized understandings of gender within the family. *Gender & Society, 14*(1), 36–61.

Ds. (2004).19. *Föräldraskap vid assisterad befruktning för homosexuella.* Stockholm: Fritzes offentliga publikationer.

Eriksson, M. (2003). *I skuggan av pappa. Familjerätten och hantering av fäders våld.* Stehag: Gondolin.

Fink, J., Lewis, G., & Clarke, J. (Eds.) (2000). *Rethinking European welfare.* London: Sage.

Haraway, D. (1991). A cyborg manifesto: Science, technology, and socialist-feminism in the late twentieth century. In *Simians, Cyborgs and Women* (pp. 149–183). London: Free Association Books.

———. (1997). Femaleman©_meets_OncoMouse™. Mice into wormholes: A technoscience figure in two parts. In *Modest_Witness@Second_Millennium. Femaleman©_meets_OncoMouse™* (pp. 46–118). New York and London: Routledge.

Haslanger, S., & Witt, C. (Eds.) (2005). *Adoption matters: Philosophical and feminist essays.* New York: Cornell University Press.

Hearn, J. (2002). Men fathers and the state: National and global relations In B. Hobson (Ed.), *Making men into fathers: Men, masculinities and the social politics of fatherhood* (pp. 245–272). Cambridge: University Press.

Hill Collins, P. (2000). It's all in the family: Intersections of gender, race and nation. In U. Narayan & S. Harding (Eds.), *Decentering the center: Philosophy for a multicultural, postcolonial, and feminist world* (pp. 156–176). Bloomington: Hypatia.

Holtzman, M. (2006). Definitions of the family as an impetus for legal change in custody decision-making: Suggestions from an empirical case study. *Law and Social Inquiry, 31*(1), 1–37.

Howarth, D. (2000). *Discourse.* Buckingham: Open University Press.

Klinth, R. (2002). *Göra pappa med barn—Den svenska pappapolitiken 1960–1995*. Umeå: Boréa bokförlag.

Larsson Sjöberg, K. (2003). Mamma, pappa, styvpappa—barn. Föräldraskap i länkade familjesystem. In M. Bäck-Wiklund & T. Johansson (Ed.), *Nätverksfamiljen* (pp. 83–99). Stockholm: Natur och Kultur.

Lewis, G., Gewirtz, S., & ClarkeJ. (2000). *Rethinking social policy*. London: Sage.

Lykke, N. (2003, September-October). Are cyborgs queer? *Biological determinism and feminist theory in the age of new reproductive technologies and reprogenetics*. Paper presented at the 4th European Feminist Research Conference, Bologna. Retrieved February 20, 2006, from http://www.women.it/cyberarchive/files/lykke.htm

Malia, S. E. C. (2005). Balancing family members' interests regarding stepparent rights and obligations: A social policy challenge family relations. *Family Relations, 54*(04), 98–319.

McClintock, A. (1995). *Imperial leather. Race, gender and sexuality in the colonial contest*. New York and London: Routledge.

Mulinari, D. (2003). Om det behövs blir vi uppkäftiga. In M. de los Reyes & Mulinari (Eds.), *Maktens (o)lika förklädnade* (pp. 93–120). Stockholm: Atlas.

Pinkney, S. (2000). Children as welfare subjects in restructured social policy. In . J. Fink, G. Lewis, & J. Clarke (Eds.), *Rethinking European welfare* (pp. 111–126). London: Sage.

Ritala-Koskinen, A. (1994). The family structures are changing—but what about the idea of the family? *Innovation: The European Journal of Social Sciences, 7*(1), 41–50.

Sandell, K. (1998). Lesbisk mor och homosexuell far ny variant av styvfamiljen. *Kvinnovetenskaplig tidskrift, 16*(1), 43–47.

Singer, A. (2002). Framtidens föräldraskap. In I. Söderlind (Ed.), *Uppväxt, familjeformer och barns bästa—Om familjeliv som offentlig angelgenhet och vardaglig praktik* (pp. 157–169). Stockholm: Institutet för framtidsstudier.

Smith, F. (2005). A child of one's own: A moral assessment of property concepts in adoption. In S. Haslanger & C. Witt (Eds.), *Adoption matters: Philosophical and feminist essays* (pp. 112–131). New York: Cornell University Press.

Stevens, J. (2005). Methods of adoption: Eliminating genetic privilege. In S. Haslanger & C. Witt (Eds.), *Adoption matters: Philosophical and feminist essays,*(pp. 68–94). New York: Cornell University Press.

Watson, S. (2000). Foucault and the study of social policy. In G. Lewis, S. Gewirtz, & J. Clarke (Eds.), *Rethinking social policy* (pp. 66–77). London: Sage.

Wheelehan, I. (2005). *Modern feminist thought. From the second wave to" postfeminism."* Edinburgh: Edinburgh University Press.

Wright, J. M. (1998). *Lesbian stepfamilies. An ethnography of love*. New York: Harrington Park Press.

6 Intimate Citizenship and the Right to Care
The Case of Breastfeeding

Lisa Smyth

Care is a central concern of human life. It is time that we began to change our political and social institutions to reflect this truth

Tronto (1993, pp.170–171)

INTRODUCTION

Parents face a raft of often contradictory advice on how best to feed and care for their newborn infants, a process that begins early in pregnancy, if not before. Mothers in particular must, during the intense and exhausting period following childbirth, negotiate the contradictory pressures of health promotion campaigns to increase rates of breastfeeding and broader cultural norms which, in the developed world, usually distinguish maternity from sexuality (Young, 1998) and subject women's sexualized bodies to critical scrutiny in ways that are sharply mediated by key social divisions, not least those of class, "race," age, and ethnicity. It should come as no surprise then to discover that methods of infant feeding (i.e., whether an infant is fed breast milk and/or infant formula) are sharply distinguished to reflect these broader social divisions (e.g., Hamlyn, Brooker, Oleinikova, & Wands, 2000). For those learning to breastfeed, they also must master what can be a technically difficult and physically painful skill (Oakley, 1986, p. 174).[1] Furthermore, official efforts to promote health through a campaign of public persuasion that "breast is best" often concentrate on educational strategies at the cost of providing more substantive support which would, for example, enable women to breastfeed without compromising their ability to inhabit public spaces or their paid employment entitlements (Carter, 1995; Galtry, 2000).

This range of contradictory pressures that new mothers face often results in relatively high rates of breastfeeding initiation following birth, but ultimately similar practices of early transfer to formula feeding, as women negotiate the health message on the one hand and their own bodily dispositions in "public" space (hospitals, "public" areas of the home, shops, work, meeting places, etc.) on the other. The practice of breastfeeding undermines the assumption that bodies and sexuality are "private" and "natural," in contrast to the "public" world of paid work and civil society (Bacchi & Beasley, 2002, p. 328; Lister, 2002, p. 191; Weeks, 1998, p. 36), raising issues of what Plummer describes as "intimate citizenship" (2001).

This chapter considers questions that breastfeeding politics and practices raise for women's citizenship, looking at how feminism in particular has responded to them. It then outlines how women's intimate citizenship can be promoted through feminist advocacy of the right to breastfeed.

FEMINISM AND BREASTFEEDING

As a number of authors have recently pointed out, feminists have paid scant attention to the social, political, and health issues raised by infant feeding, and breastfeeding more specifically, for women (Carter, 1995; Hausman, 2003; Van Esterik, 1994; Wolf, 2006).[2] This is in sharp contrast to feminist attention to issues arising in relation to pregnancy and childbirth. As Hausman argues, "It is clear that the pregnant body takes pride of place as the subject of feminist inquiry into reproduction" (2003, p. 191).

Hausman outlines the reasons for this lack of attention, not least that the practice of breastfeeding seems to diminish the autonomy of mothers, and that the apparent self-sacrifice involved seems to support conservative, maternalist accounts of motherhood. As Carter puts it, breastfeeding seems to both offer "a return to the repressed 'truth' of natural motherhood" (1995, p. 29) and provide a useful mechanism for enhancing the social control of mothers (1995, p. 34).[3] Yalom points to the ways in which images of breastfeeding have been used historically in a range of contexts for such purposes. For example, the image of the "good" maternal breast, as opposed to the "corrupted" wet nurse's breast, came to represent the promise of social regeneration during the 18th century (Yalom, 1997, p. 106). Indeed, contemporary policies that seek to increase breastfeeding rates often involve the problematization of working class, black, and other marginalized mothers (pp. 215–216).

Hausman argues, however, that the relative lack of feminist attention to breastfeeding means that there is no obvious feminist discourse through which breastfeeding women can frame what she argues is a bio-social practice (2003, p. 193). The risk with this lack of attention to the implications of infant feeding practices and politics is that it leaves the arena wide open to a conservative maternalist agenda.[4] Galtry argues, in tracing the history of feminist reluctance to take up a position on breastfeeding in New Zealand, that the concern to avoid biological determinism in developing employment rights for women has effectively resulted in the acceptance of the male worker model as the norm. This makes it difficult to gather momentum to seek to transform employment practices and expectations in ways that would facilitate gender equality, for instance, by enabling working mothers to breastfeed and enabling them to better balance the demands of infant and child care with those of paid work more generally. Furthermore, she points out that feminist avoidance of breastfeeding advocacy "reinforces the assumption that infant feeding is a matter of individual choice, with all women potentially experiencing such choice" (Galtry, 1997, p. 80). As she notes, sociological evidence indicates that this is far from the case, as constraints of class, "race," age, ethnicity, and a variety of other social divisions significantly shape infant feeding practices.

Hausman, along with others (e.g., Van Esterik, 1994), argues instead that feminists should treat breastfeeding not simply as a matter of private choice, but as an aspect of women's citizenship, and more specifically as a reproductive rights issue.[5] In what follows, I develop Hausman's claim by outlining specific citizenship issues breastfeeding does raise for women, and consider how feminists might shape a coherent political approach to them.

BREASTFEEDING, CAPABILITIES, AND CITIZENSHIP

Breastfeeding has implications beyond the usually considered issues of maximizing infant nutrition and maternal and infant health (Blum, 1999; Carter, 1995). While there is much debate about the added value of human milk in contrast to artificial milk for infants in the developed world (e.g., Blum, 1999; Earle, 2003; Hausman, 2003; Law, 2000), breastfeeding raises additional broader political and social issues, which can be analyzed as ones of intimate citizenship and are outlined in what follows.

Given that breastfeeding has become an important national and international public policy objective on grounds of the health advantages it confers (Mahon-Daly & Andrews, 2002, p. 68), it would seem that areas where rates are low raise questions about whether such policy adequately supports breastfeeding as a reproductive capability. In stating the issue in these terms, I approach it from the point of view of Nussbaum's outline of how governmentation can best develop human capabilities. As she argues, an initiative that simply seeks to maximize utility, such as infant and maternal health, or to distribute resources as evenly and fairly as possible, takes too narrow a view of the full range of human capabilities, and consequently often overlooks major inequalities in so doing. Public policies should instead be concerned with maximizing our opportunities to develop the full range of our capabilities as human beings, including that to direct our own lives, as she puts it, not least in relation to childbearing and child rearing, and to do so in our own surroundings and context (Nussbaum, 1995, p. 85). She argues that the focus of public policy should not be on whether or not particular capabilities are actually developed in practice, but instead on whether we have the *opportunities* to do so,

Government is not directed to push citizens into acting in certain valued ways; instead, it is directed to make sure that all human beings have the necessary resources and conditions for acting in those ways. It leaves the choice up to them. A person with plenty of food can always choose to fast. A person who has been given the capability for sexual expression can always choose celibacy. The person who has access to subsidized education can always decide to do something else instead. By making opportunities available, government enhances, and does not remove, choice. (Nussbaum, 1995, pp. 94–95)

Rather that treating infant feeding either as a simple matter of private choice and often practice, as feminist attention to it tends to do (Hausman, 2003), or as a matter of maximizing the health of the population, as official efforts to promote health generally see it (e.g., Department of Health and Social Services Northern Ireland, 1999), a feminist politics of breastfeeding might regard nursing as raising key questions about women's capability to nurture infants in a way that enhances rather than threatens their own sense of embodied selfhood in the physically and emotionally demanding context of such care. This would address many of the issues raised in qualitative sociological analyses of why women do or do not breastfeed (e.g., Earle, 2002; Pain, Bailey, & Mowl, 2001; Van Esterik, 2002). Thus, the ability to develop a capacity to breastfeed involves not simply that of choosing to meet the basic needs of infants for nurture and close physical contact, in response to being told that "breast is best," but also what Nussbaum describes as being able to form a conception of "the good," and "to engage in critical reflection about the planning of one's own life." In other words, public policy on breastfeeding should enable women to make well-informed and highly personal decisions about how to care for their infants in ways that enhance rather than diminish our sense of autonomous selfhood.[6] This approach would seek to take seriously the negative experiences of breastfeeding expressed, for instance, by the women in Schmeid and Lupton's (2001) study, who, despite being committed to the idea of breastfeeding, nevertheless felt alienated from their infants through the practice. Blum also articulates a less than entirely positive experience, noting that ". . . breastfeeding was one of the most intensely ambivalent experiences of my life. . ." (Blum, 1999, p. 208; see also Giles, 2003). A capabilities approach would enable women to make reasoned decisions about how to proceed, rather than in the face of physical and/or emotional difficulty, on the basis of a sense of moral obligation.[7]

Much research seeks to establish why some women breastfeed while others do not. The explanations cover a wide range of factors, including the economic and political influence of artificial milk producers (e.g., Palmer, 1993); the medicalization of pregnancy, childbearing, and infant feeding as well as the development of "scientific mothering" (e.g., Apple, 1987); the lack of significant breastfeeding role models for new mothers (e.g., Bentley, Dee, & Jensen, 2003); the sexualization of breasts and the shame and embarrassment associated with exposing breasts in public places (e.g., Bartlett, 2002; Carter, 1995); the difficulty of developing a range of "breasted experiences" (Young, 2005); a desire to shift the burden of feeding onto others, not least fathers (e.g., Earle, 2000; Maher, 1992); and the difficulty of returning to paid work and continuing to breastfeed (e.g., Hausman, 2004). As Van Esterik comments, "Research in Euro-American contexts reveals how breastfeeding has been rendered pathological, the normal medicalized, and the breastfeeding body has been turned into a site of conflict and struggle" (2002, p. 264). The range of factors at play points to the ways in which infant feeding is shaped not simply by private choice or a concern to maximize health and well being, but by a broad range of economic, political, and social forces, which orient mothers and fathers toward specific care practices. Thus, the development of breastfeeding as a human capability involves more than just giving mothers (and fathers) the chance to choose spontaneously to do so, for example, by simply informing them that "breast is best."[8] As Nussbaum argues,

> . . . the capability view insists that choice is not pure spontaneity, flourishing independent of material and social conditions. If one cares about autonomy, then one must care about the rest of the form of life that supports it, and the material conditions that enable one to live that form of life. (1995, p. 95)

Thus, a feminist agenda in relation to breastfeeding would seek substantively to promote women's autonomous decision making over infant feeding, through the enhancement of their capacity to develop a distinctive life project, which involves parenting in ways that are chosen through a process of practical reasoning, rather than simply in response to the range of pressures mentioned earlier. This would involve a decisive shift away from the feminist disavowal of the health benefits of breastfeeding noted by Hausman (2003, p. 6), while also avoiding an endorsement of biological determinism, for instance, through maternalism.

BREASTFEEDING AND CITIZENSHIP

Bacchi and Beasley argue that discussions of citizenship tend to pay little attention to bodies, despite the growing literature on the complex ways in which bodies are invested with and carry a range of social meanings (2002, p. 329). Nevertheless, considerations of the ways in which bodies and embodied relations are important distributive mechanisms for citizenship can be found in work on gender and citizenship, as well as in the emerging studies of sexual or "intimate" citizenship (Carver & Mottier, 1998; Evans, 1993; Lister, 1997, 2002; Plummer, 2001, 2003; Richardson,

1998; Walby, 1994; Weeks, 1998). Breastfeeding offers a useful example through which to consider the extent sexualized bodies, generally regarded as aspects of "private" life, can and cannot inhabit and participate in the "public" world.

A public policy that seeks to support women's capability to care for their infants by breastfeeding would need to address the ways in which the civil, social, and political aspects of citizenship, presented by Marshall (1950), are compromised (or not) by the practice. In what follows, I outline each of these in turn. Although this approach may seem overly schematic and closed (Plummer, 2001, p. 241), given the interconnections among these three aspects of citizenship, it is nevertheless useful in specifying precisely in what ways breastfeeding does bring women's citizenship into question through the sexualized and intimately maternal activities of women's bodies.

BREASTFEEDING AND CIVIL CITIZENSHIP

The freedom to breastfeed in public is far from a guaranteed civil right, raising questions about the extent to which women who do so are shielded from bodily interference in public spaces. For example, in November 2005 a woman was asked to stop the practice by police in Norfolk, England (Edemariam, 2005). Bartlett (2002) has noted similar examples that differ from state to state (Newbold, 2005). Hence, there exists a lack of guaranteed entitlement to practice breastfeeding in the "developed" world, and women can be prosecuted in some jurisdictions for so doing. For example, it was 1993 and 1994, respectively, before the United States states of Florida and New York allowed women to nurse offspring openly without fear of prosecution, and 1995 before California did likewise. A number of other states have only recently passed such legislation (e.g., Arizona in April 2006), while others still have none (e.g., Kansas, Mississippi, and West Virginia; Vance, 2006). In the United Kingdom, only the Scottish Parliament has recognized a right to feed babies and infants in public spaces (2005), although there are current proposals to enact similar entitlements in England (Kidney, 2005). Neither the Republic of Ireland nor the North of Ireland acknowledge this right.

In Northern Ireland, the Health Promotion Agency launched a "Breastfeeding Welcome Here" campaign in 2005, which recruits local businesses and other organizations to support the practice by prominently displaying a sticker with the campaign message (Health Promotion Agency, 2005). While at first glance this would appear to be a useful strategy for publicly declaring entitlement to breastfeed outside of "private" spaces, it also has the unfortunate effect of indicating that unless such a sign is on display, nursing an infant may not be welcome. Thus, it would seem that this effort carries a risk of undermining women's rights to breastfeed in public places.

Instead, private businesses and other organizations are given the arbitrary power to decide on such entitlement.

As Bartlett notes, women's *perception* that public breastfeeding is unacceptable influences their decisions in this regard (2002, p. 116). Thus, it would seem that the practice of breastfeeding places women's civil citizenship, that is, an entitlement to noninterference, conceived by Marshall (1950) as a necessary condition of freedom, in question.

BREASTFEEDING AND POLITICAL/ INTIMATE CITIZENSHIP

Breastfeeding does occasionally raise issues of political citizenship narrowly conceived, that is, women's abilities to participate in public debate and decision-making. For example, there has been much controversy over whether women Members of Parliament (United Kingdom) should be allowed to breastfeed in the debating Chamber of the Westminster House of Commons, or in Committee sessions (Sear, Miller, & Lourie, 2003). Women MPs must now make a choice between full participation in debate and decision making, or feeding their infants in specially designated "private" areas.

Breastfeeding also carries broader political significance beyond participation in political debate and decision making, notably in the way it questions the apparent distinction between sexuality and maternity (Bartlett, 2002). The sense of potential shame and embarrassment that many women express at the idea of breastfeeding (see, e.g., Earle, 2002, pp. 212–213), and the embarrassment and disgust that others express at the sight of the practice (e.g., Greene, Stewart-Knox, & Wright, 2003, pp. 56–60), raises exactly these sorts of socio-political issues about the ways in which nursing is regarded as crossing what is imagined to be quite a fixed line between private (intimate bodily) practices and public life, and between sexualized breasts and desexualized maternity. For example, in her study of women's experiences of breastfeeding in public, Cindy Stearns found that "[b]reastfeeding women fear that the exposure of their breasts will be misread as a sexual invitation to male strangers and they fear potential consequences of that misreading" (1999, p. 316). Alison Bartlett has traced the ways in which in Australia it has been politicized in precisely this way. As she notes, the practice is only acceptable when done discreetly.[9] Women perceived as breastfeeding in an "exhibitionist" way, however, are subject to much more critical and censorious political attention (Bartlett, 2002, p. 117).[10]

Thus, the often contradictory social meanings attached to maternity and women's bodies makes it difficult, often impossible, for women to decide to breastfeed and to do so in their own surroundings and context, to use Nussbaum's terms. Therefore, it often takes place "behind closed doors"

(Greene et al., 2003, p. 64). As Cindy Stearns argues, "[t]o be expected to hide breastfeeding is to hide much of the early work of mothering" for such women (1999, p. 323). Significant numbers of mothers who begin breast-feeding abandon the practice as confining it to private spaces is practically impossible (e.g., Pain et al., 2001).

Breastfeeding and Social Citizenship

The third aspect of Marshall's model of citizenship refers to one's entitle-ment to live a life in accordance with the standards prevailing in a society. This refers particularly to social rights to good health, education, and wel-fare. Policy making on breastfeeding is indeed often framed through the lens of infant, and more recently maternal, health, and is usually pursued by way of health education strategies.

Much breastfeeding advocacy, both state and nongovernmental, focuses on the health and developmental advantages that the practice can confer (Van Esterik, 2002, p. 258). However, this is usually at the expense of a broader consideration of the ways in which breastfeeding is very much shaped by the extent to which the capability to "live one's own life, and nobody else's" has been developed. It could be argued, then, that educa-tional efforts to redescribe breasts in terms of health will fail unless they take account of the ways that reproductive choices involve "both sexual capability and issues of separateness, and bind the two together in a deep and complex way" (Nussbaum, 1995, p. 85).

As noted earlier, the lack of feminist attention to the politics of breast-feeding has been shaped by, among other concerns, a sense that to endorse the practice also would risk condoning a conservative view of women's lives as "naturally" oriented toward reproduction and caring roles, in ways that would compromise their economic, physical, and emotional health and well-being (Carter, 1995, pp.19–20). As Blum puts it, "[a]rguing for breastfeed-ing is dangerous within the present ascendancy of conservatism and the threats to women's rights to bodily integrity exemplified by abortion restric-tions and 'fetal rights' cases" (1993, p. 300). Nevertheless, care policies, including these of breastfeeding, do need to be critically debated, not least because caring constitutes an important way through which we practice ethics, among other things (Tronto, 1993). As Daly argues, "[c]are is a com-plex issue for public policy. Not alone do care-related provisions frame the boundaries between family, state and market but they seek to shape intimate human motivations and relations" (2002, p. 254). She argues, nonetheless, that "emotional fulfillment, what one might term 'the intrinsic reward' [of caring], is hugely important for the well-being of the cared" (2002, p. 262). Thus, the development of policies regarding such provision needs to take seriously the orientation of the carer toward meeting the needs of the recipi-ent in specific ways. As Tronto argues, a focus on how needs might be met in ways that are just for those involved in both giving and receiving care is vital, if we are to avoid producing unequal relationships and identities through such action (1993, pp. 170–171). Infant feeding policies, and particularly official breastfeeding promotion strategies, affect not only the health and development of offspring, but also the well-being of mothers, who find themselves at the center of agendas, which often fail to take account of their emotional and practical orientations and capabilities to meet the needs of their children in officially recommended ways.

As already noted, some recent work has made the case that feminists should develop a perspective on breastfeeding precisely because it does have an impact on women's health and well-being. A number of scholars have argued that the forms of health activism in which feminists have engaged, for instance in relation to pregnancy and childbirth, where mainstream biological accounts of bodily processes and needs are taken seriously in order to be challenged, should also be extended to infant feeding (Hausman, 2003; Van Esterik, 1994; Wolf, 2006). This would enable pro-breastfeeding arguments to be reoriented toward the needs of women, rather than taking account only of professional views of these needs, along with those of babies. Hausman also argues that a feminist health advocacy approach would consider the ways in which the practice can meet a variety of necessities beyond the nutritional. Indeed, the physical, economic, and emotional costs of nursing to mothers should, she argues, be factored into policymaking at the broad societal level, in ways that would circumvent the moral pressure on mothers to breastfeed, while at the same time engage with debates about the health benefits of it (Hausman, 2003, p. 153). As she argues, "[f]eminist scholars should confront, challenge, and work with biomedical discourses about female bodies in order to help to shape the public debates that emerge from biomedical research and practice" (p. 231).

Feminism, Breastfeeding, and Intimate Citizenship

Thus, it would seem that the ambiguity over women's entitlement to breastfeed in public, the ways in which the practice throws into question a sharp distinction between sexuality and maternity, and the disconnection of related policies from the broader range of human capabilities identified by Nussbaum, compromise women's intimate citizenship in quite significant ways. In what follows, I outline how a nonmaternalist case can be made for supporting breastfeeding as a key site where women's capabilities should be developed.

GENDER AND CARE

> . . . in Korea, 1-month-old babies spend about 8% of their time alone, while American infants of a similar age spend about 67% of their time alone. (Hausman, 2003, p. 101)

Feminism has long treated care as a valuable, embodied, and relational practice, while hotly contesting its social organization. Some of the earliest alternative institutions established by feminists in the United States were child care centers (Umansky ,1996, p. 50). Motherhood in particular, and nurturing in general, have been key themes of feminist theory and politics (e.g., Daly, 2002; Ruddick, 1989; Sevenhuijsen, 1998; Tronto, 1993; Umansky, 1996). Sevenhuijsen argues, for example, that the furtherance of gender equality requires that everyone, not just women, be given the same opportunities to give and receive care (2000). While breastfeeding as a specific form of care limits the category of people who can feed the infant(s), this does not necessarily preclude active involvement of others, notably fathers, in looking after newborns.

Rima Apple has traced the historical emergence of "scientific motherhood," particularly the ways in which "scientific" practices, such as scheduled formula feeds with relatively long gaps in between and the incorporation of hospital norms and routines into everyday life, were introduced (1987). The impact of this transformation in mothering, encapsulated as it is in the move from breast to formula, has been not insignificant (Van Esterik, 1989).

Breastfeeding can contribute to the reconfiguration of the meaning of early motherhood by reshaping its practices. Indeed, the international advocacy organization, La Leche League, has long argued that housework should take a poor second place to infant feeding and care (Blum & Vandewater, 1993; Hausman, 2003). Demand breastfeeding, the method recommended by the World Health Organization (World Health Organization, 2004), makes it very difficult for mothers to "do it all" on the domestic front, and requires active participation by others, such as fathers or partners. As Hausman, puts it, "Breastfeeding. . . is an activity facilitated by flexible work, social and financial resources, and supportive professional and kin networks" (2003, p. 6). The practice thus does not undercut the need for paid paternity or parental leave, but instead underlines the necessity for it.

CONCLUSION

This chapter has sought to outline the ways in which breastfeeding policies and practices raise issues about women's intimate citizenship, which affect women's civil rights, the meanings of women's bodies, and health and welfare policies. Situating breastfeeding within a broader capabilities framework is necessary if this range of citizenship issues is to be connected in ways that enhance rather than undermine women's embodied autonomy.

As Plummer notes, citizenship is very much bound up with public spheres (2001, p. 242), and any consideration of the politics of breastfeeding must necessarily examine the gendering of public spaces (Bartlett, 2002,

Massey, 1994). "Public" (including sometimes domestic) breastfeeding often involves placing connected and dependent bodies firmly in spaces designed for disconnected and disembodied users, in ways that carry the potential to transform, or at least transgress, such gendered and sexualized meanings. A feminist approach, which situates breastfeeding in terms of women's capabilities and intimate citizenship, would seek to enable women to make reasoned decisions about how to care for their infants in ways that are as free as possible from moral, economic, and social pressures as well as enhance their abilities to parent in self-directed ways, in their own surroundings and context.

NOTES

1. As one women asks, recounting the pain and difficulty she experienced when trying to breastfeed, "Why the silence about the difficulty of breastfeeding? Why all the propaganda instead of frank talk?" Giles, F. (2003). *Fresh milk: The secret life of breasts*. New York: Simon & Schuster, 17–18.
2. This contrasts with feminism in the 1960s and early 1970s in the United States, where, as Laura Umansky illustrates, certain strands of feminism were closely connected with the countercultural movement, and its romantic ideas about "natural" forms of mothering: "Unashamed of her body, with milk flowing from her breasts and long hair flowing down her back, both nurturant and sexual, the hippie mother represented the quintessence of the counterculture". Umansky, L. (1996). *Motherhood reconceived: Feminism and the legacies of the sixties*. New York: New York University Press, p. 56.
3. Penny Van Esterik notes, for instance, that women's groups in India responded to the passing of a code regulating the marketing of infant formula as "draconian," fearing that it would damage women's careers and force them back into domesticity; Van Esterik, P. (1996). Breastfeeding and work: The situation of midwives and other women health care providers. In S. F. Murray (Ed.), *Baby friendly, mother friendly* (pp. 77–88). London: Mosby, 1996. .
4. This point is echoed in a more general sense regarding the lack of attention to bodies in work on citizenship by Bacchi, C. L., & Beasley, C. (2002). Citizen bodies: Is embodied citizenship a contradiction in terms? *Critical Social Policy, 22*(2), 324–352.
5. Hausman makes this argument in opposition to the sort of objection raised by Law, who posits that treating infant feeding as an aspect of reproduction and sexuality overlooks the key distinction between pregnancy and childbearing on the one hand, where the bodies of mother and foetus are not separate, and child rearing on the other, where they are. From his perspective, a failure to appreciate this key distinction allows breastfeeding advocacy to support a maternalist politics, which defines women in terms of motherhood and "good" motherhood in relation to self-sacrifice, including through breastfeeding; Law, J. (2000). The politics of breastfeeding: Assessing risk, dividing labor,. *Signs, 25*(2), 407–450. It seems to me that breastfeeding can be regarded as a reproductive right because it involves recognizing a continued biological connection, albeit not a necessary one, between infant and mother's bodies, which carry socio-political implications about the entitlement of those connected bodies to inhabit space as a dyad.

6. In putting the case in these terms, I reject Bacchi and Beasley's claim (Bacchi, C. L., & Beasley, C. (2002). Citizen bodies: Is embodied citizenship a contradiction in terms? *Critical Social Policy*, 22(2), 324–352–.329) that discussions of autonomy necessarily reproduce a mind/body dualism. Instead, I would follow Cornell's argument that what is often at stake in reproductive and sexual politics is women's ability to imagine ourselves as whole over time, in ways where the body is central to that imagining; Cornell, D. (1995). *The imaginary domain: Abortion, pornography & sexual harassment*. New York: Routledge.

7. As Carter argues, "Breast-feeding has been embedded in discourses of femininity, which specify what women ought to be and infer that if women are not like this it is because of some moral failing. Women are not expected to need any resources of particular conditions to perform this function since they are only after all doing what ought to come naturally"; Carter, P. (1995). *Feminism, breasts and breast-feeding*. Houndmills, Basingstoke: Macmillan, p. 70.

8. Carter argues that "[t]he absence of feminist engagement with the politics of infant feeding has left virtually untouched a dominant construction of infant feeding problems as involving an irrational, if natural, woman who needs to be told again and again why breast is best."

9. Cindy Stearns also found that the women in her study valued very highly an ability to breastfeed discreetly in public; "Being an invisible breastfeeding mother was the goal for many women. Women would describe wearing special clothing, draping a receiving blanket over the baby, sitting in obscure places, and other means of hiding the breastfeeding." Stearns, C. (1999). Breastfeeding and the good maternal body. *Gender & Society*, 13(3), 313.

10. See also Fiona Giles' selection of survey responses to a question about one thing that would have made breastfeeding easier: Giles, F. (2003). *Fresh milk: The secret life of breasts*. New York: Simon & Schuster, pp. 19–20.

REFERENCES

Apple, R. D. (1987). *Mothers and medicine: A social history of infant feeding, 1890–1950*. Madison, WI: University of Wisconsin Press.

Bacchi, C. L., & Beasley, C. (2002). Citizen bodies: Is embodied citizenship a contradiction in terms? *Critical Social Policy*, 22(2), 324–352.

Bartlett, A. (2002). Scandalous practices and political performances: Breastfeeding in the city. *Continuum: Journal of Media & Cultural Studies*, 16(1), 111–121.

Bentley, M., Dee, D., & Jensen, J. (2003). Breastfeeding among low income African-American women: Power, beliefs and decision making. *Journal of Nutrition*, 133(1), 305S–309S.

Blum, L. (1993). Mothers, babies, and breast-feeding in late capitalist America—The shifting contexts of feminist theory. *Feminist Studies*, 19(2), 291–311.

Blum, L., & Vandwater, E. (1993). Mother to mother—a maternalist organization in late capitalist America. *Social Problems*, 40(3), 285–300.

Blum, L. M. (1999). *At the breast: Ideologies of breastfeeding and motherhood in the contemporary United States*. Boston: Beacon Press.

Carter, P. (1995). *Feminism, breasts and breast-feeding*. Houndmills, Basingstoke: Macmillan.

Carver, T., & Mottier, V. (1998). *Politics of sexuality: Identity, gender, citizenship*. London and New York: Routledge.

Cornell, D. (1995). *The imaginary domain: Abortion, pornography & sexual harassment.* New York: Routledge.

Crown Copyright. (2005). *Breastfeeding, etc. (Scotland) Act.* Retrieved August 8, 2006, from www.opsi.gov.uk/legislation/scotland/acts2005/20050001.htm

Daly, M. (2002). Care as a good for social policy. *Journal of Social Policy, 31,* 251–270.

Department of Health and Social Services Northern Ireland. (1999). *Breastfeeding strategy for Northern Ireland.* Belfast: Author.

Earle, S. (2000). Why some women do not breast feed: Bottle feeding and fathers' role. *Midwifery, 16*(4), 323–330.

———. (2002). Factors affecting the initiation of breastfeeding: Implications for breastfeeding promotion. *Health Promotion International, 17*(3), 205–214.

———. (2003). Is breast best? Breastfeeding, motherhood and identity. In S. Earle & G. Letherby (Eds.), *Gender, identity and reproduction: Social perspectives* (pp. 135–150). Houndsmills: Palgrave Macmillan.

Edemariam, A. (2005, November 23). Would you mind if I breastfeed? *The Guardian,* pp. 12–13.

Evans, D. T. (1993). *Sexual citizenship: The material construction of sexualities.* London, New York: Routledge.

Galtry, J. (1997). "Sameness" and suckling: Infant feeding, feminism, and a changing labour market. *Women's Studies Journal, 13*(1), 65–88.

———. (2000). Extending the "bright line"—Feminism, breastfeeding, and the workplace in the United States. *Gender & Society, 14*(2), 295–317.

Giles, F. (2003). *Fresh milk: The secret life of breasts.* New York: Simon & Schuster.

Greene, J., Stewart-Knox, B., & Wright, M. (2003). Feeding preferences and attitudes to breastfeeding and its promotion among teenagers in Northern Ireland. *Journal of Human Lactation, 19*(1), 57–65.

Hamlyn, B., Brooker, S. Oleinikova, K., & Wands, S. (2000). *Infant feeding 2000:* A Survey conducted on behalf of the Department of Health, the Scottish Executive, the National Assembly for Wales and the Department of Health, Social Services and Public Safety in Northern Ireland. London: The Stationery Office.

Hausman, B. L. (2003). *Mother's milk: Breastfeeding controversies in American culture.* New York: Routledge.

———. (2004). The feminist politics of breastfeeding. *Australian Feminist Studies, 19*(45), 273–285.

Health Promotion Agency, N. I. (2005). Breastfeeding welcome here initiative. Launched by HPA. *Inform, 41,*1. Retrieved August 8, 2006, from http://www.healthpromotionagency.org.uk/Resources/corporate/inform/pdfs/inform41.pd

Kidney, D. (2005). *House of Commons Hansard debates for November 8.* Col. 181. Retrieved December 29, 2005, from www.publications.parliament.uk/pa/cmhansrd/cm051108/debtext/51108 .

Law, J. (2000). The politics of breastfeeding: Assessing risk, dividing labor. *Signs, 25*(2), 407–450.

Lister, R. (1997). *Citizenship: Feminist perspectives.* Washington Square, NY: New York University Press.

———. (2002). Sexual citizenship. In E. F. Isin & B. S. Turner (Eds.), *Handbook of citizenship studies* (pp. 191–207). London: Sage.

Maher, V. (1992). Breast-feeding in cross-cultural perspective: Paradoxes and proposals. In V. Maher (Ed.), *The anthropology of breast-feeding: Natural law or social construct,* (pp. 1–36). Oxford: Berg.

Mahon-Daly, P., & Andrews, G. (2002). Liminality and breastfeeding: Women negotiating space and two bodies. *Health & Place, 8*(2), 61–76.

Marshall, T. H. (1950). *Citizenship and social class, and other essays.* Cambridge: University Press.

Massey, D. B. (1994). *Space, place, and gender.* Minneapolis: University of Minnesota Press.

Newbold, D. (2005). *Breastfeeding out and about.* Australian Breastfeeding Association. Retrieved August 11, 2006, from http://www.breastfeeding.asn.au/bfinfo/out.html Nussbaum, M. C. (1995). Human capabilities, female human beings. In M. C. Nussbaum & J. Glover (Eds.), *Women, culture, and development* (pp. 61–104). Oxford: Clarendon Press.

Oakley, A. (1986). *From here to maternity: Becoming a mother.* Harmondsworth: Penguin.

Pain, R., Bailey, C., & Mowl, G. (2001). Infant feeding in North East England: Contested spaces of reproduction. *Area, 33*(3), 261–272.

Palmer, G. (1993). *The politics of breastfeeding.* Hammersmith, London: Pandora, an imprint of Harper Collins.

Plummer, K. (2001). The square of intimate citizenship: Some preliminary proposals. *Citizenship Studies, 5*(3), 237–253.

———. (2003). *Intimate citizenship: Private decisions and public dialogues.* Seattle: University of Washington Press.

Richardson, D. (1998). Sexuality and citizenship. *Sociology, 32*(1), 83–100.

Ruddick, S. (1989). *Maternal thinking: Toward a politics of peace.* Boston: Beacon Press.

Schmied, V., & Lupton, D. (2001). Blurring the boundaries: Breastfeeding and maternal subjectivity. *Sociology of Health & Illness, 23*(2), 234–250.

Sear, C., Miller, V., & Lourie, J. (2003). *Breastfeeding in Parliament.* House of Commons Library. Retrieved August 11, 2006, from http://www.parliament.uk/commons/lib/research/notes/snpc-00508.pdf

Sevenhuijsen, S. (1998). *Citizenship and the ethics of care: Feminist considerations on justice, morality, and politics.* London and New York: Routledge.

———. (2000). Caring in the third way: The relation between obligation, responsibility and care in Third Way discourse. *Critical Social Policy, 20*(1), 5–37.

Stearns, C. (1999). Breastfeeding and the good maternal body. *Gender & Society, 13*(3), 308–325.

Tronto, J. C. (1993). *Moral boundaries: A political argument for an ethic of care.* New York: Routledge.

Umansky, L. (1996). *Motherhood reconceived: Feminism and the legacies of the sixties.* New York: New York University Press.

Vance, M. R. (2006). *Summary of breastfeeding legislation in the US as of 12/05/06* La Leche League International. Retrieved August 8, 2006, from http://www.lalecheleague.org/Law/summary.html#CA

Van Esterik, P. (1989). *Beyond the breast-bottle controversy.* New Brunswick, NJ: Rutgers University Press.

———. (1994). Breastfeeding and feminism. *International Journal of Gynecol. Obstet., 47*(Suppl.), 41–54.

———. (1996). Breastfeeding and work: The situation of midwives and other women health care providers. In S. F. Murray (Ed.), *Baby friendly, mother friendly* (pp. 77–88). London: Mosby.

———. (2002). Contemporary trends in infant feeding research. *Annual Review of Anthropology, 31*, 257–278.

Walby, S. (1994). Is citizenship gendered? *Sociology, 28*(2), 379–395.

Weeks, J. (1998). The sexual citizen. *Theory Culture & Society, 15*(3–4), 35–52.

Wolf, J. H.(2006). What feminists can do for breastfeeding and what breastfeeding can do for feminists. *Signs: Journal of Women in Culture and Society, 31*(2), 397–424.

World Health Organisation. (2004). *Nutrition: Infant and young child* world health organisation. Retrieved July 19, 2005, from www.who.int/child-adolescent-health/NUTRITION/infant_exclusive.htm

Yalom, M. (1997). *A history of the breast.* New York: Alfred A. Knopf, Distributed by Random House.

Young, I. M. (1998). Breasted experience: The look and the feeling. In R. Weitz (Ed.), *The politics of women's bodies: Sexuality, appearance, and behavior.* New York: Oxford University Press.

————. (2005). *On female body experience: "Throwing like a girl" and other essays.* New York: Oxford University Press.

7 Gender, Sexuality, and Nation— Here and Now

Reflections on the Gendered and Sexualized Aspects of Contemporary Polish Nationalism

Agnieszka Graff

Poland's right-wing politicians have a great deal to say about women and sexual minorities and though their pronouncements may appear simplistic, aberrant, or obsessive, they do deserve our attention. This is because of, first, the political impact (in Poland the aberrant has a way of turning into reality, and needs to be confronted as such), and second these rhetorical excesses provide a case study in gendered nationalism of a sort rarely found in contemporary Europe (the Balkans being a possible exception). The discourse in question is obsessed with motherhood and fatherland, flags and fetuses; it is also marked by a profound anxiety about twin evils threatening to invade Poland from the West (with Holland and Germany the most likely sources), namely: homosexuality and abortion. It is a language filled with moral certainties, aversion toward "equality" and "tolerance," and a deep commitment to what it calls "normality." To offer one example, on June 18, 2005 a "Normality Parade" marched through Warsaw—the response to recent demonstrations in defense of gay and lesbian rights ("Equality Parades"). The event was a proud promotion of home-grown "natural" heterosexuality, threatened by minorities, which are perceived not only as aggressive and powerful, but also, crucially, as foreign. Among the slogans used were "Boy + girl = normal family," as well as "Pedophiles and Peder-asts are Euro-enthusiasts."[1]

In what follows, I offer two instances of gendered nationalist rhetoric, followed by an extended interpretation, which strives to situate these bits of discourse in a broader context. Gendered nationalism is, of course, no Polish invention: Its various local versions as well as underlying dynamics have been discussed in feminist scholarship for over a decade (e.g., McClintock, 1995; Mosse, 1985; Parker et al., 1992; Yuval-Davis, 1998). There is a striking overlap between ideologies of gender and nationalism: On one hand, ideas about gender roles, sexuality, and reproduction are an important part of exclusionary discourses concerning nationhood and national pride and identity; on the other hand, the very idea of nation is often gendered and sexualized. As Floya Anthias, Nira Yuval-Davis, and others have argued, women are rarely subjects/participants of national processes; their role in such projects is primarily that of biological reproducers and "bearers of culture." Nations tend to be allegorically represented as female figures (typically, a beloved woman in danger, or a mother who has lost her sons in battle), while women themselves (as reproducers of the nation) are used as markers of collective boundaries and differences (Anthias & Yuval-Davis, 1994, pp. 314–315). If, as theorists have argued, women's role in relation to the nation-state is chiefly metaphorical, while that of men tends to be metonymic (see McClintock, 1995, p. 354), then the present study explores the rhetorical and political consequences of this peculiar division of labor in the specific context of Poland's recent rise of nationalist sentiment and revival of national mythology.

We begin with two samples of right-wing rhetoric, both from the summer of 2006 and the same source: the political party that calls itself, rather tellingly, the League of Polish Families (LPR). In the two cases, the man behind the words is Roman Giertych, LPR's leader and a central figure of Poland's recent nationalistic turn. Although the party does not enjoy great voter support, 4% according to a January 2007 poll (CBOS, 2007), in 2005, it rose from marginality to participation in government, as part of the ruling right-wing coalition. Giertych, who remained largely invisible for many years and was branded with the label of "extremist," became Poland's minister of education and one of the country's most influential politicians. My first text is excerpted from a Polish Press Agency (PAP) news release found on the official website of the League of Polish Families; the second comes from a speech given in the Polish Parliament by Giertych himself:

- The League of Polish Families has appealed to all Polish Parliamentarians to support the addition to the Polish Constitution of a statement concerning the protection of human life from conception. . . . Roman Giertych emphasized that this would fulfill the legacy of cardinal Stefan Wyszyński and John Paul II. . . . According to Giertych, the killing of unborn children took on "the dimensions of a sort of holocaust, a slaughter of innocents. . ." during the 20th century. . . He assessed that abortion is a crime that can be "analogously compared" to the Holocaust of Jews. . . . In his view, the introduction of such protection into the Constitution "will be an important signal in Europe and the world that there is resistance to the view that killing the unborn is acceptable.". . . It is no accident that the appeal was made in Częstochowa, after the "renewal of the Polish nation's vows to Virgin Mary as Queen of Poland." ("LPR *apeluje*," 2006)
- [When Social Democrats were in power] Polish youngsters were being taught—on the budget of the Polish school system—that one's sex is a matter of decision, that it can be changed. . . (applause) that it can be changed several times during a lifetime. This was taught at training

camps organized by the campaign against homophobia. . . . And who was doing the teaching? German transsexuals, who came here, and were paid with our money, to teach such things to Polish children. That's what it was like in your times. (Giertych, 2006)

It takes no great interpretative effort to see that gender and sexuality intersect with concern about national identity in these statements: The link is emphasized by the speaker and constitutes an important part of his rhetorical strategy. What we have here is a peculiar mixture of melodrama and sentimentality in the service of aggressive xenophobia, an alarmist appeal to national pride articulated in terms of gender and sexuality. In both excerpts, Poland is feminized (in the first case, through association with the Madonna; in the second, via emphasis on children and school) and described as under pressure, if not siege. Both the pressure and resistance to it are gendered and sexualized. The attackers are masculine, but perversely and ruthlessly so: What motivates them is a desire to harm Poland's children (in the first case, by killing them, in the second by leading them astray, into homosexuality and sex change). Needless to say, rescue is on the way in both cases, in the shape of manly men, who follow in the footsteps of high priests (a pope and a cardinal associated with both patriotic sentiment and the cult of the Virgin).

The League's campaign to change the Constitution amounts to a complete and irreversible ban on abortion, including that performed in cases of rape, incest, and severe fetal damage. As of February 2007, the campaign had secured the government's support, while Warsaw's streets were decorated with images of enormous fetuses, advertising a website called www.nienarodzeni.pl [the unborn], the League's billboard campaign to mobilize voters. Efforts to elevate fetuses to the status of full citizenship (as the website's name suggests) may seem familiar to those who have followed antichoice efforts in the United States and elsewhere, but the press release already cited suggests that Polish antichoice activists do not rely exclusively on it. Something different, more local and far more elaborate, is implicit in this campaign's symbolic start in Częstochowa, the antiabortion vows to the Virgin, and Giertych's hope that these vows will constitute "an important signal to the world and to Europe." What we are witnessing here is a well-planned and funded public relations effort to build a solid link between antichoice politics and Polish national identity. Its effectiveness lies in the skillful use of women's metaphorical relation to the national project (i.e., the collective investment in the figure of the Madonna as a stand-in for Poland).

Of course, it is not just any Madonna involved here, but the one from Częstochowa, where the Virgin Mary reigns in her symbolic capacity as "queen of Poland." To this very local divinity—not to some abstraction drawn from Catholic dogmatic theology—local women's reproductive rights are being sacrificed. Giertych vows to put an end to abortion at the location where "Polishness" is at its most concentrated and feminized, knowing well that a politician who kneels at this shrine seems to transcend politics and enter the realm of "pure" ethnic bonding. Not altogether accidentally, he adds that abortion can be "analogously compared" to the Holocaust of Jews in Poland. This is hardly an anti-Semitic outrage at which the media might jump, but Giertych has winked at his anti-Jewish voters nonetheless. Given LPR's links with such political groups from the 1930s, its occasional slippages into such rhetoric, and the present public taboo on explicit anti-Semitism, such an allusion is understood by all: What is suggested in a somewhat evasive manner is a competition between Polish and Jewish victimhood, now finally to be won by Poles. We will return to links between anti-Semitism and gender politics later; for the present, let us focus on the role of the Virgin.

Historically, the cult of the Madonna in Poland has long been associated with threats to national integrity; it began in the 13th century in a period of grave danger, and had a way of mobilizing members of the nobility to action, the idealized vision of femininity integrating men in a sense of (national) brotherhood[2] (see Ostrowska, 2005, p. 218). As Elżbieta Ostrowska demonstrates in her study of gender in the tradition of Polish patriotism, the 19th century romantic version of this legacy involves a semantic crossover between seemingly disparate sets of ideas: (1) Poland as Mother, and (2) the Madonna, Mother of God and Poland's queen and protectress. This imaginary unity has in turn been projected onto (3) the figure of the Polish Mother, the heroic mother of sons, a sign situated between myth and stereotype, central to the country's national identity in its homosocial dimension (see also Janion, 2006, pp. 272–273; Walczewska, 1999, pp. 53–56).

The highly charged blend of maternal/national fantasies has had a varying impact on the position of Polish women, ranging from empowering, to highly ambivalent and repressive. Recent ethnographic research suggests that there exists a subversive, perhaps even feminist, subcurrent in Polish folk religiosity, evident in women's mystical encounters with the Virgin Mary, which are routinely rejected by Church authorities (Bierca, 2006). The story that interests us here, however, is the dominant one, with the Virgin surrounded by sons, not daughters. Ostrowska and Janion both argue that the bonds between Poles as "brothers" are strengthened and sanctified by the presence of the Mother; she may be elevated to a semidivine level, but this act of male bonding at the feet of the imaginary Mother requires the rejection of all significant bonds with actual women. To earn his Mother's love, the son must abandon the woman-as-lover—the omnipresence of this theme in poetry and painting has been documented well in the work of Maria Janion (2004, 2006), who also emphasizes the necrophiliac element in the brothers'/sons' devotion to Poland. The allegorical paintings and patriotic poetry produced in the wake of the country's 18th century partitions portray the beloved Polonia as either enchained, in pain, bereaved, dead or dying, buried or standing over her grave, and in one case literally crucified. All these themes can be spotted in the drama staged by Giertych at the Częstochowa opening of his antiabortion campaign: the brothers (LPR politicians) come to the suffering Mother (the Black Madonna of Częstochowa, with her famously wounded face) and vow to abandon all loyalty to the lover (reproductive rights are, after all, only needed if women engage in sexual activity).

The Virgin Mary of the LPR's "appeal to Polish Parliamentarians" is no benevolent ruler. A cruel and impatient divinity, she requires constant reassurance that the "brotherhood" remains faithful—hence the need to "renew" vows. Specifically, this faithfulness concerns the protection of the unborn. If the Virgin Mother is associated with the Child, then the child is in perennial danger. Abortion may be illegal, but the forces of evil are ever present and watchful. Roman Giertych arrives in Częstochowa to promise help: a constitutional and thus permanent ban on abortion. Thus, real women's reproductive rights are offered as a gift to the symbolic woman. It is a bloody sacrifice, because, if the campaign is successful—and there is a very real chance it will succeed—Polish women will be forced by law to give birth even at the risk of severe damage to their health. Clearly, if the female divinity presiding over Poland today is a mother, she is no great enthusiast of daughters.

What makes the improbable idea of an unconditional ban on abortion palatable to so many (including many women) is that it comes packaged in patriotic bathos. The tradition of romantic patriotism has been successfully mobilized today *against women* by the extreme right. The result is an admirably coherent nationalistic antichoice ideology, where patriotism is not just tied to but synonymous with resistance to women's rights. Poland is being imagined as a mother in distress, while those who talk of "rights" are a foreign force aiming to kill her (unborn) children. In 2003, this scenario became front-page news thanks to the visit of The Netherlands prochoice group Women on Waves, an organization that uses a Dutch ship to offer medical abortion on exterritorial waters to citizens of countries where getting rid of an unwanted pregnancy is illegal. The event caused an outburst of antifeminist nationalist rhetoric. Katarzyna Gawlicz, who studied coverage by the right-wing daily *Nasz Dziennik*, notes that feminists are referred to as invaders, while "Langenort" (the Women on Waves vessel) is described there as a "pirate ship" and a representative of "Europe, or possibly the anonymous world government" (this last phrase constituting a thinly veiled gesture honoring Polish anti-Semitism) (Gawlicz, 2005, p. 114). From this perspective, the Dutch effort to provoke debate over reproductive rights in Poland becomes an invasion, a state of national emergency.

The object of interest of Poland's antichoice campaign are not "the unborn," but the nation: Poland as a heroic mother, trying to shelter her (unborn) children from the onslaught of murderous outsiders, as well as their treacherous agents at home. Actual women are wombs, vessels that carry the nation's children and need to be protected against invaders. In 2003, this role of the violent intruder in this symbolic war was played by the feminist ship; in Giertych's 2006 Częstochowa appeal, the villain is more generalized, those "in Europe and the world" who espouse "the view that killing the unborn is acceptable" ("LPR *apeluje.*..," 2006).

Let us now turn to the second excerpt, Giertych's outburst about German transsexuals visiting Polish schools. Again, Europe is aggressive and perverse, aiming to infiltrate the boundaries of that which is innocent and childlike. It is hardly surprising that the statement was greeted by applause in Parliament, and then eagerly reprinted in the press. In just a few lines, Giertych builds a piece of melodrama, complete with corrupt and lascivious villain, pure and helpless victims, an evil traitor and, last but not least, Giertych himself—the brave defender of innocents. With the help of enemies at home (the gay-lesbian NGO Campaign against homophobia), the outsider not only infiltrates our boundaries (significantly, his homeland is Poland's historical invader), but also takes advantage of "our" money to do so. Alas, the danger is held at bay: "gone are the golden days of deviations of all kinds and they will not come back" (Giertych, 2006).

Why does a German transsexual make such an excellent villain? Why are homosexuals so persistently portrayed in Polish media as drag queens from Berlin love parades? Whence this mix of the foreign, the threatening and the sexually ambivalent? Clearly, nationalism depends on the clarity of boundaries, a neat demarcation between "us" and "them." These boundaries are often gendered and/or sexualized. In Giertych's world, the boundaries of national identity coincide with those between purity and aggressive sexuality, or between a stable, orderly, family-oriented world of men, women, and children (Polish), and a chaotic power set on disrupting this world (European, German). WE are identified with stability, purity, and clear gender differentiation, but THEY are sexually deviant, as well as devious, stealthy, and elusive; our children are innocent, but German transsexuals arrive to deprave them; our women are mothers by definition (Polish Mothers), but Dutch feminists invade our motherland to make them abort (unborn) Polish citizens. The very concept of reproductive and sexual rights—individual choices in matters concerning intimate life and fertility—is viewed as foreign to our identity as a nation.

Although my samples of gendered and sexualized nationalist rhetoric may be grotesque, the discourse they exemplify is by no means marginal, not any more. The LPR's attitudes toward women's rights and the status of gays and lesbians have increasingly filtered into what counts as "mainstream" or "common sense." Interestingly, while there is a great readiness to embrace ultranationalist rhetoric and legislation in the case of gender politics, this eagerness does not extend to foreign policy: Poland has become more isolationist and confrontational under right-wing rule, but it is not declaring any wars or planning to leave the European Union. It is as though the area of gender has become a depositary of national pride. Explanation for this peculiar dynamic is, in my view, not to be sought in Polish history, but rather in a cross-cultural perspective.

Case studies from various contexts—Kenya (Stamp, 1991), the former Yugoslavia (Mostov, 2000), Singapore (Heng & Devan, 1992), or South Africa (McClintock, 1995, pp. 352–389) to name just a few—provide abundant evidence that there exists a cross-cultural logic of gender and nation, one of idealization and control that intensifies in periods of transition, war, and real or perceived instability. The more a given collectivity elevates *Woman* (as allegory, abstraction, the nation's embodiment in the symbolic realm), the more it tends to control *women*—members of society, citizens, individual human beings with needs, desires, and aspirations of their own. Nationalism pushes women's citizenship to the margins, treating them as the "backdrop against which men determine the fate of the nation" (Mosse, 1985, p. 23). As we have seen already, this logic is followed faithfully by Poland's nationalists (e.g., in Giertych's vows to the Virgin Queen that he will eradicate what little is left of women's rights in her kingdom).

Many scholars note that the nation is often symbolically figured as a familiar domestic space, a family, with a corresponding distribution of gender roles and hierarchies. This makes nationalism a privileged site for the articulation and institutionalization of gender difference (Mayer, 2000; McClintock, 1995, pp. 357–358; Yuval-Davis, 1998). If nationalism tends to police gender boundaries, it is because the nation (as an extended kinship group) has a motivation in keeping an eye on "its" women, who are needed for reproduction: not only biological but also cultural, as bearers of the collectivity's identity and honor (Yuval-Davis, 1998, pp. 45–56). There is also a powerful interest in masculinity as well as homosociality. If, to use Benedict Anderson's celebrated term, nations are "imagined communities," then they tend to visualize themselves in heavily masculinized terms, through the metaphor of "brotherhood" (1991, p. 16). As George Mosse elaborates, European nationalism is deeply invested in maintaining a clear boundary between the sexes, itself cohering around an ideal of "manliness," punishing out all that was deemed "un-manly" (in particular, homosexuality), and often projecting sexual perversity onto the ethnic or racial other (1985, pp. 1–47, 133–153). A 1938 poster for a Nazi exhibition of "degenerate" art, reprinted by Susan Gubar in *Racechages*, makes the fascist association between homosexuality, Gypsies, Jews, blacks, and jazz (as a degenerate collaboration between the last two groups) shockingly evident (Gubar, 1997, p. 74). The effeminate (though tuxedo-clad, and hence clearly male) saxophone-playing figure in the poster is obviously and grotesquely black, with protruding lips and ape-like features, but wears in addition a Gypsy earring as well as a star of David.

It is only recently that Polish scholars have taken up such perspectives—abandoning, or at least bracketing the previously dominant framework of "transition from communism to democracy"—yet several important studies have already appeared. Some examine the historical development of the gendered dimension of our national identity (Hauser, 1995; Janion, 2004, 2006; Ostrowska, 2004; Walczewska, 1999); others focus on specific contemporary embodiments of gendered and sexualized nationalism (Gawlicz, 2005; Ostolski, 2007; Sypniewski & Warkocki, 2004). The nationalist association between Jews and homosexuals, which Mosse observed in the German context, has been documented for Poland by Adam Ostolski. Comparing the homophobia of present-day right wingers (in particular, the ultraconservative daily *Nasz Dziennik*) with anti-Semitic discourse of the 1930s, Ostolski found striking parallels, which suggest an underlying deep structure of stigmatization and exclusion at the heart of Poland's nationalist discourse, one based on paranoia and fear rather than a sense of well-established entitlement. Both groups are stigmatized in their respective contexts as scheming, devious, and treacherous, a powerful "lobby" and a "threat to civilization," guilty of their own exclusion as well as the violence they supposedly "provoke" by "imposing themselves" on the majority (Ostolski, 2007; see also Graff, 2006).

My own contribution to this growing genre of cultural criticism—an article about Polish media in the period of Poland's European Union accession—is worth mentioning here, because of the context it provides for the "excesses" analyzed earlier (Graff, 2007). My analysis of gender-focused texts and images published in three mainstream weeklies (*Wprost, Newsweek Polska,* and *Polityka*) in the years 2003 through 2005 brings to light two interconnected phenomena: an unprecedented preoccupation with gender difference and the status of sexual minorities as well as the appearance of a sexualized discourse about European Union accession. The European Union was described by conservative commentators as weak and effeminate and contrasted to the more virile United States; suggestions were made that the Polish attitude toward the European Union should be more manly, and so on. The magazines could not get enough of "real men" and "real women," and lavished their attention on biological differences between the sexes. Yet, there was also plenty of room for the opposite of "nature": the gay/lesbian movement often personified by images of drag-queens. These three periodicals were no exceptions in this regard, for a broad spectrum of Polish media turned to discussions of gender difference in this transitional period. Repeatedly, readers of Polish papers, radio-listeners, and viewers of Polish television were shocked by news of the imminent demise of sex differences, followed by soothing reassurance: Difference is doing fine, after all, for it is eternal, natural, universal. Men are men and women are women, especially here, in Poland, due to the remarkable commitment of "our women" to femininity.

My argument about this material was that the conservative discourse about gender was linked to anxiety about national identity, an anxiety caused by European Union accession. The narrative of "gender crisis" (in particular that of masculinity, a favorite topic with journalists in 2003) was followed by the "return of the real man" (announced on the cover of the conservative *Wprost* on May 30, 2004, a few weeks after Poland joined the Union). I argue that the obsessive "gender talk" of this period is best understood as displaced narrative about national identity: an effort to contain ambivalence about change and construct a notion of Polishness stable enough to accommodate, or perhaps even outweigh, European Union accession. It is hardly surprising, in the light of the theories of gender and nation cited earlier, that the "bearer" of this stability was an idealized vision of femininity.

If women are required to carry the burden of representing Poland's supposedly timeless and unchanging identity, men are positioned as defenders of women who fulfill this role. The paradox of the masculine situation is that it requires the formation of a male collectivity (the homosocial), but this need comes with a prohibition against intimacy among the men involved (the homosexual). As we have seen earlier, the "brotherhood" of conservative politicians imagines itself as protecting Poland-as-mother from invaders: German transsexuals, Dutch feminists. Interestingly, both groups of villains appear to want one thing only, the blood of Polish babies. The persistent blurring of lines in conservative Polish media between homosexuality and pedophilia is an effort to portray "perverts" as a danger to children, a theme of sex panics analyzed by Gayle Rubin in her seminal essay "Thinking Sex" (1993, pp. 25, 39). Another reading, however, may also be suggested here: that with the popular myth of folk anti-Semitism about Jews as blood-thirsty child-snatchers. Arguably, however, the focus on children has still another function, that of a screen or mask against the homosexual aspect of nationalism itself. As Maria Janion puts it, "A patriotism in process of becoming nationalism cannot be free from what it considers the greatest danger. Nationalism exacerbates homophobic sentiment because—spectacularly based on the homosocial bonding of men—it is extremely vulnerable to homosexual desire" (2006, p. 273).

The intersection between gender and nation becomes particularly potent in times of war and (real or imagined) crisis. During conflict, nationalist ideologies call on men—a "brotherhood" now bound even more closely together as "brothers in arms"—to protect "womenandchildren" (Enloe, 1990). As Tamar Mayer observes, among the dominant themes of national narratives of gender are "purity," "modesty," and "chastity" (2000, p. 10). Radical nationalist mobilization is that of men in defense of these values: It projects the ideal feminine as the embodiment of national identity (pure, modest, and hence in need of protection), but is deeply suspicious of actual women (who now need to be watched more closely than ever, because they might be captured or themselves conspire with the enemy). Needless to say, there is a world of difference between "our women" and "their women," as far as purity is concerned. Furthermore, not all of "our women" are really ours. According to *Nasz Dziennik*, for instance, a Polish feminist is an oxymoron; feminists are by definition "enemies of our nation" (Gawlicz, 2005, p. 113).

The sinister reality behind these abstractions is, of course, war-rape. In an essay about the destructive infantilism of nationalist masculinity in the Balkans, Dubravka Ugresic writes: "The war in Yugoslavia is a masculine war. In the war, women are post-boxes used to send messages to those other men, *the enemy*. And *enemies* who were their *brothers* until a short time before, at that" (1998, p. 122). Her point is that war-rape is a means of communication between groups of men; the intensity of the hatred that follows "brotherly" love calls for an equally intense form of communication. The rape of the "other's" women is a message about domination and territorial claims. When the homosocial turns homicidal, women's lives are reduced to containers for men's meanings.

Today's Poland is, of course, not at war, but if you consider the alarmist tone of nationalist discourse, its omnipresence in the media and impact on the legislative process, we might as well be at war. Until about 2003, mainstream media spoke of "transition" and (European Union) "accession." Since then, and especially after the right-wing populist coalition took power in 2006, the prevailing category has been "crisis" and need of "renewal," as well as "moral purification," with Poland's leaders bemoaning the nation's role as a victim of history. We are witnessing the institutionalization of an obsessive discourse of victimhood, described by ethnographer Joanna Tokarska-Bakir in her much-discussed essay about the logic of Polish anti-Semitism as a mindset marked by pathological inability to accept Poland's role as perpetrator of any harm to others, especially if those others happen to be Jews (2004, pp. 13–22). The "brotherhood" of Polish national identity is a masculinity based on victimhood and a sense of being unjustly accused by ungrateful others, a manliness under siege, in constant danger of losing its virility. None of this is really news, for, as Ostrowska demonstrates, there is a long history of Polish "crisis of masculinity" associated with the country's loss of independence in the late 18th century. Ours is a homosociality in perpetual crisis, at times evolving into panic, a masculinity based on the idea of inevitable loss, betrayal, and tragic defeat, a "brotherhood" that imagines itself trapped in a matriarchy. What makes the present situation distinct is that today the homosexual "threat" is a real public presence, and occasionally spectacle, which needs to be confronted, as it was in the already mentioned "Normality Parade." The rise of nationalism coincides with—and responds to—both women's emancipation and a massive coming-out of Poland's gays and lesbians (see Graff, 2006).

The present study participates in what I consider a major methodological shift in the study of gender in Polish culture and society. It is a move away from postsocialist categories, which were central to much Polish sociology of the last decade, as well as English-language studies of the "transformation" under way in Eastern Europe, including those focusing on gender (e.g., Einhorn, 1993; Gal & Kligman, 2000; Watson, 1997)—a move to postcolonial perspectives. Clearly, to compare Poland to India or Ireland is an altogether different project than that of viewing it as a culture "catching up" with Germany, France, and Britain, that is, a bit behind due to time spent in the communist "freezer," but fundamentally "Western" and liberal at heart. One of the most outspoken proponents of such a shift in perspective is Ewa Thompson, who writes in the United States, but often addresses a Polish audience. She suggests that those who doubt Poland's colonial past take a stroll by the enormous estate still owned by the former colonial power in the center of Warsaw—the Russian (formerly Soviet) embassy—and consider both its vastness and the arrogance with which the owners treat their host country (trash containers left in full view of passers-by). Thompson concludes, "Poland is a postcolonial country, and in order to repair the damage done to our Republic, we need to compare ourselves with Algeria, India and Ireland, and not with countries that were never subjugated in this way" (2006, p.11). Maria Janion appears to agree with Thompson, when, echoing Clare Cavanagh, she insists that "Poland's history deserves its place in post-colonial studies" (Janion, 2006, p. 323). According to Janion, however, it is a matter of great importance that Poland was not only colonized but also a colonizer of its eastern neighbors, Ukraine and Belarus. Hence, there exist the bizarre combination of megalomania and inferiority in our attitudes toward "the East," and the bizarre mix of gendered analogies in our collective imagination: Poland both as enchained woman and a manly and valiant being, penetrating its effeminate neighbors (Janion, 2006, p. 327).

What is the significance of the growing interest in postcolonial theory among scholars of Polish literature and culture, and what is its relevance to feminist scholarship and activism? Until recently, proponents of women's rights, myself included, have had their hopes set on Poland's gradual entry into, and acceptance of, the future-oriented liberal discourse, which dominates in the European Union—a way of thinking about collective identity that pays little heed to blood ties and defines nation as a civic project, sometimes referred to as *Staatsnation* (Yuval-Davis, 1989, p. 21). Feminist theorists in the West remain somewhat skeptical of the classical liberal construction of citizenship, for it starts with the hasty assumption that citizens have equal status, and often, in the name of "neutrality", remains blind to existing inequalities: those derived from gender, class, or other contexts (see, e.g., Hobson & Lister, 2002, 36–39). This is true enough, but still I am convinced that only within a public realm dominated by a broadly defined liberalism can one even begin to formulate a gender-conscious notion of citizenship. Feminist interventions may be critical of this framework and aim to modify it, but they take it as a starting point.

Now, such a starting point—until recently taken for granted by many as in the making, if not a given—is slipping out of our reach. It has also been argued that efforts to introduce certain debates into Eastern Europe were doomed from the start, for the region has its own, far more communitarian tradition of liberalism (Funk, 2004), while Polish culture in particular has "translated" Western doctrines into a local brand of the philosophy, heavily influenced by antiliberal strands of Catholicism (Szacki, 1993, pp. 230–238). Recent developments suggest that this may be true. Poland's Prime Minister Jarosław Kaczyński went on record saying that he considers the very concept of citizenship foreign to the Polish tradition. The statement is worth quoting: "[I]t is harmful to use in public life political-ideological concepts which are completely devoid of meaning, have no tradition behind them, such as for instance 'citizenship'" (cited in Paradowska, 2006, p. 12).

In short, until recently Polish political culture appeared to be in "transition" to a liberal democracy, and feminists were working under the illusion that the still fluid framework might be modified, citizenship made more inclusive. Today, "citizenship" is a "foreign" and "harmful" word, while the dominant narrative speaks of "struggle" against the very values we were striving to embrace. The reproductive rights of women along with the rights of sexual minorities are in a symbolic position: the embodiment of precisely those aspects of "citizenship" those in power consider most "foreign" to our tradition. Giertych's vows to the Virgin Mary may seem theatrical and grotesque, but the event is emblematic of a major shift in Polish political culture. In such a context, the shift from the postcommunist to the postcolonial in feminist analysis is a pessimistic but perhaps necessarily corrective.

NOTES

1. All translations from Polish by A. Graff. In Polish these slogans are: "*Chłopak, dziewczyna, normalna rodzina,*" "*Pedofile, pederaści, to są Unii entuzjaści.*" Images from the parade as experienced by its organizers can be viewed at http://www.lpr.pl/?sr=lista&dz=galeria&id=38. See also photographs of the League's antichoice exhibit at the European Union Parliament: http://www.lpr.pl/?sr=lista&dz=galeria&id=41. What is striking in both sets of images is the prominence of men, the focus on children (the fetuses featured mature ones, invariably referred to as "children"), and the almost complete absence of women.
2. Before the famous battle of Grunwald (1410) against the Knights of the Teutonic Order, Polish fighters sang "Bogarodzica"—a sacred song about the Mother of God, which for a long time functioned as Poland's national anthem, and is still a poem all school children memorize. The Częstochowa monastery's significance for the national mythology has roots in the 17th century, when it became a fort and a pocket of resistance against the Swedish invasion.

REFERENCES

Anderson, B. (1991). *Imagined communities: Reflections on the origin and spread of nationalism.* London: Verso.

Anthias, F., & Yuval-Davis, N. (1994). Women and the nation state. In J. Hutchinson & A. D. Smith (Eds.), *Nationalism: The reader* (pp. 312–316). Oxford: Oxford University Press.

Bierca, M. (2006). Mistyka typu ludowego. Kobieca pobożność maryjna w świetle teologii feministycznej. In K. Leszczyńska & A. Kościańska (Eds.), *Kobiety i religie*, ed (pp. 119–138). Kraków: Nomos.

CBOS. (2007). Preferencje partyjne w styczniu, komunikat z badania aktualnych problemów kraju. Centrum Badania Opinii Publicznej, Warszawa www.cbos.pl/SPISKOM.POL/2007/K_006_07.PDF

Einhorn, B. (1993). *Cinderella goes to market. Citizenship, gender and women's movements in East Central Europe.* London: Verso.

Enloe, C. (1989). *Bananas beaches and bases: Making feminist sense of international politics.* Berkeley: University of California Press.

Funk, N. (2004). Feminist critiques of liberalism: Can they travel East? Their relevance in Eastern and Central Europe and the former Soviet Union. *Signs, 29,* 695–726.

Gal, S., & Kligman, G. (Eds.). (2000). *Reproducing gender. Politics, publics and everyday life after socialism.* Princeton, NJ: Princeton University Press.

Gawlicz, K. (2005). Płeć i naród. Dyskurs dotyczący aborcji w 'Naszym Dzienniku' a konstruowanie tożsamości narodowej. In E. Zierkiewicz & I. Kowalczyk (Eds.), Kobiety, Feminizm Media (pp. 99–116). Poznań: Konsola.

Giertych, R. (2006a). Speech in Polish Sejm on 7.19.2006 (5 kadencja, 22 posiedzenie, 2 dzień, 13 punkt porządku dziennego: 7.19.2006. Retrieved August 14, 2006, from http://www.sejm.gov.pl/archiwum/prace/kadencja1/prace1.htm. (2006b).

Graff, A. (2006). We are (not all) homophobes: A report from Poland. *Feminist Studies, 32*(2), 434–450.

———. (2008). The return of real men and real women: Gender and E.U. accession in three Polish weeklies. In C. Elliott (Ed.), *Global empowerment of women: Responses to globalization, politicized religions and gender violence.* London: Routledge.

Gubar, S. (1997). *Race changes. White skin, black face in American culture.* New York: Oxford University Press.

Hauser, E. (1995). Traditions of patriotism, questions of gender: The case of Poland. In E. E. Berry (Ed.), *Postcommunism and the body politic.* New York: New York University Press.

Heng, G., & Devan, J. (1992). State fatherhood: The politics of nationalism, sexuality, and race in Singapore. In A. Parker, M. Russo, D. Sommer, & P. Yaeger (Eds.), *Nationalisms and sexualities* (pp. 343–363). New York: Routledge.

Hobson, B., & Lister, R. (2002). Citizenship. In B. Hobson et al. (Ed.), *Contested concepts in gender and social politics* (pp. 23–53). Cheltenham, UK: Edward Elgar.

Janion, M. (2004). Pożegnanie z Polską. Jeszcze Polska nie umarła. *Krytyka Polityczna,* (6), 141–151.

———. (2006). *Niesamowita Słowiańszczyzna. Fantazmaty literatury.* Kraków: Wydawnictwo Literackie.

LPR apeluje o poparcie dla konstytucyjnej ochrony życia. (2006). Polish Press Agency (PAP) release 8–26–2006. Retrieved August 28, 2006, from available at: http://www.lpr.pl/?sr=!czytaj&id=5105&dz=kraj&x=1&pocz=0&gr=

Matynia, E. (2003, Summer). Provinicializing global feminism: The Polish case. *Social Research, 70*(2), 499–530.

Mayer, T. (2000). Gender ironies of nationalism. Setting the stage. In T. Mayer (Ed.), *Gender ironies of nationalism. Sexing the nation.* London: Routledge.

McClintock, A. (1995). *Imperial leather. Race, gender and sexuality in the colonial context.* London: Routledge.

Mosse, G. (1985). *Nationalism and sexuality. Middle class morality and sexual norms in modern Europe.* Madison: University of Wisconsin Press.

Mostov, J. (2000). Sexing the nation/ Desexing the body. Politics of national identity in the former Yugoslavia. In T. Mayer (Ed.), *Gender ironies of nationalism. Sexing the nation.* London: Routledge.

Ostolski, A. (2007). Spiskowcy i gorszyciele. Judaizowanie gejów w polskim dyskursie prawicowym. In M.Głowacka Grajper & E. Nowicka (Eds.), *Jak się dzielimy i co nas łączy.* Przemiany wartości i więzi we współczesnym społeczeństwie *polskim,.* Kraków: Nomos.

Ostrowska, E. (2004). Matki Polki i ich synowie. Kilka uwag o genezie obrazów kobiecości i męskości w kulturze polskiej. In M. Radkiewicz (Ed.), *Gender. Konteksty.* Kraków: Rabid.

Paradowska, J. (2006). Wizje prezesa. Co Jarosław Kaczyński powiedział w Salonie Polityki" już po wyłączeniu kamer. *Polityka, 12*(1547), *25*(3) 22.

Rubin, G. (1993). Thinking sex: Notes for a radical theory of the politics of sexuality. In L. S. Kaufman (Ed.), *American feminist thought at century's end. A reader* (pp. 3–62). Cambridge MA: Blackwell.

Stamp, P. (1991). Burying Otieno: The politics of gender and ethnicity in Kenya. *Signs, 16*(4), 351–388.

Sypniewski, Z., & Warkocki, B. (Eds.). (2004). *Homofobia po polsku.* Warszawa: *Sic!*

Szacki, J. (1994). *Liberalizm po komunizmie.* Kraków: Znak.

Thompson, E. (2006). Sarmatyzm i postkolonializm. O naturze polskich resentymentów. *Europa, 137*/2006–11–18, 11.

Tokarska-Bakir, J. (2004). *Rzeczy mgliste: Eseje i studia.* Sejny: Pogranicze.

Ugresic, D. (1998). *The culture of lies: Antipolitical essays* (C. Hawkesworth, Trans). University Park: The Pennsylvania State University Press.

Walczewska, S. (1999). *Damy, rycerze i feministki. Kobiecy dyskurs emancypacyjny w Polsce.* Kraków: eFKa.

Watson, P. (1997). (Anti)feminism after communism. In A. Oakley & J. Mitchell (Eds.), *Who's afraid of feminism? Seeing through the backlash* (pp. 144–161). New York: The New Press.

Yuval-Davis, N. (1998). *Gender and nation.* London: Sage.

8   Defining Pornography, Defining Gender

Sexual Citizenship in the Discourse of Czech Sexology and Criminology

Kateřina Lišková

Questions of gender and sexuality are currently being addressed by discourses of science and law enforcement with the ultimate aim of defining and controlling sexual citizenship. Criminological discourse in particular relies heavily on presumably shared notions of cultural norms regarding what constitutes nonoffensive and moral sexuality. Interconnected with the scientific notions of natural, healthy, and mature sexuality that are offered by sexology, they together constitute a disciplinary power, which attributes normalcy and legality to the conduct of some, and pathology or criminality to others.

My chapter is a sociological analysis of the discourses of pornography produced by both sexology and criminology in the contemporary Czech Republic. Its aim is to analyze two recent books dealing with pornography written by well-known Czech sexologists and criminologists. My study is organized around three main topics: (1) sexuality, morality, and social cohesion; (2) scientific discourses and their liberatory versus status quo preserving potential concerning (gender) normality; and (3) the resonance of sexological and criminological discourse with antiporn feminism. The two exemplary texts are *Morality, Pornography, and Criminal Vice* by a collective of authors, including criminologist Jan Chmelík and sexologist Petr Weiss (Chmelík, 2003), and *Pornography or Provoking Nakedness* by the sexologist Radim Uzel (2004).

SEXUALITY, MORALITY, AND SOCIAL COHESION

Sexuality is, not surprisingly, a main topic of both worries. For Chmelík and his collective, it is twofold. Good and healthy sexuality is a key society-building element, "human sexuality is at the beginning of the deepest connection between people and is basic for the well-being of individuals, couples, families, and society" (Chmelík, 2003, p. 12).

Nevertheless, there is bad and dangerous sexuality which, according to this text, constitutes an enormous threat to society; sexual debauchery should be criminalized, especially if youth (supposedly sexually innocent) are involved—because according to the authors, including the well-known Czech sexologist Petr Weiss, "society is interested in the proper moral education of youth" and "youth must be protected against all negative influences including undoubtedly lack of sexual restraint" (Chmelík, 2003, p. 12). Pornography is framed by Chmelík as the polar opposite of morality, "Everything immoral is mostly connected to pornography" (p. 41). Their definition of porn is, "Sexual acts depicted in an obtrusive, distorted and unreal manner, sexual contact with exaggerated violence and perversity such as showing anal and oral intercourse, etc. . . . Through pornography, human beings are reduced to the very physiological core—overemphasizing reactions to basic sexual stimuli" (p. 43). In this influential criminological account (praised by the chairman of the Supreme Court Senate), pornography stands in for the "skewing of moral values," is "degrading to human dignity," "eliciting feelings of shame and repulsiveness"—all of which are contrary to "natural sexuality free of commercial efforts, aggression and perversity" (p. 43). In conclusion, these authors view pornography as a potentially criminal sociopathological element, which is especially dangerous to youth.

Given all this, the question remains—how to reconcile the presupposed criminal essence of porn with another claim, "Pornography is induced by a natural need to cover one of the basic life needs of humans"? (p. 47). Generally, Chmelík et al. are very close to other acclaimed Czech sexologists and psychologists (Hubálek & Pondělíček) who posit, "Recently, the liberalization process has reached an extent which is unparalleled within the last two millenniums. Time is up, thus, for a change of direction" (Brzek, 1993, pp. 35–36).

The views of sexologist Radim Uzel seem to be totally opposite—at least at first glance. He perceives the attacks against porn as negative stances toward nakedness and sex as such (Uzel, 2004, p. 26). For Uzel, pornography stands in for sexual openness, which in his account is very much needed; it aids in the prevention of sexual exploitation (p. 80), the everyday sublimation which keeps a man going (p. 189). In short, pornography is "socially and individually beneficial" (p. 103). According to Uzel, it is "not true that pornography subverts social ties" (p. 104); on the contrary, it is the "confused fight for a legal ban on porn which is siphoning off the means to fight the real crime," but most of all it is "a governmental attempt at legally enacting morality" (p. 104). He calls for the liberalization of sexuality and for sexual education, "We should try to revise the deeply rooted view that sexual feelings and sexual knowledge are inappropriate and unhealthy for youth" (p. 166).

This sexologist's positive and affirming stances toward sexuality and pornography would be welcome if they were unambiguous. However, that is not the case. The first discrepancy worth noting is when he claims that "consuming pornography is not a dark side of human being but his adequate part, the expression of which is inappropriate to be ashamed of" (p. 189)—so why does he claim "under oath" in the very introduction of the book that he is not "a reader or a consumer" of porn himself? (p. 11). The more important inconsistency has to do with the character of pornography. Uzel attributes several fundamentally different qualities to porn, apparently not realizing their mutually exclusive character. First, he argues that porn is a fantasy, "bought mainly because it is different from real life, it is an idealized reality" (p. 141). Second, only 10 pages later he claims, "pornography is a mirror hall of human sexuality. . . , it defines humans as sexual animals. . . , it is a concise metaphor for sex" (p. 151). Third, porn ceases to be either fantasy or metaphor, because "porn deals with sex in its true essence, that's why pornography is being neglected" (p. 151). These seemingly contradictory views concerning idealized reality, animal drives, fantasy and even the essence of sex might appear simply vague, but in fact are used to serve specific purposes, which will be examined later in the chapter.

Further problems are revealed when we focus on Uzel's broader notions of sexuality. Although he claims that "porn is not all that horrible" (p. 21), sex for him falls in with breeding, because he adds, "couples having sex are not ruining the earth, they are rather populating it" (p. 21). This explanation more than anything else carries a latent message about sex being exclusively coupled, heterosexual, and reproductive. Uzel's heteronormativity is obvious despite his manifest support of rights for sexual minorities. In a passage critical of social conservatism, he states, "we know very well our numerous countrymen who would want to have this country free of homosexuals, prostitution, drug addicts, abortion and alcohol" (p. 21); inexplicably, this statement is followed by a comment, which essentially endorses the conservative argument, "Well, I think many problems would disappear then" (p. 21). Here he gets very close to the notion of homosexuality as something "bizarre" or "sickly distorted," which would sound like "common-sense" homophobia if it were not also the standpoint of other well-known Czech scholars, such as psychologist Slavomil Hubálek and sexologist Ivo Pondělíček (Brzek, 1993, p. 6).

Thus, two ideal types define the Czech scientific continuum regarding porn. At one end is the seemingly liberal sexologist Uzel, who cheers for porn as a means of social cohesion, sexual liberation, or at least an educational tool, and at the other end is the criminologist Chmelík, who cautions against the perils of sexual chaos caused by the usage of pornography.

SCIENTIFIC DISCOURSES DEFINING (GENDER) NORMALITY

Sexologists might be conservative or liberal, perceiving sex as a threat to society or as a means to individual liberation and social emancipation—but they all claim to be scientific. Let us analyze their scientific merit and the means for reaching it.

Sexology has historically made claims about nature and naturalness. The former has been deployed to justify our innate violence as well as peacefulness. It and the supposed truth about "Man" meet in sex; a founding father of sexology put it clearly, stating that "a man is what his sex is" (Weeks 1985). Claims about what is "natural" are powerful—and we should not miss one important feature, namely that they are always both about nature and society. Sexologists thus perform a double-step, consisting first of biologizing sexuality (and the social) and second socializing nature.

Sexuality is biologized mostly via notions of sexual dimorphism. People are not only categorized according to their genitalia (and invisible hormones and chromosomes) into women and men, but this division is perceived to pervade every aspect of life. Thus, Weiss identifies "tertiary characteristics, which consist of differences between men and women in the realm of thinking, feeling, emotions and behavior—both verbal and nonverbal, the latter playing an important role in sexual conduct" (Chmelík, 2003, p. 137). Uzel holds that "differences between men and women often preclude mutual understanding" (2004, p. 139). Differences are, according to him, coded biologically and their common denominator is sexuality,

The main difference between male and female sexuality is the fact that male sexuality is bodily focused, men are characterized by a bodily lust, they are often satisfied by unabiding and anonymous physical gratification; whereas a woman is oriented toward a spiritual experience, love, and ongoing relationship requiring certainty and protection (p. 139).

Contrary to his seemingly progressive scientific rhetoric that deprecates irrational arrangements, he reproduces the most conventional gender clichés.

The study of sexuality has become a search for the origin of "sexual instincts" and the exploration of relations between men and women, which have been seen as intertwined in biological imperatives. Uzel claims "sex to be as natural as food" (p. 25). He goes on to invoke socio-biological explanations of the differences between the sexes, saying, "The higher promiscuity of men is given evolutionarily through the effort to spread their genetic material as much as possible; the higher stability of women's relationships is the result of them seeking higher security for their progeny" (p. 25). This is the very same reasoning used by the founding fathers of sociobiology. This highly contested discipline has been accused of serious methodological as well as political problems. The latter includes seeking—and finding—evolutionary, and thus unavoidable bases for social events like war or rape. Strangely, however, these naturalistic and supposedly neutral metaphors all say the same thing: society as we know it is the only possible and right one, because it has been evolving into this state for tens of thousands of years; moreover, because atavism and instincts guide human action and genes dictate social inequalities, any change in the social structure is highly unlikely and undesirable. In the words of Edward O. Wilson, the founder of sociobiology, "The genetic bias is intense enough to cause a substantial division even in the most free and most egalitarian of future societies. . . men are likely to play a disproportionate role in political life, business and science" (Fausto-Sterling, 1992, p. 72).

Biology comes in handy whenever sexologists need to find an indisputable cause for sexual differences. One of Uzel's "slippery slope" arguments goes as follows, "Besides proven differences between the sexes displayed in the higher consumption of energy by men, even for breathing, men need more protein, iron, beef and zinc, and repeated research has also shown they consume more pornographic materials" (Uzel, 2004, p. 134). However, the question of nature and "naturalness" might be very confusing for Uzel himself—he writes, "What is natural for one person, does not have to be natural for the other" (p. 113). These are all clear examples of using the natural in order to legitimize the status quo. In other words, nature is used to uphold culture.

The complementary half of the biologization of sexuality is to be found in the socialization of nature, describing the life of animals in terms of social institutions. Chmelík offers one such example, "Prostitution-like behavior can be traced in some primates. A female ape with a tasty bite, fleeing from a hungry male positions her genitals in front of him and while the male is having fun the female can calmly finish her snack" (Chmelik, 2003, p. 55). Because it is *natural,* socialized nature serves as an example of the proper organization of society. The whole biological and naturalist discourse serves one and only one purpose—to reproduce society in its present form, inequalities included, and provide a logical explanation for the deeply normative assumptions of sexologists.

Since its early stages, sexology has been focused on the definition and classification of sexual pathologies. In this fashion, Weiss keeps using the term deviation, although he himself notes that the scientific community has already accepted terms like "paraphilia" or "sexual variation" precisely for their neutrality. So the terminology he uses is marked by deep normativity, he talks about "defects in sexual preference" (p. 138), the "psychosexual development of deviants" (p. 139), or he describes that "a sick direction of sexual activities leads to preferring improper sexual objects or ways of gratification which are contrary to the moral and aesthetic norms of society" (p. 139). Among such activities, he identifies cross-dressing or watching porn. The latter is seated within his taxonomy under the rubric of deviations in activity, specifically a kind of voyeurism called pictophilia. A passion for taxonomic labeling, a trait that has accompanied sexology since its inception, is still typical of Czech sexologists today.

All "deviations" are judged against the norm, which is coupled sexual activities, implicitly perceived as heterosexual. In the sexologist's eyes, even these heterosexual activities are themselves normalized. Normal heterosexual intercourse is divided into phases following one after another in precise order—Weiss, when diagnosing masochism as a deviation, finds "important from the sexological point of view the omission of foreplay and cuddling, skipping the phases" (p. 163). In a case study, he describes a man who began showing "deviant tendencies" only after "he had watched an audiovisual pornographic piece representing s/m practices" (p. 159). However, this man had been previously "notable" because of his interest in being present at the birth of his own child (p. 160). The sexologists' interest in "deviant" and "pathological" behaviors reversely stresses the importance of norms and normality. Moreover, it points to a tenuous line dividing the "normals" from the "deviants"; "If a heterosexual reacts to homosexual pornographic stimuli, we can reliably indicate this person to be homosexual, even in the case of no previous homosexual intercourse" (p. 45). Not only is sexuality being normalized and pathologized, the same applies to gender identities and their holders. Thus, sexologist Pondělíček labels men with "some feminine characteristics" and women "characterized as traditional men" as being "partially disturbed" (Brzek, 1993, p. 24). He follows that "in the great majority, they are normally sexually oriented individuals" but adds hastily that "sexologists cannot perceive them as completely sexually normal" (p. 24). In a reality perceived as a clear-cut binary, there is not much room left: You are either a heterosexual man, or a heterosexual woman. A small percentage is left for the "homosexual deviants" as heterosexuality's constitutive outside, but there is absolutely no shifting or fluidity allowed—it is simply either/or.

Sexology is connected to medicine in order to make itself look more serious and scientific, in a word, respectable. Early sexologists exclusively used Latin in their treatises; their aim was twofold: to exert their scientific merit and to prevent the general public from misusing their science for masturbatory purposes (and thus as pornography itself). Similarly, Czech sexologist Ivo Pondělíček has always expressed himself in esoteric language, employing a lot of philosophical terminology. Recently, he has added a moralizing tone—thus, pornography for him is similar to explosives and drugs and as such should be censored. For some scholars, open information about sexuality is deemed harmful. The ex-rector of Charles University in Prague, Radim Palouš, "called for open information in all areas of human knowledge—with the exception of sexuality" (Uzel, 2004, p. 49). Uzel criticizes such backwardness and indoctrination. In the center of fights over pornography, he identifies sexuality as such, and irrational attitudes toward it are "rooted in Christian tradition," especially its Catholic rendition (pp. 113–114). Uzel is clearly against what he calls "the bigotry and intolerance of the church" (pp. 128–129, 167). The ultimate belief in science and scientific progress leads Uzel to skepticism toward irrationality and traditional values that backed "witch-hunts, holy inquisition, and religious persecution" (p. 29). He sees the present and future in bright colors, thanks to science, "With the progress of science and general education, the new generation is in a much better position compared to our ancestors" (p. 30). As Weeks points out, sexologists always perceived themselves as "engaged in a symbolic struggle between darkness and light, ignorance and enlightenment, and this 'science' was their surest weapon" (Weeks, 1985, p. 69). Moreover, sexologists have always used the modernist rhetoric of progress and a better future. Krafft-Ebing, like others, hoped that his work might "prove of utility in the service of science, justice and humanity" (p. 72). Similarly, Uzel states that his "book is trying to remove the labels" (Uzel, 2004, p.10), and "its aim is to disrupt anti-sexual myths and to contribute in a humble way to human happiness" (p. 45).

Sexuality is described in biological terms; the gender division is imposed socially, for example, by "scientific" descriptions like the one by Weiss and Uzel. These provide the rationale for preexisting commonsense perceptions about men and women being incomplete halves, which can only find wholeness when united with the other, further reproducing heterosexist bias. Science, which enjoys such high status in our society, thus contributes to the legitimization of rigid binary gender roles—and all this in the name of progress and human happiness. Not only is "modern sexuality" an "invention of sexological pens" (Weeks, 1985, p. 63), but it also defines what are and are not normal gender roles and identities.

THE RESONANCE OF SEXOLOGICAL
AND CRIMINOLOGICAL DISCOURSE
WITH ANTIPORN FEMINISM

This criminologist's understanding of porn resonates with the way in which it is understood by antiporn feminists. According to Chmelík, sexual arousal involves a risk of aggressive behavior, which is prone to increase as a result of watching porn. Porn "stimulates the idea that women are docile victims" (Chmelik, 2003, p. 45). The criminologist and antiporn feminists are in agreement, however unreflected upon, regarding the supposed dehumanization and objectification of women through porn, "Woman in pornographic materials is being dealt with mostly in an inhuman way, she is perceived as a useless thing serving a man for satisfying his sexual filthiness" (p. 48). The same has been argued by feminists opposed to pornography such as Andrea Dworkin (1987, 1989), Catharine MacKinnon (1987, 1993), Susan Brownmiller (1975), Laura Lederer (1980), Diana Russell (1980, 1993), and many others, as well as by some current European feminists (Baer, 1996; Itzin, 1996; MacRae, 2003). The central criminological category in defining pornography, however, is morality; contrariwise antiporn feminists focus on discrimination (MacKinnon).

Pornography, in the view of both this Czech criminologist and antiporn feminists, is closely linked to violence against women. Chmelík presents it as synonymous with abuse and traffic in women—as well as does feminist

Kathleen Barry, who calls porn female sexual slavery (Barry, 1979). In the criminologist's perception, as well, pornography triggers violence against women. When he describes rape, however, his consonance with feminists comes to an end. Chmelík focuses on the rape victim, stressing four distinctive features:

- "the victim's masochism" ("some masochistic women find it sexually stimulating to be abused, so that they compel men to do it");
- "the victim's role in guilt" ("provoking conduct on the part of the victim, women who provoke men by flirtatiousness, loudness, slinkiness, baring parts of their bodies and thus work up sexual desire in him. . . this category contains cases where the victim consented to intercourse only to change her mind immediately before the act");
- "the aggressor's small role in guilt" (when a man is under the influence of drugs or alcohol);
- "the hyperbolizing of repercussions" ("the damage on the victim is minimal, the woman does not have any visible marks on her body, has previously had intercourse with the man in question etc.").— (Chmelík, 2003, p. 50)

This list reproduces all the classical rape myths as they were identified and unraveled by feminists in the late 1970s. However, this contemporary Czech criminologist repeats them all as a scientific truth, unaware of their falsity. Since this also is the approach informing the attitudes of judges, it is not surprising that Czech courts do not sentence drunk rapists whose victims are "flirtatious" prostitutes (City Court of Brno, Czech Republic, July 2006).

It is paradoxical that this criminologist, who reproduces rape myths exposed by feminists, shares with the same feminists a condemnation of pornography. This focus in common of a mainstream criminologist and an influential stream of feminism on pornography is not random. It reveals a socially conservative tone, one to be expected from criminology as a status-quo-preserving discipline; nevertheless, this is undesirable within feminism, which is and should be a socially dynamic power.

However, the sexologist Uzel does not hold antiporn attitudes and claims that men, women, and society in general benefit from its existence. Still, some of his arguments resonate with those of antiporn feminists. This becomes apparent when he writes about the insurmountable differences between men and women, an opinion also held by Susan Griffin, who argues that men and women cannot communicate because the latter speak the language of nature (1978); Mary Daly, who advocates the creation a new gynomorphic vocabulary for women which, according to her, is very much needed in a polarized society (1978); and Carol Gilligan, who claims women have an essentially different way of thinking and moral reasoning than men (1982).

Despite these similarities, Uzel himself is explicitly antifeminist. What he despises about feminism is its focus on equality and political goals. Uzel states that, "The fuel to all feminist movements is basically hatred towards men, often skillfully masked" (2004, 133). According to him, "All feminists are unified in this hatred." Thus, while positioning himself as the liberal alternative to standard scientific antiporn discourse, he at the same time maintains deeply conservative views.

Uzel's knowledge of feminism, however, is fairly limited. According to him, antiporn feminists "disapprove of oral sex" and allegedly perceive porn as "a conspiratorial perversion jeopardizing family and nation" (p. 146). He is particularly horrified by Susan Brownmiller and Laura Lederer, prominent antiporn feminists. However, there is a congruity between their opinions and his, one that he is not aware of. Brownmiller argues that sexuality is biologically given and men are predators by nature (1975). Similarly, Uzel stresses the naturalness of hard, promiscuous, predator-like, bodily-oriented sexuality for men, and a softer, relationship and love-oriented sexuality for women (Uzel, 2004). These characteristics of feminine sexuality are shared by most antiporn feminists: Robin Morgan (1978), Kathleen Barry (1979), Adrienne Rich (1983), and Andrea Dworkin (1982).

Antiporn feminists regard pornography as discrimination against women, but sexologist Uzel claims that as long as the majority of porn consumers are men, feminist campaigns against it are oppressive to males. These feminists also hold that porn causes violence against women, while Uzel presents violence in sex using the example of praying mantises—given his antifeminism, it is hardly pure chance that he chose a species in which a female commits violence against the male (Uzel, 2004, p. 66). Given widespread sexualized violence against women in society, Uzel might have instead chosen a "violent-male-species" example—but that would not have resonated with his political beliefs.

CONCLUSION

The continuum of approaches to pornography is defined by uncompromising deprecation on one side—according to these authors; pornography usage is immoral and results in increased aggressiveness and general sociopathy (Chmelik, 2003). On the other side of the Czech scientific continuum of porn, there are sexologists who do not hastily condemn porn users, but who instead stress the essential biological difference between female and male sexuality (Uzel, 2004), thus reproducing and reinforcing the gender binary. The irony here is that the "conservative" antiporn writer utilizes language actually employed by at least one section of the feminist movement, while the "liberal" wing of scholars espouses an explicitly antifeminist agenda. This framing of the debate excludes from the realm of Czech science the possibility of a nonantiporn, pro-sex feminist position.

REFERENCES

Baer, S. (1996). Pornography and sexual harassment in the EU. In R. A. Elman (Ed.), *Sexual politics and the European Union. The new feminist challenge* (pp. 51—66). Providence: Berghahn Books.

Barry, K. (1979). *Female sexual slavery.* New York: New York University Press.

Brownmiller, S. (1975). *Against our will. Men, women and rape.* New York: Bantam Book.

Brzek, A. (1993). *Průvodce sexualitou člověka.* Praha: Státní pedagogické nakladatelství.

Chmelík, J. (2003). *Mravnost, pornografie a mravnostní kriminalita.* Praha: Portál.

Daly, M. (1978). *Gyn/Ecology. The metaethics of radical feminism.* Boston: Beacon Press.

Dworkin, A. (1982). *Pornography: Men possessing women.* London: Women's Press.

———. (1988). *Letters from a war zone.* New York: Lawrence Hill.

Fausto-Sterling, A. (1992). *Myths of gender: Biological theories about women and men.* New York: Basic Books.

Gilligan, C. (1982). *In a different voice: Psychological theory and women's development.* Cambridge: Harvard University Press.

Griffin, S. (1978). *Woman and nature. The roaring inside her.* New York: Harper & Row.

Itzin, C. (1996). Pornography, harm, and human rights: The UK in the European context. In R. A. Elman (Ed.), *Sexual politics and the European Union: The new feminist challenge* (pp. 67–82). Providence: Berghahn Books.

Lederer, L., (Ed.). (1980). *Take back the night: Women on pornography.* New York: William Morrow.

MacKinnon, C. A. (1987). *Feminism unmodified. Discourses on life and law.* Cambridge: Harvard University Press.

———. (1993). *Only words.* Cambridge: Harvard University Press.

MacRae, H. (2003). Morality, censorship, and discrimination: Reframing the pornography debate in Germany and Europe. *Social Politics, 10,* 314–345.

Morgan, R. (1978). *Going too far.* New York: Vintage Books.

Rich, A. (1983). Compulsory heterosexuality and lesbian existence. In A. Snitow, C. Stansell, & S. Thompson (Eds.), *Powers of desire: The politics of sexuality* (pp. 177–205). New York: Monthly Review Press.

Russell, D. (1980). Pornography and violence: What does the new research say. In L. Lederer (Ed.), *Take back the night. Women on pornography* (pp. 218–238). New York: William Morrow.

Russell, D. E. H. (Ed). (1993). *Making violence sexy: Feminist views on pornography.* New York: Teachers College Press.

Uzel, R. (2004). *Pornografie aneb Provokující nahota.* Praha: Ikar.

Weeks, J. (1985). *Sexuality and its discontents: Meanings, myths and modern sexualities.* London and New York: Routledge Kegan Paul.

9 Lesbian Representation and Postcolonial Allegory

Anikó Imre

POSTCOLONIAL ALLEGORY, NATIONALISM, AND GENDER

Fredric Jameson, in a text that launched a widespread discussion in post-colonial studies in 1986, argued for the specificity of "third world" literary (and, by extension, cinematic) texts with regard to the ratio and the relationship between the personal and the political. In an admittedly cursory comparison, he claimed that instead of the radical gap that exists in the first world between the private and the public, the poetic and the political, and sexuality and the sphere of politics and economics, in third world national cultures, the libidinal and the political are inseparably tied together—a bond that makes all third world cultural products inevitably allegorical (Jameson, 1986, p. 77).

Jameson's work catalyzed a debate about postcolonial allegory, which has since become acknowledged as "an especially charged site for the discursive manifestations of what is at heart a form of cultural struggle" in a world of postcoloniality (Slemon, 1987, pp. 11–12). It has led to explorations of similarity and exchange between "third" and "first world" allegories (Shohat & Stam, 1994, p. 271). It has become evident that postcolonial allegories represent a variety of forms and purposes. Furthermore, there has been an aesthetic shift in postcolonial cultures from the teleological, Marxist-inflected allegories of earlier, immediate post-Independence phases of nationhood to a more self-deconstructive postmodernist use of allegory (p. 271). In post-Independence national cultures, allegory was initially called upon to legitimate the sacredness and unity of new nations. However, as Reda Bensmaia argues, drawing on Homi Bhabha's work, the division between the *pedagogical* and *performative* functions of allegory has become increasingly apparent in more recent postcolonial literary and cinematic texts. The latter tend explicitly to acknowledge the crisis of the hermeneutic stability of national history and allegory. As a result, it is no longer possible to read third world allegories as "self-righteous and predetermined discourses on good and evil, on the pure and the impure, on true and false identity, on the glorious past scorned by colonialism. . ." (Bensmaia, 1999, p. 2).

In the essay "DissemiNation: Time, Narrative and the Margins of the Modern Nation," Bhabha discusses the ambivalence of the nation as a narrative strategy, manifest in the divide between the performative and pedagogical functions of nationalism. He explains, "In the production of the nation as narration there is a split between the continuist, accumulative temporality of the pedagogical, and the repetitious, recursive strategy of the performative. It is through this process of splitting that the conceptual ambivalence of modern society becomes the site of *writing the nation*" (Bhabha, 1994, p. 145). Rather than the homogeneous and horizontal view proposed by nationalist historiography, whose reference point is an unchanging "people," the "people" is a complex rhetorical strategy of social reference repetitively produced and confirmed within a set of discourses.

We then have a contested conceptual territory where the nation's people must be thought in double-time; the people are the historical "objects" of a nationalist pedagogy, giving the discourse an authority that is based on the pre-given or constituted historical origin *in the past*; the people are also the "subjects" of a process of signification that must erase any prior or originary presence of the nation-people to demonstrate the prodigious, living principles of the people as contemporaneity: as a sign of the *present* through which national life is redeemed and iterated as a reproductive process. (p. 145)

The paradox of the dual time of nationalism, manifest in a pedagogical mission that attempts repetitively to *reinscribe* and perform what it *represents* as horizontal, homogeneous, and unchanging, "surmounting" the traces of such continual construction has an explicit gendered reference. Anne McClintock captures this reference in her own description of the temporal contradiction of nationalism between a frozen past and a dynamic future, which is resolved through the idea of the hierarchical racial family of nations on the one hand and through a gendered distribution of time within nationalism on the other. Nationalism is split between an active, forward-thrusting masculine future and an unchanging feminine past frozen into official histories, symbols, and canonized texts (McClintock, 1995, pp. 358–359).

All nations have evolved gendered and sexualized, depend on specific constructions of normative gender and sexuality, and make use of gendered and sexualized allegories to perpetuate those constructions. Nationalism favors a homosocial form of male bonding and includes women only symbolically, most prominently in the trope of the mother as the embodiment of ideal femininity (Parker, Russo, Sommer, & Yaeger, 1992, p. 6). Since all nationalisms privilege men as their proper liberal subjects, in times of national instability, "nationalist discourses turn history and destiny into sexualized scenarios. If the right working of the nation is the right working of masculinity, enforced threats to the nation are represented as emasculating" (Smith & Brinker-Gabler, 1997, p. 15).

"Emasculated" postcolonial nations or those in transition, whose historical foundations are particularly tenuous, exclude with great zeal all sexualities perceived as nonreproductive from representation, in both the aesthetic and political senses of the term. Regarding political representation, lesbianism has been far less visible than even male homosexuality in Euro-American civic discourses. "As an expression of female sexuality, lesbianism was not merely a 'love that dare not speak its name' until the twentieth century—it did not even have a name." Even in the early 20th century, when women appeared in the public sphere as workers, consumers, and political leaders, the representations of lesbianism in national discourse remained largely offstage in what Teresa de Lauretis describes as "socio-sexual (in)difference" (Parker et al., 1992, p. 7). In the sphere of aesthetic representation, nationalism channels desires through sanctioned and gendered aesthetic avenues such as poetry and tragedy, and is threatened by forms of love that are not those of nationalism.[1] The nonheterosexual woman, who cannot be forced into the binary paths of heteronormative reproduction, is thus poised to disrupt the discursive economy of nationalism.

Teresa de Lauretis suggests that lesbian representation in the cinema necessarily calls attention to the (inherently heterosexual) conditions of vision. She makes an analytical distinction between "films that represent lesbians" and "films that represent the problem of representation" (de Lauretis, 1991, p. 224). Elsewhere, she discusses "guerrilla practices" in women's cinema of the 1980s, films that propose lesbianism as *a question of representation*, of what can be seen," where,

> [l]esbianism is not merely a subtext of the film, nor simply a content to be represented or "portrayed," but is the very problem of its form: how to represent a female, lesbian desire that is neither a masculine usurpation of male heterosexual desire, nor a feminine, narcissistic identification with the other woman. (de Lauretis, 1990, p. 22, emphasis in original)

However, this otherwise useful distinction presupposes a certain kind of national context where "lesbianism" and "outness" are viable choices.

I want to ask what happens to lesbian representation when it is subjected to the merciless allegorization at the heart of postcolonial national historiography. Hence, I offer a comparative analysis that juxtaposes three film texts, from Argentina, India, and Hungary, respectively. All the films try to work out a compromise between the pedagogical and performative functions of postcolonial national allegory in remarkably similar ways. Homi Bhabha's account of the ambivalence between the performative and pedagogical functions of nationalism will be helpful in attempting such a synthesis, even if it is not specific to gendered and sexualized identities; the same will be the case for Teresa de Lauretis's incorporation of the concept of allegory into her gendered poststructuralist framework, even if it has no specific concern with nationalism and national identities. As I will show, the lesbian figures at the center of the three works inevitably mobilize the performative dimension of allegorical interpretations, which are bound by specific nationalisms and national cultures.

THREE ALLEGORIES OF POSTCOLONIAL LESBIANISM

Feminist and queer studies scholars of a poststructuralist orientation tend to focus on films and other visual practices that have emerged side by side with Western feminist movements and theories. Such practices are equipped with tools of radical deconstruction to carve out a theoretical and activist space for the female subject for whom the conventions of looking within Hollywood cinema constitute more relevant master narratives than do those of nationalism. As a result, lesbian and queer theories have paid very little attention to the ambivalences of nationalist affiliation.

Deepa Mehta's *Fire* (1996, India/Canada), María Luisa Bemberg's *Yo, lo peor de todas* (*I, the Worst of All*, 1990, Argentina), and Károly Makk's *Egymásra nézve* (*Another Way*, 1982, Hungary) are three films about lesbianism made in postcolonial national contexts. While the relationship between the two women at the center of each film is unmistakably homoerotic, lesbian acts tend to remain almost entirely invisible and nameless; also lesbian representation is disavowed or minimized by the directors and the majority of the critics. The works are very different from each other, rooted as they are in their specific contexts of origin, but they pose similar dilemmas of classification and critical processing in the West. On the most mundane front, when available at all, they tend to be placed in the "drama" or "foreign film" just as often as in the "gay and lesbian" sections of video stores and libraries. Indeed, there is something foreign about the tentative lesbianism of these representations: they are all grim, tragic, or pessimistic in their outcome, ostensibly devoid of the kind of excess, play, and performance of sexuality that tends to characterize North American and Western European lesbian films of the past few decades.

Yo, lo peor de todas, a historical costume drama directed by María Luisa Bemberg, is based on Octavio Paz's allegorical novel *Las trampas de la fe* (1982)/*The Traps of Fate* (1988). It focuses on the figure of the legendary Mexican nun-poet Sor Juana Inés de la Cruz and her passionate relationship with the wife of the Spanish Viceroy, the Condesa de Paredes María Luisa, in the context of the colonization of Mexico by Spain and the Inquisition in the 17th century. Indian-born Canadian Deepa Mehta's melodramatic *Fire* centers on the sexual and emotional bond that develops between two neglected and abused wives trapped in a traditional Hindu family in contemporary Delhi. The Hungarian film *Another Way*, a historical drama made by director Károly Makk and co-written by lesbian writer Erzsébet Galgóczi, is about a tragic affair between lesbian journalist Éva and her married colleague Lívia, which takes place in the Budapest of 1958, 2 years after the failed uprising against the Soviet-communist invasion.

Unlike in most Western films about lesbians, the nation looms as the center of narrative coherence in all three works. They allegorize female homosexuality, refusing even to speak its name and effacing its representations by directing attention to larger, "universal" issues, which are putting collective pressure on the nation, such as colonial oppression, religious fundamentalism, and women's inequality in the public sphere. The relationships that secretly develop in the shadow of oppression are inherently tragic—symbolic of the individual's fate in hopeless collective situations. As each director insists, their lesbians are postcolonial allegories. Nevertheless, their representations of lesbian desire, however effaced, caused controversy within the films' national environments, provoking silence and unease (in the cases of *Another Way* and *I the Worst of All*), condemnation and even banning by the defensive nation-state and conservative groups (in the case of *Fire*), yet also galvanizing lesbian activism (in the cases of *Fire* and *Another Way*).

In all three cases, however, one can discover instances of performativity both in the texts themselves and the way they were subsequently mobilized in their respective contexts of reception. This performative dimension undermines the allegorical straitjacket of national seriousness into which the lesbian representations are forced. The moments of play, humor, and irony—"homotextuality," to borrow Judith Mayne's term for lesbian disturbances in spectacle and the structure of the look (1990, pp. 26–27)—appear in the film texts in different disguises: as excessive symmetry of visual details, which reflects ironically on allegories of gender and nationalism; as theatrical acting and exuberant, "feminine" décor; or as a recurring thematic reference to cross-dressing, dancing, and other forms of play. As a result, in different ways, the representation of lesbianism visualizes and critiques the arbitrary foundations of the nation and its supportive fundamentalist ideologies, grounded as those are in the ostensibly neutral binary divisions inherent to representation itself. In none of these cases can the lesbian representation be contained as a teleological national allegory.

Both of *Fire*'s protagonists are married women. However, the husband, whom the younger Sita is arranged to marry at the beginning of the film, unabashedly prefers his Chinese lover; the older Radha's husband is devoted to the religious guidance of a swami, who is helping him purge himself of worldly desires. The neglected women experience joy and happiness together until they are finally betrayed by a jealous man-servant. In the eventual confrontation with her husband, Radha's clothes catch on fire. After her husband chooses to remove his helpless mother from the fire instead of helping Radha, she leaves the house with Sita. The film ends as the lovers begin a—no doubt uncertain—life together. The title refers to the last, climactic event: Radha's burning sari presents an ironic, reversed performance of the myth of Sita, Lord Rama's wife, the epitome of the obedient and loyal spouse in Hindu mythology, who had to walk through trial by fire (*agni-pariksha*) to prove her fidelity to her husband (see Syed, Kapur, Katrak, Panesar).

While the film follows the conventions of a stifling social melodrama, which takes place almost entirely in the cramped spaces of the shared family home, its spectacularity—the two gorgeous women themselves, the color and composition harmonies of the clothes and furniture, Radha's memory sequences, and the man-servant's elaborate, Bollywood-style sexual fantasies—subtly introduce an element of camp. Explicit instances of humor and play repeatedly puncture the seriousness of the familial and religious limits imposed on the women. In Sita's first solitary moment after she arrives in her new husband's home, she tries on a pair of men's jeans and dances in front of a mirror to a pop tune. At the height of the women's newfound happiness, they perform another dance together, this time dressed as a heterosexual couple. This queer tone is further amplified by the insertion of a rather inorganic scene-within-the-scene, a visualization of Mundu's, the servant's narcissistic fantasy, in which his secret infatuation with Radha is reciprocated, and in which all the family members appear in various kinds of drag performing roles assigned by Mundu's desire for power and love.

The framing look is importantly transnational, informed by the director's diasporic perspective. It reveals the extent to which the oppressive religious nationalism urged by the Hindu Right, which officially banned the film's exhibition in India after its release, was already a desperate performance of authority, fighting a losing battle against the forces of globalization to secure a strictly national space purified by nationalism. This is also evident in Jatin's, the younger brother's affair with a Chinese woman, or in the presence of the porn video outlet the brothers operate, literally at the side of their respectable family restaurant business. As Ratna Kapur argues, *Fire* needs to be located in the broader cultural wars that have been exploding across the country, setting up Indian culture in opposition to an "outsider," "the West" (Kapur, 1999).

Thomas Waugh goes so far as to say the censorship battle between the film and the anxious Hindu Right, represented by the then leading Shiv Sena Party, the self-appointed moral and cultural guardians of the nation, was itself a desperate performance of politics, a "censorship brouhaha" similar to those that surrounded other diasporic films such as *Bandit Queen* or *Kama Sutra*, inefficient in the face of a long tradition of queer representations. The attacks on such works are reminders that state censorship can hardly keep pace with, let alone contain, the proliferating sexual discourses in films such as these, much less in Bollywood and regional popular cinemas. Waugh explains that Indian cinema has traditionally been very open to same-sex desire—regardless of the fact that homosexuality has never been so named—within institutions of publicity, stardom, fan culture, and reception, as well as within narrative worlds where the borders around homosociality have been quite ambiguous. Although the queer cinema scene in India is not as prominent as it is in Taiwan or the Philippines, in the past decade, the "liberalization" of the Indian economy and the transnationalization of the media have increased the cross-border importation of erotic commodities (Waugh, 2001, pp. 280–281).[2] Deepa Mehta herself declares that she wanted to capture a society in transition, where cultural transformation is being fostered from the outside, by globalization (Kapur, 1999).

The Hindu Right's quest to "protect" Indian tradition from contamination is deeply grounded in local tradition. It constitutes a patriarchal and religious convergence with Gandhi's appeal to "female" virtues such as chastity, purity, and self-sacrifice, embodied by the figure of the eversuffering virtuous Sita (Katrak, 1992, pp. 398–399). The dimension of Hindu mythology that recognizes the spiritual in the physical also socializes women to subsume sexuality in the spiritual realm, leaving behind desire and pleasure. According to Gandhi, women could only be pure and noble if they renounced sex altogether; moreover they are to assume a public role only for the national cause (Katrak, 1992, p. 401). Nevertheless, the historical roots of this oppressive ideal go even deeper, as they also represent points of convergence between Gandhian and 19th century British colonial attitudes, both of which reinforced women's subordinate position in patriarchal family structures.

Fire's power to perform the heteronormativity of nationalism to itself and imagine alternative arrangements among the sexes was harnessed by lesbian activist organizations based in India. The Campaign for Lesbian Rights was instrumental in organizing broad-based protests against the Shiv Sena's attacks on the film. *Fire*, a feature film, became a key point of reference for activists, the subject of reports and discussions, in which the two senses of representation—aesthetic and political—crossed and supported each other. As part of the activist effort that developed from the defense of the work, the organization Lesbian Emergence wrote two Hindi street plays and a version of the Rajasthani folk tale *Teeja-Beeja*, which narrates the story of love between two women. They also distributed leaflets and educational materials in order to debunk negative myths about and increase the visibility of lesbianism.

María Luisa Bemberg's film, *I, the Worst of All*, revolves around Sor Juana Inés de la Cruz and her relationship with the Vicereine of Spain, María Luisa. Upon their arrival in *"Nueva España,"* the viceroy and his wife decide to "adopt" the erudite and beautiful nun. This involves providing ideological protection from the religious excesses of the misogynist archbishop, the representative of the Inquisition. Years later, when the viceroy is recalled to Spain, pressures from the Inquisition and the condesa's absence manage to destroy Sor Juana emotionally. At the very end of the work, after being forced to renounce her books and other possessions, she dies caring for people decimated by cholera.

The film does not speculate about whether Sor Juana is a lesbian and if so, what kind she is. Like Sita and Radha, she is rather a woman who cannot find happiness in the severely constrained roles assigned to females in a colonized society—a context that no doubt stands as an allegory of conditions created by postcolonial nationalisms in South America. In this case, the Spanish Inquisition in colonial Mexico provides a backdrop of repression and stagnation, not unlike the Rosas dictatorship, the military regimes of 1930s, or the Dirty War of the 1970s. Such a broad allegorical interpretation is reinforced by the transnational aspect of the production: Bemberg, a director from Argentina, insisted on making a film about a Mexican subject and shooting it on site—a plan that eventually failed for financial and political reasons (Williams, 2002, p. 137). Octavio Paz' *Traps of Faith*, the novel from which the film was adapted, has itself been convincingly read as an allegory of the ideological traps in which Soviet intellectuals found themselves during Stalinism (Bergmann, 1998, pp. 246–247).

While the Indian women run away from their family prison of unhappiness perpetuated by religious fundamentalism, Sor Juana joins the convent because, as a woman of humble origin, she is forced out of the public world of the intellect where she rightly perceives her place to be. In both cases, it appears that more freedom might prompt these women to make different, perhaps heterosexual choices. There is no taken-for-granted, let alone natural, lesbian identity in either film; rather, women seem obliged to take on men's roles because males themselves cannot adequately perform them. While Radha is unable to bear children, which is seen in *Fire* as something that contributes to her husband's religious abstinence and her own openness to embracing the joy Sita has to offer, the condesa, who sees motherhood as women's most natural and noble mission, bears a child while in Mexico after repeated miscarriages. In his discussion of the role of lesbianism in the film, Bruce Williams argues that such desire is integral to the text, but is obscured or tamed by the work's ostensible aim to depict women seeking to assert their autonomy at key moments of an oppressive national history and by Bemberg's own comments, which open up the film's significance toward a universal atemporal rejection of repression, fanaticism, and fundamentalism while downplaying lesbianism as friendship (Williams, 2002, p. 139).

The gendered colonial dynamic, however, is subversively performed and allegorized within the relationship of the two women themselves. Sor Juana is visually and verbally identified in their interaction as an allegory of Mexico, while the condesa is symbolic of Spain. Their communication is determined by colonial dominance and submission. Nevertheless, it is performed by the wrong subjects. During the condesa's last visit to the convent, she asks Juana to remove her veil—an act that compels a joint postcolonial and queer reading of drag. She insists on seeing the "real" Juana under the habit. When Juana resists, the condesa employs her colonial authority and "commands" Juana to expose herself to the latter's dominant gaze. This familiar dialectic of domination–submission, however, is wrested from its colonial moorings in the course of its all-female performance and yields the most intimate and erotic moment of the film, the first and only kiss between the two women. "This Juana is mine. Only mine," the condesa declares, to Juana's silent ecstasy. Shortly thereafter, when the Viceroy is dismissed from his post as colonial administrator, he visits the convent to say good-bye to Juana and on his wife's behalf as well. As he and Juana sit across the bars that separate her from visitors, he explains that returning to Spain is very painful for his wife because "she fell in love with Mexico." "And Mexico will miss her," Juana responds, devastated. "It will sink into a lake."

The gendered binary scaffolding of colonial desire crumbles when women on the two sides of the colonial divide use the very allegorical language that renders them tools of symbolic traffic among men and assert their own desire for each other. Such binary divisions are turned theatrical, performative in several other subtle ways. The very first encounter among Sor Juana, the Viceroy, and the condesa takes place in the convent after the first of several performances of Juana's plays. Amidst the applause, the Viceroy turns to his wife, "How does her poem go, the one that makes fun of men?" The condesa begins reciting, while Juana approaches unnoticed, adding the last lines of the poem. "I was eager to meet you," the condesa greets her. "There must be few cultured women in Mexico." "Or elsewhere, Madam," Juana says reversing her inadvertent condescension. "Shall we adopt her, María Luisa?" the Viceroy asks joining the erotically charged conversation, turning it into a love triangle in which it is the women who use the man in the middle. The desire between the women turns each utterance into a performance queered away from its proper function: The Viceroy proves his worldly sophistication by citing a poem written by a nun that makes fun of men; the first exchange between the colonizer woman and the colonized female subject is wrapped in flirtation, which makes the Viceroy's allusion to the child-like condition of the colonial subject to be saved and protected by the colonizer carnivalesque. No wonder the outraged Archbishop whispers to a priest upon witnessing all this, "This is not a convent, this is a bordello."

Indeed, the Archbishop's narrative function is to make visible and attempt to reestablish the "proper" allegorical workings of gender constitution, religion, and colonization. He is in the business of dividing and separating, of rendering distinct and discrete. The first thing he demands of the nuns during their introductory meeting is that they veil themselves. He wants more "discretion" in the convent and battles "laxity" on every front, including the regulation of Sor Juana's desires and creative output. In an initiative that requires "utmost discretion," he creates a rift among the nuns by bribing some of them with additional internal power in exchange for enforcing his rules. "Secrecy is the key to the Church's ascendancy," he utters in justification of the surveillance and control mechanisms he installs.

However, in this historical costume drama, "historical" and "costume" push against each other as forcefully they do in *Orlando* and other feminist reappropriations of the genre. The setting and mise-en-scène are allegorical, stylized, abstract, and often ahistorical. The tone of theatricality is set in the very first scene, introduced by the intertitle "Mexico, 17th century/Méjico, Siglo XVII." The brightly lit composition in the foreground, set in front of a stationary camera against a dark background, is perfectly symmetrical. A long table divides the frame horizontally, on which stand two, straight tall glasses. A stage-like rectangular structure in the background creates additional parallel horizontal lines, while tall candle-holders add vertical ones. The bars of the dim window on the back wall repeat the crossing lines and introduce the motif of prison-bars, which divide and connect, both literally and figuratively, colonial subjects, sexes, and genders throughout the film. Two hands reach into the artificially lit center of the frame from left and right in synchronized movement and remove the glasses. A cut to a longer shot reveals the new Viceroy and Archbishop of "New Spain" sitting at the table facing each other and foreshadows the power struggle that develops between them. Two allegorical figures, they identify themselves as the representatives of state and church authority, "Caesar and God," respectively.

Their struggle is for the right kind of colonization, fought over the bodies and souls of the colonized. As the Archbishop puts it, "Our responsibility, yours and mine sire, is to save this new Spain, this innocent people, which Heaven sent to us." Their ensuing sparse, evenly paced dialogue outlines their ideological differences about how to perform the task. The chiaroscuro lighting, the symmetrical structure of the setting, and the rhythmical lifting of the glasses that accompanies the measured dialogue provide a dialectical pattern, which is repeated at all levels of the film. It boils over only in the final confrontation between the two of them toward the end of the work, when they openly clash in an argument to decide under whose "jurisdiction" or "protection" Sor Juana's poetry and desires fall.

Cross-dressing, once again, is represented as a manifestation of lesbian subversion: The Vicereine does not only unveil but also dresses Juana, giving her a spectacular headdress made out of the plumes of the quetzal, the "Mexican bird," which Juana puts on immediately, accompanied by a playful curtsy that carries out and simultaneously undermines her performance as a colonized love object. Another instance of cross-dressing takes place in Juana's imagination as she sits by the bedside of her dying mother, realizing that her aversion to marriage and other forms of proper femininity had caused a never-healing rift between the two of them. She then sees herself as a young girl, dressed in male drag to be able to go to university but facing her mother's derision and rejection. Juana's memory-double playfully whispers to her, "Since I couldn't dress as a man, I dressed as a nun."

The Hungarian *Another Way*, the only film made in Soviet-controlled Eastern Europe during communism that openly depicts lesbianism, is similar to *Fire* and *I, the Worst of All* in that the film's own discursive strategies, the creators themselves, and the critical community all converged in interpreting the lesbian protagonists as mere allegories of larger, national, and universal, issues. Felice Newman, one of the English translators of the novel *Törvényen belül* (1980; "Within the Law," English title *Another Love*, 1991), from which novelist Erzsébet Galgóczi and director Károly Makk developed the film, writes,

> In how many novels written in the "free" and "liberated" West does a lesbian character represent the soul of the nation?. . . In Galgóczi's view, Hungary is a nation caught in an Orwellian squeeze. And Éva is Hungary's national spirit. *Another Love* is Erzsébet Galgóczi's State of the Union address, and she has chosen a fiercely independent (albeit emotionally battered) lesbian to carry the message. . . Such guts, Galgóczi! (Newman, 1991, p. 17)

The misunderstanding here is profound even though the ethnocentrism at its core is unintended. No East European writer can "choose" a lesbian character within cultures where there is no such thing as a lesbian. Galgóczi, who was a closeted lesbian until the untimely end of her troubled life, struck out in this one novel to bring her own unrepresentable subjectivity into representation. The only way she could do so, however, was by pulling the smokescreen of national allegory in front of the highly autobiographical story of the tragic lesbian.

This strategy worked for the film version, too. At the 1982 Cannes Festival, Polish actress Jadwiga Jankowska-Cieślak, who played the role of Éva—in the absence of Hungarian actresses who would have taken on such a role—won the Award for Best Actress. The work received the FIPRESCI Award "for its clarity," for the "originality of its libertarian message," and for its struggle for "individual freedom." European reviews praised it for the "extraordinary richness with which Makk and Galgóczi linked two disparate themes: the human right to another kind of love, namely lesbian love, and the search for political freedom" (Zsugán, 1982, p. 16). American film critics and academics have been just as uncritically thrilled, ignoring the contradiction that a lesbian should allegorically stand for the cause of the nation, in whose official discourses lesbianism is inconceivable.[3]

What makes this contradiction possible to miss is precisely that the film's aesthetic successfully sublimates the lesbian theme in the realm of political allegory and suppresses a potentially lesbian look. Éva is the only "real" lesbian in the three works—still without a name, but with a certain harassed lesbian self-awareness. "She is that way," declares a male character in the film, indicating that her sexuality does not fall within the normative categories of language. She "suffers from two perversions," as the director puts it in an interview; she "loves her own sex," and is "unable to lie" (Szilágyi, 1982, p. 12). Her sexual "perversion" is never directly identified in the film, yet the circumscriptions, empty pronouns, and pronominal adjectives that refer to lesbianism point to a collective understanding of the secret (Moss, 1995, p. 245). This "understanding" crystallizes in the stereotype of the male-identified and mannish lesbian, who cannot resist the seductions of traditional femininity and competes with men for women.

Tragic lesbian love is a feasible allegory for signifying the failure of heroism in the face of complicity and oppression because Éva, an East European lesbian, is constructed as an anomaly, an aberration, a contradiction in terms, as someone not viable other than a trope from the start. Shortly after she begins her job on the staff of the Budapest daily *Igazság* (*Truth*) as a reporter in 1958, she falls in love with a married colleague, Lívia, a markedly feminine blonde (Polish actress Grazyna Szapolowska). Lívia, much like Radha in *Fire*, seeks an outlet from her eventless and emotionally deprived life on the side of her military officer husband and finds it in the new erotic energy that Éva radiates. After several dates and much emotional agony, she yields to temptation. Following their single sexual encounter, however, everything comes crashing down on the lovers: Lívia's jealous husband shoots his wife so that she remains wheelchair-bound and bitter toward Éva, a living memorial of regret and just punishment, whose greatest fear is that nobody will want to make her pregnant. Éva, whose reporting about communist atrocities has made her situation simultaneously impossible at the newspaper, gives in to despair. The scene that opens and closes the film (whose plot is told in retrospective narration) finds her at the Austro-Hungarian border, hinting at the possibility that she may have intended to emigrate illegally. Nevertheless, she does not hide from the border guards when they try to stop her, and is shot dead.

Unlike in *Fire* or even in *I, the Worst of All*, the camera refuses to eroticize contact between the women, including the sex scene, and medicalizes the crippled, naked infertile body of Lívia in the narrative introduction, which warns us of the consequence of "perversion" before the story begins. The film starts out with Éva's removal from the plot and ends the same way, teaching a lesson to those (like Lívia) who diverge from the correct path of livable choices. A sigh of relief accompanies her exit, as she is not a point of identification to begin with. She is useful only to the extent that her sacrifice can posthumously be converted into political capital.

Despite Makk's and Galgóczi's efforts to allegorize lesbianism, the pressure put on national allegory's apparently self-contained referential system by the representation of lesbian desire released allegory's ghostly, inherently self-reflective side. Although the performative dimension that lesbianism opens up within national allegory is not as explicit as it is in *Fire* and *I, the Worst of All*, a retrospective reading has highlighted the ways in which Éva's refusal to choose between available feminine and masculine identities makes such allegory unravel. Both the novel and the film have proven to be crucial identificatory resources for Hungarian lesbians, who have gradually appeared from the closet since the official end of communism. Éva Szalánczki's plight has become perhaps the most important historical and discursive record of lesbian visibility, on which these activists have drawn to construct their own very different kind of emergence into postcommunist representation.[4]

The first postcommunist novel about lesbianism, *Goat Lipstick* (*Kecskerúzs*, Budapest: Magvetö, 1997), by a lesbian writer who uses the pseudonym Agáta Gordon, engages in conversation with its single predecessor to stake out a different kind of lesbian subjectivity "within" but also "outside" the law, one no longer constituted in isolation. There is a conscious effort in *Goat Lipstick* to create a literary tradition, a "minor literature" of sorts in the Deleuzian sense, which deterritorializes language, connects the individual to political immediacy, and produces a collective assemblage of enunciation, turning a most personal story political (Sándor, 1999, pp. 10–12). This kind of allegorization, however, is deployed for the purposes of lesbian identification, resisting allegorical incorporation by the national body.

The continuities between the two novels, landmarks in the constitution of a lesbian community, are numerous and intentional, going far beyond the overt references in *Goat Lipstick* to passages in Galgóczi's novel. Both texts are caught in the ambivalence between a capitulation to and a critique of nationalistic ideologies of gender and sexuality. However, Galgóczi's tragic isolated lesbian commits suicide—importantly, on the border of the nation, by border guards' guns. Gordon's protagonist, even though she sinks into paranoia and depression and ends up in the psychiatric institution where she writes her autobiographical text, nevertheless belongs to a secret collectivity and is able to inhabit a lesbian space built from a collection of found images and texts. Whereas Galgóczi's lesbians inevitably and tragically come up against absolute borders and binaries determined by the allegorizing logic of nationalism, Gordon's heroines hide among texts, quotations, and images that represent these demarcations as malleable. Even more important, Gordon's lesbians take pleasure in this textual hiding. "Hiding, the incorporation of a role and the incorporation of a self is almost luxurious in this novel, an enjoyed and excessive game" (Sándor, 1999, p. 12).

Goat Lipstick is a paradigmatic text of postcommunist, lesbian feminist emergence in that it both identifies with the earlier text and transforms it in the course of a collective critical process of postcommunist reinterpretation. Gordon and her interpretive community take a critical poststructuralist stand toward the same categories. Éva's search for what she calls lesbian "nature" was bound to fail within the patriotic parameters imposed by the search itself. Gordon, by contrast, foregrounds the way her heroine constructs lesbian subjectivity as a patchwork of allegories of reading (Balogh, 2002). While Éva's story is retrospectively constructed in a realistic manner by a fascinated male police officer, the embodiment of state power, in

Gordon's text the hiding protagonist's self-fashioning is communicated in a fragmented way through found poetry and punctuation-free floating sentences without clear boundaries, evoking a "playfully dislocated, placeless subject" (Sándor, 1999, pp. 11). Beáta Sándor characterizes this discursive repetitive self-creation as playful, rendering borders and limits much less permanent than they are in Galgóczi's novel and Makk's film. Even being "in and out" are just subtle distinctions. "Small signs gain their meaning gradually and playfully, and through spatialized performances: they make a certain sense in one space and at a certain time and are without "meaning" at another." Even the body of the lesbian is malleable, androgynous, metaphorically mixing with animals such as centaurs and goats. This self-creation corresponds to the poststructuralist notion of the subject as something precarious, formed in a process of repetitive contradiction, "irreducible to the humanist essence of subjectivity" that characterizes the male subject of modernism (Sándor, 1999, p. 12).

Galgóczi's *Another Love*, its film adaptation *Another Way*, and Gordon's *Goat Lipstick* have been crucial texts of lesbian self-constitution in a postcommunist national culture in the work of the Budapest Lesbian Filmmaking Collective, a group of semiprofessional cineastes who represent the vanguard of feminist theorizing and activism in Hungary. Their debt to the film and the two novels is acknowledged in the documentary made by the Committee subsequent to *Goat Lipstick*'s publication, *Pilgrimage to the Land of Goat Lipstick* (2005). The video follows a group of women, including Agáta Gordon herself, as they revisit the places and events of the novel. It goes back and forth between occurrences of the day, including a bus ride from Budapest and a hike up to the cottage that saw the secret beginning of a lesbian community, and those of the night, as the group sits around the fire and Agáta and her former lover, the two main protagonists of the novel, take turns recollecting how lesbians from Budapest gradually and secretly inhabited the area. The storytelling is pleasurable and witty, interrupted by frequent and intimate laughter, conjuring up lesbian identities in a discursive process that refers not only to the actual happenings but also to their mythical and lyrical legitimization in Gordon's book, from which the film's intertitles quote to introduce new sections. Lesbian storytelling functions as a complex game of recognition, in which participants employ the mainstream national community's fear of naming lesbianism and turn it into a pleasurable game of hide and seek: The first couple "lived here in a way that no one knows about them and still doesn't," as Gordon begins the tale.

Pilgrimage's mythical semireligious travel to and repetitive resettling of the "land" discursively identified in the novel *Goat Lipstick,* performs and foregrounds the very process Bhabha describes, whereby the nation's people are continually recreated in a process of "dissemination" rather than originated as such at a specific point in time. The "people" who are being created in the film are united precisely in a critical consciousness of heterosexual norms and assumptions, and in an intentional effort to conjure up a retrospective tradition that begins with *Another Love* and *Another Way* and continues with *Goat Lipstick* and *Pilgrimage*.

CONCLUSION

The allegorical tendency of nationalistic discourse continues to be a strong force within postcolonial nations, which makes many women prioritize their national identities above all other affiliations. Representations of lesbianism, however, are likely to foreground the self-deconstructive aspect of allegorization. Because of its dual character—pedagogical and performative, simultaneously lending itself to essentialist and poststructuralist conceptions of identity and nation—the concept of allegory itself can be seen as a link between postcolonial and feminist theories' concerns with binary discursive mechanisms. In both areas, allegory has been deployed to establish a connection between essentialist and poststructuralist models of identity and representation. The very concept that helps us understand important differences between first and third/second world representations of lesbianism also aids to emphasize the continuity among them.

Ultimately, I would like my comparative analysis of the three postcolonial lesbian films to contribute to the ongoing work of rethinking lesbian representation, queer theory, and theories of visuality and gender as they cross studies of nationalism, postcoloniality, and globalization. As Judith Butler puts it, sexual difference *within* homosexuality has yet to be theorized in its complexity as the vocabulary of describing play, crossing, and the destabilization of masculine and feminine identifications within homosexuality that has only begun to emerge (1993, p. 240). "The inquiry into both homosexuality and gender will need to cede the priority of both terms in the service of a more complex mapping of power that interrogates the formation of each in specified racial regimes and geopolitical spatializations" (Butler, 1993, p. 241).

NOTES

1. British colonialism criminalized and suppressed same-sex desire in a way that had not been the case in the earlier Mughal era. With the ideological aid of colonial theological Puritanism, the British influenced the suppression and erasure of same-sex desires not only through their cultural, economic, and legal systems, but also through the anticolonial nationalistic movements they necessitated (see Syed, 2002).
2. Paola Bacchetta discusses the activities of "Campaign for Lesbian Rights," a coalition among lesbian and feminist groups as well as leftist individuals and organizations throughout India, which came about as a result of the Hindu Right's attacks on *Fire* in December of 1998; see Bacchetta, P. (1999). New campaign for lesbian rights in India. *Off Our Backs*, 2(4), 6. See also Kulla,

B. (2002). Why has "water" evaporated? The controversy over Indian film-maker Deepa Mehta" *Off Our Backs, 32*(3/4) 51–52.
3. David Paul writes, "At first glance the issues of lesbianism and censorship may strike one as unlikely twins, but a brilliant idea links them in this story. For Éva, sexual and political nonconformity are of one piece. Since she cannot accept the Party line on matters of sexual preference. . . she can equally well reject the Party line on journalistic scandals" (p. 192). Kevin Moss similarly accepts the filmmaker's explicit allegorical intentions without examining the discursive violence committed against the lesbian character: "In *Another Way*, then, Makk takes advantage of the similarities between political and sexual dissidence and constructs his film around the intersections of the two. Éva is both politically and sexually dissident, and the film shows how similar the devices used to conceal and reveal such dissidence are" (p. 246).
4. For this information, I am grateful to members of the Lesbian Film Committee, Katrin Kremmler, Magdi Timár and Eszter Muszter, with whom I conversed at the Lesbian Film Festival in Budapest, July 4, 2004.

REFERENCES

Bacchetta, P. (1999). New campaign for lesbian rights in India. *Off Our Backs, 29*(4), 6.
Balogh, A. P. (2002). A leszbikus lét utópiái és realitásai Gordon Agáta *Kecskerúzs* című regényében [Utopias and realities of a lesbian existence in Agáta Gordon's Kecskerúzs]. Unpublished paper.
Bensmaia, R. (1999). Postcolonial nations: Political or poetic allegories? *Research in African Literatures, 30*(3), 151–163.
Bergmann, E. (1998). Lesbian desire in *Yo, la Peor de Todas*. In S. Molloy & R. Irwin (Eds.), *Hispanisms and homosexualities* (pp. 229–247). Durham: Duke University Press.
Bhabha, H. K. (1994). DissemiNation: Time, narrative and the margins of the modern nation. In *The Location of culture*. New York: Routledge.
Brinker-Gabler, G., & Smith, S. (Ed.). (1997). *Writing new identities: Gender, nation, and immigration in contemporary Europe.* Minneapolis: University of Minnesota Press.
Butler, J. (1993). *Bodies that matter: On the discursive limits of "sex."'* London and New York: Routledge.
De Lauretis, T. (1990). Guerrilla in the midst: Women's cinema in the 1980s. *Screen, 31*(1), 12–25.
———. (1991). Film and the visible. In Bad Object-Choices (Ed.) *How do I look? Queer film and video*, (pp. 223–263). Seattle: Bay Press.
Györgyi, A. (2001). Feminizmus gyerekcipöben [Feminism in baby shoes]. *Heti Válasz*. Retrieved May 15, 2005, from http://lektur.transindex.ro/?cikk=526
Jameson, F. (1986). Third world literature in the era of multinational capitalism. *Social Text, 15*, 65–88.
Kalocsai, C. (1998). Leszbikus és meleg elméletek: identitások és identitáspolitikák [Lesbian and gay theories: Identities and identity politics]. *Replika*, 33–34. Retrieved May 16, 2005, from http://www.c3.hu/scripta/replika/3334/18kalo.htm
Kamani, G. (1997). Burning bright: A conversation with Deepa Mehta about *Fire. Trikone Magazine, 12*(4), 11–12.
Kapur, R. (1999). Cultural politics of fire. *Economic and political weekly*. Retrieved June 2, 2006, from http://www.cscsarchive.org

Katrak, K. H. (1992). Indian nationalism, Gandhian "Satyagraha", and representations of female sexuality. In A. Parker, M. Russo, D. Sommer, & P. Yaeger, (Eds.), *Nationalisms and sexualitites* (pp. 395–406). New York: Routledge.

Kulla, B. (2002). Why has "water" evaporated? The controversy over Indian filmmaker Deepa Mehta. *Off Our Backs, 32(3/4)* 51–52.

Mayne, J. (1990). *The woman at the keyhole.* Bloomington: Indiana University Press.

McClintock, A. (1995). *Imperial leather: Race, gender and sexuality in the colonial context.* London: Routledge.

Moss, K. (1995). The underground closet: Political and sexual dissidence in East European culture. In E. E. Berry (Ed.), *Postcommunism and the body politic* (pp. 229–251). New York: New York University Press.

Newman, F. (1991). The passionate landscape of Eva Szalanczky: An introduction to *Another Love.* In *Another Love.* Erzsébet Galgóczi. Pittsburgh: Cleis Press.

Panesar, R. (1999). Ballyhoo in Bollywood: *Fire* ignites controversy in India. *Fabula, 3(1),* 11.

Parker, A., Russo, M., Sommer, D., & Yaeger, P. (Eds). (1992). *Nationalism and sexualitites.* New York: Routledge.

Paul, D. W. (1989). Hungary: The Magyar on the bridge. In D. J. Goulding (Ed.), *Post new wave cinema in the Soviet Union and Eastern Europe* (pp. 172–213). Bloomington: Indiana University Press.

Sándor, B. (1999). *Constantly rewriting herself: Lesbian representations and representations of lesbians in Hungary from the 1980s to the present.* Master's Thesis, Central European University.

Shohat, E. & Stam, R, (1994). *Unthinking eurocentrism: Multiculturalism and the media.* New York: Routledge.

Slemon, S. (1987). Monuments of empire: Allegory/counter-discourse/post-colonial writing. *Kunapipi, 93,* 1–16.

Syed, J.(2002). Queering India. *Trikone Magazine, 13(3),* 1–18.

Szilágyi, Á. (1982). Kettös szorítottság kínjában. Beszélgetés Makk Károllyal [In the agony of a double bind: A conversation with Károly Makk] *Filmvilág, 22(5),* 11–14.

Szin, P. (2001). Romániai meleg-leszbikus öröm [Gay and lesbian joy in Romania]. *Transindex.ro.* Retrieved from http://itthon.transindex.ro/?cikk=538

Takács, J. (1997). (Homo)sexual politics: Theory and practice. *Replika.* Retrieved May 17, 2005, from http://www.replika.c3.hu/english/02/07/takacs.htm

Waugh, T. (2001). Queer Bollywood, or "I'm the player, you're the naïve one?" Patterns of sexual subversion in recent Indian popular cinema. In A. Villajero & M. Tinkcom (Eds.), *Keyframes* (pp. 280–290). London and New York: Routledge.

Williams, B. (2002). A mirror of desire: Looking lesbian in María Luisa Bemberg's *I, the worst of all. Quarterly Review of Film and Video, 19,* 133–143.

Zsugán, I. (1982). Riport a cannes-i filmfesztiválról [Report from the Cannes Film Festival. *Filmvilág, 25(7),* 15–19.

Part III

Men and Masculinities

New Identities, Emerging Subjectivities

10 Patriarchies, Transpatriarchies, and Intersectionalities

Jeff Hearn

GETTING HERE. . .

It is not just a question of personal reflexivity to ask how does one get here. . . that is, how do we get to where we happen to be in terms of the political and analytical questions that seem important to us? This is a matter of biography, history, geography, and perhaps even fashion.

Indeed, it is also of interest to note how words, concepts, theories, and styles of doing academia go in and out of fashion, that is, they are subject to temporal processes of differentiation, promotion, popularization, ideology, critique, and sometimes reinvention in the frame of "new" words and concepts; this can also be so in studies on gender. The word and concept of "patriarchy," and some of the theoretical traditions deployed in its use and development, have been for some time rather out of fashion. I have been sorry about that.

For me, the concept of patriarchy is and has been a useful way of focusing on the societal and broadly structural forms and flows of men's gendered powers, even if the structuralism now has to make way for insights of post-structuralism and some other "posts." So, although I have been engaged in debates on the concept of patriarchy for a long time, I still do not think we have finished with it.

From the late 1970s, I have been trying to make "sense" of patriarchy, for some that time in terms of sexuality, reproduction, generativeness/care, and violence (Hearn, 1983, 1987, 1991); during about the same period several, probably many, others were doing something similar. This was, and is still, a very contradictory project in terms of an awareness of the short-comings of an over-simple structuralism or of monolithic analyses, and yet recognizing the need to move well beyond the lures of the more immediate and individual.

I now jump forward some years. . . . . Increasingly, and especially over the last decade or so, I have been involved with a variety of colleagues in a range of transnational studies. These have included principally studies on men and masculinities in Europe, as part of the EU Framework 5 Critical Research on Men in Europe (CROME) project (Hearn, 2003;

Hearn & Pringle, 2006a, 2006b; Pringle et al. 2006), and the subsequent Sub-network of the EU Framework 6 Coordination Action on Human Rights Violation (CAHRV) endeavor (Hearn, Novikova, et al., 2006); gender divisions and policies of large transnational corporations (Hearn et al., 2002; Hearn & Pringle, 2006a; Hearn et al. 2007; Hearn & Piekkari, 2005); men's gender-conscious national and transnational organizing (Hearn & Holmgren, 2006; Hearn & Niemi, 2006); and sex trade, ICTs and pornographization in the media (Hearn, 2006; Hearn et al., 2007; Hearn & Parkin, 2001).

In different ways, these various inquiries all raise questions regarding transnationalization, whether in terms of transnational organizations, movement and migration, virtual communication, or some other social form (Hearn, 2004c). They highlight the need to theorize and problematize not only men, gender, and sexuality, but also the nation, nationality, and nationalism, race/ "race" and ethnicity, language, intersectionalities, and multiple oppressions (Hearn & Parkin 1993). This is the territory of transnational postcolonial feminism (Desai, 2006; and in my case profeminism) and transversal politics (Cockburn, 1998; Cockburn & Hunter, 1999; Yuval-Davis, 1997). It is a field that problematizes the nation and other "centers" and "given" units of analysis (Hearn, 1992, 1996), one that speaks politics across difference, as well as raising questions for my own and others' shifting personal, political, and spatial positionings (Hearn, 2005). In turn, these transnational studies have taken me back to some very long established debates on the nature of patriarchy or patriarchies.

PATRIARCHY

From the 1960s, theories of patriarchy have emphasized different forms and aspects of men's social relations (especially structural social relations) to women. Scholars, especially feminist ones, have focused on biology (Firestone, 1970); politics and culture (Millett, 1970); the domestic mode of production (Delphy, 1977, 1984); kinship patterns (Weinbaum, 1978); family (Kuhn, 1978); economic systems (Eisenstein, 1979; Hartmann, 1979); "the politics of reproduction" (biological reproduction and the care of dependent children; O'Brien, 1981, 1990); "sex-affective production" (the production of sexuality, bonding, and affection as the core processes of society; Ferguson, 1989; Ferguson & Folbre, 1981); sexuality (MacKinnon, 1982, 1983); love power (Jónasdóttir, 1988); and various combinations thereof.

Many of these feminist theorists analyzed "something(s)" that are routinely taken-for-granted and sometimes even seen as beyond words. To take the last listed example, Anna Jónasdóttir has brought the full powers of critical and feminist interrogation to focus critically on love and love power, the power of "socially organized love (as an interhuman, creative and practical activity)", 1988, p. 220). This is not to belittle "love," and of course there are many different kinds and contexts of it (and also presumably love power). Rather, even the most positive, or indeed contradictory, of emotions and social practices are open to and part of analysis, power, and politics, especially in this case gender analysis, power, and politics. In particular, I have much sympathy with Jónasdóttir's (2007) examination of what is usually called "reproduction" as "production," although in some ways I think it is equally interesting to think of "production" as "reproduction": sexual, biological, generative, violent, and more generally materialist discursive in character (Hearn, 1987, 1992; Hearn & Parkin, 1987).

Much, though not all, feminist work on patriarchy theory has sought a clear and critical engagement with marxism, dialectical and historical materialism, and structuralism, in a manner that attends to some of the "empty spaces" of most of that body of thought. The nonmaterialism of much so-called materialist theory has been highlighted by such feminist scholars. In these various works, I recognize many linkages to questions, which have concerned me for a long time. I think of these political and analytical points of contact as "familiar friends." I see them as part of a broader range of attempts to rethink materialism more thoroughly, more accurately. For my own part, I have been concerned to make materialist theory more materialist, including recognizing the materiality of the body.

Feminist reworkings of patriarchy have sought to approach on patriarchy from a strong critical and materialist perspective, and to foreground the place of sexualities, intimacy, and care in this process. In this way, it may be seen what might follow if sex were to be "taken seriously" in political and social theory. I strongly think there is not enough materialist or materially grounded analysis of patriarchy or, if you prefer, viriarchy (rule of adult men), androcracy, patriarchal society, patriarchally organized society, or the male-dominated gender order (Stacey, 1986).

Throughout, the main interest and "red thread" of these debates, for me, has come and comes from how in various theories of patriarchy, men, and different categories and practices of them, have been analyzed societally, structurally, and collectively, and what that means politically and practically.

CRITIQUING PATRIARCHY, RECOGNIZING PATRIARCHIES

Much of the work on patriarchy discussed in the preceding section has shown that it is necessary to focus rigorously on gender, not just as a variable but as a fundamental analytical and political category. Whatever the discussions on inter- or multi- or transdisciplinarity, different fields vary significantly in how much (or how many of) their leading practitioners seem bothered by this kind of question. For example, I have been struck how the dominant male scholars and articulations by them in economics and political science have appeared to be even more resistant to studying gender in some areas of sociology or social psychology. Patriarchy has an uneven life in and between the disciplines.

However, even by the late 1970s, a number of feminist and profeminist critics (e.g., Atkinson, 1978; Beechey, 1979; Rowbotham, 1979; as opposed to mainstream, malestream, or even antifeminist critics) were suggesting that the concept of "patriarchy" was too monolithic, ahistorical, ethnocentric, biologically overdetermined, and dismissive of women's resistance and agency (see Hearn, 1987, 1992). One set of critiques has been that patriarchy does not have a logic, as capitalism is suggested to have. This argument, defending capitalist logic, now seems to need to be more complex, especially with the apparent mergings and blurrings of the economic and the political (Hardt & Negri, 2000), as in the massive industrial profiteering of the Iraq War ("War profiteering," 2006), in ways that were so often formerly recognized in the supposed determining autonomy of the economic (see Smith, 2004). Nevertheless, it could be argued that there are logics to patriarchy (such as the continuance of men's power and domination, processes of recouping such power and persistence of uneven combinations of forms of power), just as much as there are to the diversity of capitalism(s).

One can, of course, also critique the term patriarchy for not being exactly accurate in "this kind of society," as there is no legal or moral rule and/or control of possessions by fathers or adult men similar to past or, at least locally, in some other places. In this respect, some critical anthropologists point out that the term patriarchy may be confused with partrilineal, patrilocal, and patrifocal societies. Here again, however, taking the term literally, we would have also have to abandon such terms as monarchy, democracy, perhaps even pluralism and autocracy, along with many others. Similarly, capitalism is no longer, or perhaps more accurately no longer understood as, such a unified social formation. Recent theorizations of capitalism and its contemporary globalized and neoimperialist forms often stress the interplay of the economic and the political as well as the blurring of the boundary between the two.

Moreover, if one finds it more acceptable to refer to male-dominated (or probably more accurately, men-dominated) gender order or system or contract (Hirdman, 1988), then so be it! Either or anyway, in the light of these discussions, greater attention has been given to:

- first, the historicizing and periodizing of "patriarchy" (e.g., from private to public patriarchy; Brown, 1981);
- second, other structural gender systems, such as androcracy, fratriarchy, and viriarchy (Remy, 1990; Waters, 1989); and
- third, the presence of multiple arenas, sites, structures, and oppressions of patriarchy.

In the last case, Walby (1986, 1990) has specified the following sets of patriarchal structures: capitalist work, the family, the state, violence, sexuality, and culture, while I specified reproduction of labor power, procreation, regeneration/degeneration, violence, sexuality, and ideology (Hearn, 1987, 1992).

In the latter work (1992), I argued for a concept of *patriarchies*. This pluralizing of patriarchy to patriarchies, like that of sexuality to sexualities and of masculinity to masculinities, opened up for me some new avenues of exploration. It is helpful to think of "patriarchy" in this way, as there are both very different forms of it across time and space, as well as that operate simultaneously according to social arena and with varied scopes, scales, and historical trajectories. These can be of different extents or domains, unevenly developed and overlapping.

Particularly, in these historical developments, the public domain and organizational forms have become increasingly and centrally important, as we move toward a world in which and a time when all is public and the private is abolished (Hearn, 1992). Indeed, organizational (and management) studies are central in theorizing current forms of public patriarchies.

RETHINKING PATRIARCHIES THROUGH INTERSECTIONALITIES

In developing these various ideas and analyses, however, there were two things that revolve around the matter of intersectionalities (see, e.g., Crenshaw, 1991; McCall, 2006), something not so clear at the time of the "heart" of the patriarchy debate as now.

First, the distinctions noted about historical periodizing of patriarchy, other versions of gender systems, multiple arenas and structures, and the pluralizing of patriarchy to patriarchies are also debates on intersectionalities (e.g., family/generation; work/class; sexuality). Indeed, they could be said to be discussions on intersectionalities given different social or spatial form.

Second, the focus in earlier work on patriarchy, by others and myself, has been largely on the national societal of cultural context, rather than whatever lies between and beyond. There have been discussions on global or world patriarchy (see, e.g.,Connell, 1993, 1998, 2005; Mies,1986), but they seem to me to be too monolithic, not sufficiently differentiated, or perhaps intersectionalized. Hence, this perspective introduces a second kind or realm of intersectionalities.

Let me take the first of these points. Historicizations, arenas, and structures, as identified earlier, are also about intersectionalities. The intersection of social divisions has been a very important area of theorizing in critical race studies, black studies, postcolonial studies, and related fields. In terms of my own experience, I have been particularly interested in how various kinds of intersectional approaches complicate the analysis and politics of men and masculinities (e.g., hooks, 1984; Morrell & Swart, 2005; Ouzgane & Coleman, 1998).

The move from private to public patriarchy is one from the intersections of family, age, generation, sexuality, and indeed work, with gender, to intersections of work, class, employment, occupation, and organization with gender. Both also entail intersections of gender with relations to law and the state—in terms of citizenship, nationality, ethnicity/"race"—and arguably also to religion, albeit of very different kinds.

The identification of what where thought of in the 1980s as various structures and arenas of patriarchy can also be rethought in terms of intersectionalities, for example:

- capitalist work (work, class, occupation);
- reproduction of labor power (work, family, sexuality);
- the family (age, generation, sexuality, work, religion);
- procreation (age, generation, sexuality);
- the state (citizenship, ethnicity/race, family, nationality, religion, violence);
- regeneration/degeneration (age, body, generation, disability);
- violence (violence);
- sexuality (sexuality);
- culture/ideology (identity, culture, multiple).

These listings are indicative and, of course, not exhaustive.

In each case, connections can be made between the intersections of gender and one or more social divisions and differences, in the form of multiple oppressions, and thence the analysis and theorizing of patriarchy. For example, in the first listed case, capitalist, and indeed socialist or other noncapitalist, work and its social organization, through relations of class, occupations, rewards, and wealth, can be examined through intersections of gender and class, as in Marxist feminism and feminist marxism. In such approaches, the combinations of class and gender power can in turn be understood to be more or less determinate of other social relations, such as ethnic relations.

Similarly, intersections of family or state or some other social arena with gender relations can be seen as affecting a wide variety of other social divisions and differences, such as citizenship, ethnicity/race, family, nationality, religion, and violence. Moreover, both the state (as well as supra-states, such as the European Union [EU]) and the family operate closely and sometimes in contradiction, with societally dominant gender relations forming complex combinations of contingent intersections at the levels of societal structure, collective social movements, and individual identity.

Indeed, one of the key issues of intersectional analysis, whether of patriarchy or not, is the extent to which two or more social divisions and differences are understood as determinate of other such divisions and differences. In all the forms of patriarchal arena listed earlier, there is the question of to what extent they are determinate of patriarchy or patriarchal relations, not only in the social arena in question, but also more generally at the societal level of analysis. To put this another way, one can ask to what extent such social, patriarchal arenas are separate from each other or are interconnected in the formation of patriarchy as a society-wide form.

TRANSPATRIARCHIES

The second point, that of moving beyond national, societal cultural contexts, has been prompted by various transnational studies over recent years. In these, I have found it useful to refer to patriarchy in transnational contexts as transpatriarchies, as a way of talking about patriarchies, intersectionalities, and transnationalization at the same time (Hearn, 2004a, 2005, 2006).

Limiting patriarchy to a *particular* society, nation, or "culture" is now increasingly problematic, with both greater awareness of global linkages and the assertion of new forms of nationalism in that context. Indeed, global transformation, as well as regional restructurings such as Europeanization via the European Union and its expansion after the break-up of the Soviet bloc, may be part of the changing hegemony of men (Novikova et. al., 2003, 2005). Formulations of patriarchy, like those of hegemony, have been characteristically based on domination within a particular society or nation (Hearn 2004a). Indeed, the nation has often been represented in the modern political era as one of the most powerful forms of hegemony. A significant aspect of this increasing complexity is contemporary global challenges, albeit probably more limited than often supposed, to the nation-state. This is seen in what may appear currently to be opposed transnational forces: On the one hand, the United States (and its allies) represents Christian, military capitalist neoimperialism, while, on the other, exist multinational Islamic power bases, of both the oil-rich postfeudal capitalist and the diasporic jihadist varieties.

Nevertheless, there is now a considerable literature that, from quite diverse positions, questions the theoretical usefulness and empirical accuracy of the very notion of globalization (Banerjee & Linstead, 2001; Hirst & Thompson, 1999; Petras & Veltmeyer, 2001; Rugman, 2000). One aspect of the critique is the need to give much more emphasis to the ways that nation-states, national boundaries, and organized labor at the national level remain important within political economy (Alasuutari, 2000; Edwards & Elger, 1999; Gibson-Graham, 1999; Kite, 2004; Waddington, 1999). Indeed, for this and other reasons, transnationalization seems a more accurate concept than globalization (Hearn, 2004c).

Whatever the balance of power seen between the nation-state and forces that transcend it, transnational processes do introduce a variety of intersectional issues into analysis, including patriarchies or transpatriarchies. At the very least, they raise questions of the intersections of gender relations with *inter alia* citizenship, nationality, ethnicity, racialization, locality and spatiality, identity, and religion. These (transnational) intersectionalities complicate the previous set of intersectionalities identified in the previous section in terms of social arenas or structures with patriarchies.

TRANSPATRIARCHIES AND INTERSECTIONALITIES IN PRACTICE

This kind of conceptualization of transpatriarchies may raise a number of major underexamined questions. This is especially so when one considers men on a global or transnational scale, within and constituting trans(national)patriarchies, or more economically, transpatriarchies. There are urgent studies and actions needed in relation to men and transpatriarchies in international and multinational business corporations; sex trade; information and communication technologies; militarism; international finance; oil and other energy policy; global circulation of representations; and governmental and transgovernmental machineries of various kinds.

At the same time, one might consider whether there a need to abandon "transpatriarchies" in favor of conceptualizations of transnational dominations of all kinds. This may be so conceptually, but gender/patriarchal transnational domination does seem peculiarly persistent.

Let us take two examples, multinational corporations and the sex trade. First, the largest multinational corporations are economically larger than many of the smaller or less developed nations. Of the 100 largest economies, some estimates place half as corporations, half as countries (Anderson & Cavanagh, 2000). In 2006, Nokia had sales of 41.1 billion euros [53.4 billion United States dollars], for the first time eclipsing Finland's national budget ("Nokia profits. . ." 2007). These companies are very heavily dominated by men, especially at the highest levels. Organizational research has developed methods for studying men and masculinities in corporations and other such groups (Cockburn, 1983, 1991; Collinson & Hearn, 1996, 2005; Kanter, 1977; Ogasawara, 1998).

It is not difficult to see how this kind of approach could be applied to transnational operations, including capitalist corporations and military organizations, although it will call for creative international cooperation. Yet men, masculinities, and their social construction and social power are generally left unspoken in discussions of global business (Hearn et al., 2005); they are, in that sense, invisible, an "absent presence" (Hearn, 1998), despite (and perhaps because of) their dominance, especially at the highest levels, within expatriate policy, practice, and discourse. The "transnational capitalist class" (Sklair, 2001) is in practice very much a male one. The critical study of ruling class men is a very fertile and politically important area for future research and politics (Donaldson & Poynting, 2005, 2006).

Moreover, there is also immense scope for far greater attention to these issues in the gendering of international business-to-business activity, alliances, partnerships, supply chains, financial dependencies, and other intercorporate relations, formal or informal, and often involving men at the highest levels. In these situations, there have been initial attempts to analyze "transnational business masculinity" (Connell, 1998) and "business masculinities" (Connell & Wood, 2005). These are the true "men of the world" (Hearn, 1996), who command major individual, corporate, and institutional power and influence, locally, nationally, and transnationally. The concentrations of capital, along with various technological and governmental changes, also suggest great accumulation of power in the hands of this very gendered capitalist ruling class. This can be seen as an example of the extension of certain men's powers beyond the nation, through historically changing forms of their inclusive as well as exclusive.

Another example is the sex trade. To contextualize this, we may note Povinelli and Chauncey's (1999) critique of many globalization texts for often proceeding,

> . . . as if tracking and mapping the facticity of economic, population, and population flows, circuits and linkages were sufficient to account for current cultural forms and subjective interiorities, or as if an accurate map of the space and time of post-Fordist accumulation could provide an accurate map of the subject and her embodiment and desires. (p. 445)

In other words, to express this differently and simply—sexuality, the sex trade, and sexual violence count, in and of themselves.

Just as cities are characteristically organized sexual-spatially, so is the world, as in the association of European and United States imperialism and militarism, mass prostitution, and sex tourism in South East Asia (Enloe, 1983). The international scale of trafficking and prostitution is difficult to appreciate. In the face of globalizing forces, sexuality is subject to considerable historical transformation. For example, even in the mid-1990s in Thailand estimates of women in prostitution ranged from 300,000 to 2.8 million, with a third of them minors. Thai women are also in prostitution in many other countries. The Center for the Protection of Children's Rights estimated there are 200,000 masseuses in Bangkok, half 20 years old or less (Bindel, 1996, p. 29). Global processes are thus sexualized in specific identifiable ways.

If we turn to the media-based, or in some senses virtual, part of the sex trade, then it is perhaps even clearer that we are living in the middle of a major transformation of social relations of sexuality. The types of sexual exploitation and violence documented on the Internet include: prostitution, bride and sex trafficking, sex tours and tourism, pornography, information services and exchange of information on prostitution, and live sex shows through videoconferencing. Donna Hughes has summarized the global situation,

> The Internet has become the latest place for promoting the global trafficking and sexual exploitation of women. This global communication network is being used to promote and engage in the buying and selling of women and children. Agents offer catalogues of mail order brides, with girls as young as 13. Commercial sex tours are advertised. Men exchange information on where to find prostitutes and describe how they can be used. After their trips men write reports on how much they paid for women and children and write pornographic descriptions of what they did to those they bought. Videoconferencing is bringing live sex shows to the Internet. . . . The profits are high and there are few effective barriers. . . . (Hughes, 1997; see also Hughes, 2002)

The scale of change is indeed remarkable. The annual number of hardcore pornographic video rentals in the United States has risen from 79 million in 1985 to 759 million in 2001. In 1997, there were about 22,000 pornographic websites; the number in 2003 was about 300,000 (Campbell, 2003). A spokesman for N2H2, a filtering software company, reported a 350% increase in pornography sites from 2001 to 2002, and it filtered about 300,000 such sites.

Information and communication technologies (ICTS) may solve one of the historical problems of prostitution and the sex trade, which has long often involved extensive travel by women to be within reach of the men (Hearn, 2006; Wellman, 2001, p. 232). Males are the main producers and consumers of sexualized violence and sexual exploitation, on ICTs as elsewhere. ICTs need to be understood as collective and individual actions of particular groups of men, as well as the historically specific development of specific forms of masculinities, such as, local pimping masculinities. Such shifts over time can thus be seen as new and changing forms of transpatriarchies. Thus, in these kinds of development there are rather indeterminate flows of gendered power of men, part physical, part virtual, part bodily material, and part representational. One might indeed argue that these binary divisions of forms of men's powers, impacts, and experiences are being eroded within such transpatriarchal moves and movements. Such changes raise possibilities of new forms of male hegemony (Hearn, 2004), different in kind to the more immediate ones in private patriarchy and even the institutional powers in public patriarchy.

CONCLUDING, OR NOT CONCLUDING, DISCUSSION

In this chapter, I have sought to develop some preliminary thoughts on what is clearly a huge subject. As such, these final comments are not so much conclusions as some indications of how further work from this perspective might be developed.

In many transnational movements, both physical and virtual, particular groups of men are the most powerful actors (Connell, 1998; Hearn, 1996). There are very many ways in which transpatriarchies and transpatriarchal powers and processes develop and change through various forms of transnationalizations. These may include *processes of extensions of transnational patriarchal power*, whether through new technologies or corporate concentrations. Such extensions can easily facilitate *processes of transnational individual and collective nonresponsibility* of men, whereby social problems created are held to be the business of others, be they women, other men, governments, or other parts of the world. This disconnection is, of course, part of a long history of patriarchal imperialism and colonialism.

Interestingly, such changes bring with them *processes of loss of expected security and privilege* for some men. This can be seen at least as partly an historical and geographical set of processes, from the individual to the state to transnational institutions. At the same time, losses, or perceived losses, of power among certain males can interplay with *processes of recouping patriarchal power*. More specifically, there are growing *processes of surveillance*, along with reciprocal, even symbiotic, *processes of their disruption*, for example, through technological hacking or terrorism; *transnational movements and formation of transnational social, political, cultural spaces*; and even *transnational impacts of emotions* (Hearn, 2007a). Together, these make for very complex contradictions, as, for example, in those *of sexual and other forms of citizenship* (Hearn, 2006).

It is clear that the term transpatriarchies is open to various interpretations. Perhaps surprisingly to some it may also invoke the idea of transgender. This at first may seem an odd way of thinking about patriarchies or transpatriarchies, as after all, the notion of patriarchy, as in transpatriarchies, refers to the rule of men, or at least certain men. The prefix trans can also be seen more broadly than only the transnational in reference to both transgender and, indeed, what I call transsectionalities (Hearn, 2007b). Regarding transgenderism, there are some incipient signs that patriarchal domination might be entering a new historical phase, with some women in leading positions adopting patriarchal styles, yet men in power adopting less obvious ones *while still retaining patriarchal power*. This could usher in changing forms of transgender patriarchal power.

As regards transsectionalities, I mean the "transformulation" of social categories, rather than just their mutual constitution and interrelations (as with intersectionalities). It seems increasingly difficult to discuss gender or any other social division in isolation from others. Although this may have always been so historically, it does not seem to have been much noticed until recently. Social change, such as toward virtualities and information societies, may contribute to the increasing elaboration of intersectionalities among social divisions. The very formation of "people" as persons, bodies, and individuals may be in the process of profound historical transformation. Rather than people being formed primarily as fixed embodied *members* of given collectivities, defined by single social divisions, they may increasingly appear to exist and develop in social relations, spaces, and practices among multiple oppressions and power differentials. Persons and bodies no longer appear so easily as equivalents (Hearn, 2004b, p. 207). At the same time, however, these intersectionalities may be treated with caution, as they may also be part of contemporary hegemonic ways of obscuring gender, men, and their powers. Transsectional patriarchal power could be another way of recouping power for certain males.

Finally, this contribution is, in some ways, a plea to return to the political and analytical terrain of dialectical, historical, materialist approaches to patriarchy, but now in the contexts of transnationalizations, intersectionalities, and transsectionalities. In other ways, it is a modest proposal for the use of a new word.

ACKNOWLEDGMENTS

This chapter is a development of earlier background presentations at Free University of Amsterdam, November 2002 (Hearn, 2004c); University of Stockholm, May 2003; Umeå University, September 2003; and more closely related papers at the Finnish National Women's Studies Conference, Helsinki, November 2005; the 6th European Feminist Research Conference, University of Lodz, August 2006; and University of Uppsala, October 2006. I am very grateful to all those who commented at these sessions.

REFERENCES

Alasuutari, P. (2000). Globalization and the nation-state: An appraisal of the discussion. *Acta Sociologica, 43*(3), 259–269.

Anderson, S., & Cavanagh, J. (2000). Top 200: *The rise of global corporate power.* Institute of Policy Studies. Retrieved October 29, 2007, from http://www.debtwatch.org/altres_idms/docs/observatoris/trans/top_200.pdf

Atkinson, P. (1979). The problem with patriarchy. *Achilles Heel, 2,* 18–22.

Banerjee, S. B., & Linstead, S. (2001). Globalization, multiculturalism and other fictions: Colonialism for the new millenium?. *Organization: The Interdisciplinary Journal of Organisation, Theory and Society 8*(4), 683–722.

Beechey, V. (1979). On patriarchy. *Feminist Review, 3,* 66–82.

Bindel, J. (Ed.). (1996). *Women overcoming violence & abuse (Research paper no. 15).* Bradford: Research Unit on Violence, Abuse and Gender Relations, University of Bradford.

Brown, C. (1981). Mothers, fathers, and children: From private to public patriarchy. In L. Sargent (Ed.), *Women and revolution: The unhappy marriage of marxism and feminism* (pp. 239–267). New York: Maple; London: Pluto.

Campbell, D. (2003, May). With pot and porn outstripping corn, America's black economy is flying high. *The Guardian,* p. 3.

Cockburn, C. K. (1983). *Brothers*. London: Pluto.

———. (1991). *In the way of women*. London: Macmillan.

———. (1998). *The space between us: Negotiating gender and national identities in conflict*. London: Zed Press.

Cockburn, C. K., & Hunter, L. (Eds.). (1999). *Soundings 12 transversal politics*. London: Lawrence & Wishart.

Collinson, D. L., & Hearn, J. (Eds.). (1996). *Men as managers, managers as men: Critical perspectives on men, masculinities and managements*. London: Sage.

———. (2005). Men and masculinities in work, organizations and management. In M. Kimmel, J. Hearn, & R. W. Connell (Eds.), *Handbook of studies on men and masculinities* (pp. 289–310). Thousand Oaks, CA: Sage.

Connell, R. W. (1993). The big picture: Masculinities in recent world history. *Theory and Society, 22*(5), 597–623.

———. (1998). Masculinities and globalization. *Men and Masculinities, 1*(1), 3–23.

Connell, R. W., & Wood, J. (2005). Globalization and business masculinities. *Men and Masculinities, 7*(4), 347–364.

Crenshaw, K. (1989). Demarginalizing the intersection of race and sex: A black feminist critique of antidiscrimination doctrine, feminist theory and antiracist politics. *University of Chicago Legal Forum*, 139–167.

———. (1991). Mapping the margins: Intersectionality, identity politics, and violence against women of color. *Stanford Law Review, 43*(6), 1241–1299.

Delphy, C. (1977). *The main enemy*. London: WRRC.

———. (1984). *Close to home*. London: Hutchinson.

Desai, M. (2006). From autonomy to solidarities: Transnational feminist political strategies. In K. Davis, M. S. Evans, & J. Lorber (Eds.), *Handbook on gender and women's studies* (pp. 457–468). Thousand Oaks, CA.: Sage.

Donaldson, M., & Poynting, S. (2005). Snakes and leaders: Hegemonic masculinity in ruling-class boys' boarding schools. *Men and Masculinities, 7*(4), 325–346.

———. (2006). *Ruling class men, money, sex. power*. Bern: Peter Lang.

Edwards, P., & Elger, T. (Eds.). (1999). *The global economy, national states, and the regulation of labour*. London: Mansell.

Eisenstein, Z. (Ed.) (1979). *Capitalist patriarchy and the case for socialist feminism*. New York: Monthly Review Press.

Enloe, C. (1983). *Does khaki become you? The militarisation of women's lives*. London: Pluto Press.

Ferguson, A. (1989). *Blood at the root*. London: Pandora.

Ferguson, A., & Folbre, N. (1981). The unhappy marriage of patriarchy and capitalism. In L. Sargent (Ed.), *Women and revolution: The unhappy marriage of marxism and feminism* (pp. 313–318). New York: Maple; London: Pluto.

Firestone, S. (1970). *The dialectic of sex*. London: Jonathan Cape.

Gibson-Graham, J. K. (1999). *The end of capitalism (as we knew it)*. Cambridge, MA: Blackwell.

Hardt, M., & Negri, A. (2000). *Empire*. Cambridge, MA.: Harvard University Press.

Hartmann, H. (1979). The unhappy marriage of marxism and feminism: Towards a more progressive union. *Capital and Class, 8*, 1–33.

Hearn, J. (1983). *Birth and afterbirth: A materialist account*. London: Achilles Heel.

———. (1987). *The gender of oppression. Men, masculinity and the critique of marxism*. New York, Wheatsheaf, Brighton: St. Martin's Press.

———. (1991). Gender: Biology, nature and capitalism. In T. Carver (Ed.), *The Cambridge companion to Marx* (pp. 222–245). New York: Cambridge University Press.

————. (1992). *Men in the public eye: The construction and deconstruction of public men and public patriarchies.* London and New York: Routledge.

————. (1996). Deconstructing the dominant: Making the one(s) the other(s). *Organization: The Interdisciplinary Journal of Organization, Theory and Society, 3*(4), 611–626.

————. (1998). Theorizing men and men's theorizing: Men's discursive practices in theorizing men. *Theory and Society, 27*(6), 781–816.

————. (2003). Men: Power, challenges of power and the "big picture" of globalization. In I. Novikova & D. Kambourov (Eds.), *Men and masculinities in the global world: Integrating postsocialist perspectives* (pp. 45–74). Helsinki: Kikimora Publishers, Aleksantteri Institute.

————. (2004a). From hegemonic masculinity to the hegemony of men. *Feminist Theory, 5*(1), 49–72.

————. (2004b). Information societies are still societies. In T. Heiskanen & J. Hearn (Eds.), *Information society and the workplace* (pp. 205–208). London: Routledge.

————. (2004c). Tracking "the transnational": Studying transnational organizations and managements, and the management of cohesion. *Culture and Organization, 10*(4), 273–290.

————. (2005). Autobiography, nation, postcolonialism and gender: Reflecting on men in England, Finland and Ireland. *Irish Journal of Sociology, 14*(2), 66–93.

————. (2006). The implications of information and communication technologies for sexualities and sexualized violences: Contradictions of sexual citizenships. *Political Geography, 25*(8), 944–963.

————. (2007a). Feeling out of place? Towards the transnationalizations of emotions. In S. Fineman (Ed.), *The emotional organization: Passion and Power* (pp. 187–201). Oxford: Blackwell.

————. (2007b). Sexualities future, present, past. . . Towards transsectionalities. *Sexualities: Studies in Culture and Society, 10.*

Hearn, J., Hirdman, A., Jyrkinen, M., & Knudsen, S. V. (2007). *Unge, kjønn og pornografi i Norden—mediestudier [Media research on young people, gender and pornography in the Nordic region.* Oslo: Nordic Council of Ministers.

Hearn, J., & Holmgren, L. E. (2006). Männliche Positionierungen zur Gleichstellung der Geschlechter und zum Feminismus: Theoretische Bezüge und praktische Passings'[Locating men's diverse gender-conscious positionings on gender equality and feminism: Theoretical frameworks and practical passings]. *Feministische Studien, 24*(2), 224–241.

Hearn, J., Jyrkinen, M., Piekkari, R., & Oinonen, E. (2007). Women home and away: Transnational managerial work and gender relations. *The Journal of Business Ethics, 70.*

Hearn, J., Metcalfe, B., & Piekkari, R. (2006). Gender in international human resource management. In G. Ståhl & I. Björkman (Eds.), *Handbook of research on international human resource management* (pp. 502–522). Cheltenham, UK: Edward Elgar.

Hearn, J., & Niemi, H. (2006). Is there a "men's movement" in Finland?: The state of men's gender-conscious organising. *NORMA: Nordic Journal of Masculinity Studies, 1*(1), 63–81.

Hearn, J., Novikova, I., Pringle, K., Šmídová, I., Bjerén, G., Jyrkinen, M., et al. (2006). *D32 Methodological Framework Report SN2.* CAHRV Project, Helsinki: Swedish School of Economics.

Hearn, J., & Parkin, W. (1987). *"Sex" at "work": The power and paradox of organisation sexuality.* Brighton: Wheatsheaf; New York: St. Martin's Press.

———. (1993). Organizations, multiple oppressions and postmodernism. In J. Hassard & M. Parker (Eds.), *Postmodernism and organizations* (pp. 148–162). London & Newbury Park, CA.: Sage.

———. (2001). *Gender, sexuality and violence in organizations: The unspoken forces of organization violations.* London: Sage.

Hearn, J., & Piekkari, R. (2005). Gendered leaderships and leaderships on gender policy: National context, corporate structures, and chief human resources managers in transnational corporations. *Leadership, 1*(4), 429–454.

Hearn, J., & Pringle, K. (with members of Critical Research on Men in Europe). (2006a). *European perspectives on men and masculinities.* Houndmills & New York: Palgrave Macmillan.

———. (2006b). Men, masculinities and children: Some European perspectives. *Critical Social Policy, 26*(2), 365–389.

Hirdman, Y. (1988). Genussystemet—reflexioner kring kvinnors sociala underordning. *Kvinnnovetenskaplig Tidskrift, 3,* 49–63.

Hirst, P. Q., & Thompson, G. (1999). *Globalization in question.* Cambridge: Polity.

hooks, b. (1984). *Feminist theory: From margin to center.* Boston: South End Press.

Hughes, D. M. (1997). Trafficking and sexual exploitation on the Internet. *Feminista!, 1*(8). Retrieved from http://www.feminista.com/archives/v1n8/hughes.html

———. (2002). The use of new communication and information technologies for the sexual exploitation of women and children. *Hastings Women's Law Journal, 13*(1), 127–146.

———. (2003). Prostitution online. *Journal of Trauma Practice, 2*(3/4), 115–131.

Jónasdóttir, A. G. (1988). On the concept of interest, women's interests, and the limitations of interest theory. In K. B. Jones & A. G. Jónasdóttir (Eds.), *The political interests of gender* (pp. 33–65). London: Sage.

———. (1991). *Love power and political interests: Towards a theory of patriarchy in contemporary Western societies.* Örebro: Örebro Studies 7.

———. (1994). *Why women are oppressed.* Philadelphia, PA: Temple University Press.

———. (2007). Feminist questions, Marx's method, and the actualization of "love power." In C. di Stephano (Ed.), *Feminist interpretations of Karl Marx.* University Park, PA.: University of Pennsylvania Press.

Jones, K. B., & Jónasdóttir, A. G. (Eds.). (1988). *The political interests of gender.* London: Sage.

Kanter, R.M. (1977). *Men and women of the corporation.* Boston: Basic.

Kite, C. (2004). The stability of the globalized welfare state. In B. Södersten (Ed.), *Globalization and the welfare state* (pp. 213–238). Houndmills: Palgrave Macmillan.

Kuhn, A. (1978). Structures of patriarchy and capital in the family. In A. Kuhn & A. M. Wolpe (Eds.), *Feminism and materialism* (pp. 41–67). London: Routledge & Kegan Paul.

McCall, L. (2005). The complexity of intersectionality. *Signs, 30,* 1771–1800.

MacKinnon, C. A. (1982). Feminism, marxism, method, and the state: An agenda for theory. *Signs, 7*(2), 515–544.

———. (1983). Feminism, marxism, method and the state: Towards feminist jurisprudence. *Signs, 8*(4), 635–658.

Mies, M. (1986). *Patriarchy and accumulation on a world scale: Women in the international division of labour.* London: Zed

Millett, K. (19700. *Sexual politics.* New York: Doubleday.

Morrell, R., & Swart, S. (2005). Men in the Third World: Postcolonial perspectives on masculinity. In M. Kimmel, J. Hearn, & R.W. Connell (Eds.), *Handbook of studies on men and masculinities* (pp. 90–113). Thousand Oaks, CA.: Sage.

Nokia profits in Q4 rise on growing sales. (2007, January 26). Associated Press. Retrieved January 29, 2007, from http://www.telecomasia.net/article.php?type=article&id_article=3345 .

Novikova, I., Pringle, K., Hearn, J., Müller, U., Oleksy, E. H., Chernova, J., et al. (2003). Men, Europe and post-socialism. In I. Novikova & D. Kambourov (Eds.), *Men and masculinities in the global world: Integrating postsocialist perspectives* (pp. 75–102). Helsinki: Kikimora Publishers, Aleksanteri Institute.

———. (2005). Men, masculinities and Europe. In M. Kimmel, J. Hearn, & R.W. Connell (Eds.), *Handbook of studies on men and masculinities* (pp. 141–162). Thousand Oaks, CA: Sage.

O'Brien, M. (1981). *The politics of reproduction*. London: Routledge & Kegan Paul.

———. (1990). *Reproducing the world*. Boulder, CO.: Westview.

Ogasawara, Y. (1998). *Office ladies and salaried men: Power, gender, and work in Japanese companies*. Berkeley: University of California Press.

Ouzgane, L., & Coleman, D. (1998). Postcolonial masculinities: Introduction. *Jouvert: A Journal of Postcolonial Studies*, 2(1). Retrieved January 29, 2007, from http://social.chass.ncsu.edu/jouvert/v2i1/int21.htm

Petras, J., & Veltmeyer, H. (2001). *Globalization unmasked: Imperialism in the 21st century*. London: Zed.

Povinelli, E.A., & Chauncey, G. (1999). Thinking sexuality transnationally: An introduction. *glq: A Journal of Lesbian and Gay Studies*, 5(4), 439–449.

Pringle, K., Hearn, J., Ferguson, H., Kambourov, D., Kolga, V., Lattu, E., et al.,(2006). *Men and masculinities in Europe*. London: Whiting & Birch.

Remy, J. (1990). Patriarchy and fratriarchy as forms of androcracy. In J. Hearn & D. Morgan (Eds.), *Men, masculinities and social theory* (pp. 43–54). London: Unwin Hyman/Routledge.

Rowbotham, S. (1979). The trouble with patriarchy. *New Statesman*, 98, 970–971.

Rugman, A. (2000). *The end of globalization*. London: Random House.

Sklair, L. (2001). *The transnational capitalist class*. Oxford: Blackwell.

Smith, D. E. (2004). Ideology, science and social relations: A reinterpretation of Marx's epistemology. *European Journal of Social Theory*, 7, 445–462.

Stacey, M. (1986). Gender and stratification: One central issue or two. In R. Crompton & M. Mann, *Gender and stratification* (pp. 214–223). Cambridge: Polity.

Waddington, J. (Ed.). (1999). *Globalization and patterns of labour resistance*. London: Mansell.

Walby, S. (1986). *Patriarchy at work*. Cambridge: Polity.

———. (1990). *Theorising patriarchy*. Oxford: Blackwell.

War profiteering. (2006). SourceWatch, Center for Media and Democracy, December 5, 2006. Retrieved January 29, 2007, from http://www.sourcewatch.org/index.php?title=War_profiteering

Waters, M. (1989). Patriarchy and viriarchy: An exploration and reconstruction of concepts of masculine domination. *Sociology*, 23(2), 193–211.

Weinbaum, B. (1978). *The curious courtship of women's liberation and socialism*. Boston: South End Press.

Wellman, B. (2001). Physical space and cyberspace: The rise of personalized networking. *International Journal of Urban and Regional Research*, 25(2), 227–252.

Yuval-Davis, N. (1997). *Gender and nation*. London: Sage.

11 Changing Czech Masculinities?
Beyond "Environment- and Children-Friendly" Men

Iva Šmídová

Policy debates concerning gender equality and work–life balance initiated in the Czech Republic during the European Union accession process have stimulated research attention directed toward reproduction and potentials for change in gender relations. Public campaigns started to promote *desired* models of parental involvement of men, plead equal opportunities for women and men in all spheres of life, and point to the necessity of changing old exploitative patterns of interpersonal relationships. Besides these policy-supported programs, Czech society continues on its path of transformation, keeping some remnants of the totalitarian past, modifying others, and departing from yet another group of attitudes.

TOTALITARIAN[1] PAST: DIS/CONTINUITY OF MASCULINITIES

What are the processes that representations of masculinities are currently facing and undergoing in the region of the Czech Republic? This chapter will not explore potential historical specificities of Czech masculinities[2] in detail; rather it will point to an argument made by Havelková (1997, p. 61) identifying two major mistakes at our level of particular historical experience: first, the status of women and men in the totalitarian era imposed from above—it would be an error to regard it as an independent self-assertive process; and second, the underestimation of "the impact of long-term persisting structures, those from the pre-Communist past, which influenced Communist society and those acquired under socialism that also affect the face of the present societal transformation" (1997, p. 61). Having this particular historical context as background, it remains clear that public images of gender relations in the Czech Republic after 1989 have gained more traits conforming to traditional breadwinner-housewife arrangements. In the mid-1990s, this was accompanied with the "At last we can!" relief call. This was partly a side effect of the fast economic transformation process toward a market economy with welfare policies lagging behind; nevertheless, expectations of this trend preceded its realization as in praxis most women remained employed full-time, both because of the necessity of a dual household income as well as a result of experienced financial independence.

It is nevertheless important to consider certain specific aspects of gender relations in the Czech Republic before moving toward a discussion of representations of alternative masculinities. Images of men from the totalitarian period of Czech (and Slovak) history share traits of a certain forced/involuntary feminization (Frišová, 1993, Havelková, 1997; Šiklová in Funk, 1993); men did not have the possibility of independent self-assertion in "masculine" spheres, such as a professional career or politics. However, their position was similar to men in the West in the sense of having higher salaries (*Sociologický časopis*, 1/95, 4/97) and being present in public sphere representative positions, as some patriarchal structures worked their advantage (*Politika s ženami či bez žen?* 1996; *Žena a muž v médiích*, 1998). They were (and were perceived as) those in power. Yet, it was contradictory in another sense; the only possibility for a professional career was "to bend your back" for the communist party, not a favorable condition for playing the macho type.

Havelková (1997) describes the totalitarian period as an odd blend of traditional patriarchy, one in which both women and men were in the same position, and a weak version of fraternal patriarchy regarding relations between women and men. After 1989, she argues, an interesting development arose; men entered with enthusiasm their lost but traditional public domain, whereas women have feared men's domination neither in private nor in public spheres.

Gender relations in the totalitarian Czech past are sometimes framed by a retreat to the family, where interfacial relationships gained crucial importance (Šiklová, 1996), and men's presence in the home was higher than before and than in Western countries (Wagnerová, 1995). However, at the same time, the regime as such has disempowered men substantially. Wagnerová argues,

> Their price fell. . . . The consequences of such development were also in the loss of importance of traditional masculine role models as obligatory criteria of human action and behaviour in general. . . . Majority of men were not able to financially support their families as sole breadwinners, their self-confidence fell and together with that their willingness and ability to care about their families and feel responsible for it. (1995, pp. 80–82)

In compliance with this statement, Havelková (1997) points to a reduced level of responsibility or even irresponsibility of men in totalitarian countries and uses this as a reason for the fact that women in these nations have considered their own empowerment after 1989 as less urgent than the restoration of responsibilities for men. This lack of polarization was elaborated by Šiklová (1996), who proposed an explanation related to a "common enemy" represented by the totalitarian regime (encountered more times in the Czech history). This has supported solidarity among men and women. The situation was characterized by the figure of 97% of women fit for work were employed, and Šiklová describes it as an atmosphere in which men did not exhibit their dominance but rather acted like colleagues who bore the same kind of oppression (Šiklová, 1996, p. 17). Also, Wagnerová (1995, p. 82) concludes by pointing to the state of affairs in the society and its regime as quite decidedly provoking unity among women and men.

Regardless of an optimistic, rather naive, bias present in some of these analyses, the mood of restoration of colonized masculinity was present in the 1990s. It was accompanied by an ignorance of practices indicating continual masculine structural dominance. Public initiatives pointing to hierarchical, unequal gender relations were often misunderstood and sometimes even rejected and ridiculed.

In the period before 1989, the paradox of men's presence at home and loss of responsibility deserves a closer look. Recent totalitarian Czech history created the perception of a family as the only fortress of relative freedom, autonomy, and security. People spent considerable amounts of time "working" for the family, and just "having been" employed. Thus, the traditional public domain and breadwinning responsibility for men was distorted. After 1989, new opportunities emerged for self-realization, the scope of which has broadened substantially but also acquired limiting contours. The tendency toward support of a conventional gendered division of labor remained manifest: a man—breadwinner, a woman—caregiver and housewife.

Empirical data indicate, however, that in spite of sticking to the dual concept of gender roles, there is a disparity between ideal (attitudes and preferences) and real (action) division of men's and women's activities within the family structure (IVVM, 1998). The former tend to be more conservative in regard to changing the status quo (Maříková, 1999, p. 64). This corresponds with models of conventional masculinities elsewhere in Western societies.

The totalitarian past and its rapid breakdown have affected gender relations in the sense of dual promotion of individualism. Individualization is perceived as a spontaneous reversal of the imposed collectivism before 1989 as well as a consequence of developments after that year while catching up with Western democracies. In respect to masculinities, this has brought clashes between individual men's actions, the rhetoric of a self-made career, and a particularly individualistic approach (achievement oriented), which conceals structural conditioning regarding gender issues. These are mostly unreflected, and gender as a structural element connected to normative cultural representations of femininities and masculinities clashes with the public discourse, with a strong presence of essentializing legitimizations for the gender divide. It is important to note that the natural differences between men's and women's views are also sustained and supported by Czech women. Moreover I point again later to the inconsistency of the recent totalitarian experience of relative equality between men and women in their practices in certain respects, and the hierarchical, polarized, naturalized dual perception of femininity and masculinity present in public images of gender relations.

OFF THE BEATEN TRACK

My argument is based on two small-scale empirical studies, which offer insight into the process of reproduction and changes of masculine identities in the Czech context. The first, referred to here,[3] explored themes in and dimensions of Czech masculinities, identifying its symbolic domains. Based on life histories of several men located seemingly outside the mainstream of career-oriented, competitive masculinity, it looked for definitions of "different men." These were chosen in compliance with two confluent criteria: men employed in environment protection and/or education and those identified by informants as active fathers. The first factor referred to a concern about the weaker in contrast to the egoistic, individualist orientation often associated with masculinity; the latter was bound to the concept of family-involved fatherhood in opposition to absent or distant forms of parental involvement. Both of these criteria also were intended to indicate equalizing gender relations in practices of these men. The second research project studies families with fathers as nurturers.[4] In their everyday practices, these couples break the stereotypical public image, powerfully supported by popular psychology, of men's incapacity and women's natural ability to nurture a baby. Not only the men, but also their spouses break the same rules from the other side—they try to redefine the image of an "unnatural mother." The ideal of woman's 24-hour availability to her offspring is again the demand of mainstream representations of early motherhood in the Czech Republic. The strategy of mothers in our small sample indicated attempts to challenge the contents of the so-called "raven mother" negative label, in the Czech language, by pointing to the prosperous existence of ravens and/or to their own individual satisfaction with such family arrangements. These couples oppose connotations associated with the label of "unnatural mother" as well as redefine fatherhood.

ENVIRONMENT-FRIENDLY MEN

The study exploring Czech masculinities, based on interviews with men involved in environmental protection and active fatherhood, aimed to document gender sensitive forms of masculine identity. However, the analysis pointed strongly to the fact that even though these men defend the environment and want to change the world in this respect, they do not reflect its gendered structure. Their struggle to overcome dominance of people over nature lacks the dimension that would acknowledge the existence of domination of masculinity over femininity. Even in their role as teachers and fathers, they have hardly challenged the gendered division of labor. They presented the pattern of masculinity that is active and present for children as they are shown the world (Parsons, 1951), reproducing and sustaining the status quo of polarized conservative expectations concerning women's and men's role in society.

Gender relations were presented as contextual and thus varying substantially through the life experiences and biographies of the interviewed men. Nevertheless, even though these individuals presented openness regarding value orientations and humanitarian development of the world (feminism, too, was acknowledged by some of them as relevant and important), their presented life histories document rather unmodified gender relations. The Czech green movement does not share roots with strong social movements of the 1960s in the West and thus lacks incorporation of feminist and women's arguments, which was the case documented here (Connell, 1995, 1999).

This research study pointed to the patriarchal model of masculine identity in the Czech Republic by documenting the stress on polar division of gender roles, especially in the private sphere. Despite modifications during the course of life, the role of women remained limited to her "unique natural maternal role," and this was presented regardless of participants' own strong involvement in family life as well as the successful professional careers of their wives. So, even though these men's life histories detour in a promising way from the mainstream stereotypical track, Badinter's (1992) concept of androgynous contended masculinity does not necessarily have to be met. A man who *protects* nature (or even protects women and children) does not necessarily share (feminine) *care* (when nurturing children, housekeeping, or avoiding patriarchal relationships, etc.). These men remain hegemonic, profiting from the patriarchal dividend (Connell, 1995), despite actions by which they also produce settings where men give up their domination. The existing structures of gendered expectations on individual actors in particularly gendered settings work regardless of deconstruction of power relations in other domains.

Despite the pessimism presented here, these men were in many respects brave by breaking other fences guarding "tolerable" masculinity. Their narrative strategies were also caught in the symbolic trap of gendered language and lack of availability of alternative terminology in order to overcome the evergreen, essentializing socio-biological discourse.

FAMILY-FRIENDLY MEN

Nurturing fathers, subjects of the second study, consistently break, in many respects, the gender divide regarding division of labor (Harding, 1987; Pateman, 1988). Nevertheless, the practices of these couples that modify the commonsense understanding of women's and men's "duties" sometimes clash with their symbolic representations, and hence the arrangement of chores in these households was not a role reversal. Rather, practices of parents described in this study could present a challenge and list of improvements for the "unreversed" mainstream practice of women staying on parental leave, as an outcome of consideration and helpfulness for men in an "unnatural" role. Thus, both possible changes and the absence of changes in the gender relations of these couples offer an insight into processes sustaining and challenging the gendered structure of society. The analysis presented three main challenges by uncovering: (1) a coexistence of both a rigid and fluid or blending understanding of gender social identities, (2) a discrepancy between rhetoric and practice, and (3) clashing conceptualizations of the "new" identity for (nurturing) fatherhood and ("raven") motherhood.

The nurturing forms of fatherhood encountered both went beyond and reproduce the status quo of gender relations. The dilemma of whether there already exist new patterns of actions that these people adopt or whether their actions are the process of change itself is then set among these contours. Images of "active" and "good" have had a very strong voice in the recent years in the context of "equal opportunities" or "gender mainstreaming." However, these "desired" role models can be adopted in a quite rigid way concerning gender relations: The status is temporary; care for children can be sharply distinguished from all other sorts of housework duties. These couples, however, enter *terra incognita* and their descriptions of everyday actions also indicate the process of "gender blending" or "doing gender" (Connell, 2002; Šmausová, 2002; West & Zimmermann, 1991), for example, the type of (routine) practice that challenges attitudes and representations.

SYMBOLIC ORDER AND CHANGING MASCULINITIES

The phenomenon of gender relations is extremely complex, and thus, the findings were meant to contribute to the very amplified of interpretations of meanings associated with contemporary changes of gendered practices in our societies in the context of much broader processes of individualization, globalization, and so on (Bauman, 2002, 2004; Beck, 1992; Giddens, 1998). I argue in correspondence with Acker (1992) that it is the institutions that are already gendered, and so in order to conform to the rules of anyone of them, we (men and women) accept their gendered patterns.

Moreover, as an individual man or woman, we situate ourselves and are being situated in the structures of masculine domination, meaning domination of the hegemonic form of masculinity. Our everyday practice, our habitus (Bourdieu, 1994), is confronted with the symbolic representations of adequate and expected gender attitudes. I adopt here the approaches to the gendered structure of society offered by Harding (1983), documenting its three realms (e.g., individual life trajectories, division of labor, and the symbolic level); I also refer to the basic split between the public and private spheres (Bourdieu, 2002; Elshtain, 1999).

Based on relevant outcomes, this section outlines (1) the symbolic power of language concerning gender relations encountered in both studies, and (2) the reproduction of structures of masculine domination and their challenges present in narratives of the research participants. These two points are meant to offer examples of masculine domination reproduction as well as a potential niche for substantial change toward more equal gender relations.

LANGUAGE AND MEANS TO GRASP ALTERNATIVE EXPERIENCES

Language expressions describing gender relations followed the dual split of responsibilities for women and men in both the research projects to which the text refers. The dominant public explanatory discourse on gender relations in the Czech Republic is essentializing popular psychology driven by a strong influence of developmental psychology. Since the late 1960s, the Czech sexological school has dominated the field of competent experts who publish such handbooks. Due to the iron curtain, the flow of relevant academic publications on the topic was very limited, and thus any development concerning the application of recent theories was distorted and stalled before 1989. This was especially problematic in the sense that no alternative explanation (e.g., not based on chromosomes or later genes but on historical, social, and cultural conditions) was accessible to the public. It was thus also absent from the educational process at schools. As a mirror of this context, it is not surprising that explanations, legitimizations, and strategies of participants in the studies produced have followed the essentializing line, as the only language codes available (Bourdieu, 1998).

"Naturalizing" explanations were sometimes used in participants' narratives like the side note, "but we all know, right," reconfirming the normality of their lives courses and described experiences. However, they also frequently have kept encountering problems with the terminology to be used and the experience they were trying to grasp with it.

It was clear that language kept betraying these men in their narratives. In the research exploring environment-friendly masculinities, incomprehensive terms concerning gender relations were targeted. Expressions such as feminism and gender inequality connected to negative stereotypes were often "unloaded" in their acceptance as relevant for public debates concerning "the building of civil society"; this has presented a challenge in the context of corresponding discussions of the late 1990s. Silence or briefness around certain issues, especially narrative disproportion about profession and civic activities in comparison to involvement in the home (housework and baby care), indicates localization of the participants into a particularly gendered world. Nevertheless, a considerable amount of interview time was spent on their recent health and aging problems as well as on their perception of a reflected "mid-life crisis."

The analyses of interview transcripts indicated three strategies the participants had employed when reporting on gender relations, roles, and identities. The first was to distance themselves from the essentializing terms—but still use them for the sake of comprehensibility and lack of (awareness of) a better term. Examples include describing their relationships as teachers to kids as "pedophilia," referring to themselves as "deviants" having "infantile" fancies, and presenting their "individual deviations." Another strategy was an attempt to modify the content and thus change the connotation of existing terminology. Such was the case of their own "character" or redefinition of the "raven" mother. The third method was avoidance of the essentializing terms in cases when the participant had encountered social constructivist explanations (e.g., a previous awareness and knowledge of alternative approaches). Also, in the presentation of their own experiences on a detailed descriptive level of everyday routine practices (how I learned to love my child; it was a time-consuming process; how I got accustomed to my status of a housekeeper, etc.), the "naturalness" of gender relations was challenged.

In the case of the study on environment-friendly masculinities, answers concerning gender relations were sometimes diverted to general questions of "humanity," thus concealing its gendered aspects. They also declared that the everyday praxis of relations between women and men should be opened to public discussion, as "recent social developments clearly indicate unsustainability" regarding gender relations. In the everyday practices of these men, though, polarized duality and the essentialist approach to gender were not reflected. Thus, it seems more likely that the environment-friendly men would work on changing the world and still keep the principle of dual "nature-based" gender roles on the level of everyday life. Here again, however, controversies were not reflected: "natural maternal instinct" (caring essential for women) presented in one interview passage was contrasted in another section with a description of the daily personal care of a dying father, and not commented on as un/natural for the man himself.

Narrations of the family-friendly men also offer situations describing a necessity to grasp their practices via the existing codes in order to be understood. Also there was a clear clash between the presentation of conformity to dual family roles and the practice described in undertaking daily chores. So, the declared expressive role of mothers and instrumental role of fathers

(Parsons, 1951, 1955) just simply did not correspond with their actions. This fact was not reflected or considered problematic in their narratives. This could be interpreted with the help of the concept offered, for example, by Pierre Bourdieu (1998), who describes the existence of dominant language structures within the social structures of masculine domination, in which all the actors (both dominating and dominated) have to use the same language codes, that is, of those in power, because there are no alternatives for grasping individuals' experience.

Even here, however, fathers kept certain privileges. Their power in the situation could be demonstrated by a different evaluation of their family "roles." Their fatherhood was described as a success story; they are heroes who have proven ability to overcome so-called "biological unsuitability." There was much more silence surrounding their spouses' motherhood. Even though these mothers should have shared the success, they did not publicly reveal their family arrangements. These women opened their traditional domain for their partners' entry, and they sometimes felt left out of the public (media and research) attention. At the same time, they expressed worry about being labeled "bad mothers." Nevertheless, they also offered redefinitions of their motherhood, modifying not only the existing stereotype of the "unnatural raven" mother but also the "Super Mom" and "Super Woman" images. Their parental arrangements incorporate the condition of private aspects of gender equality and public silence.

The language betrays nurturing masculinities' accounts via a lack of terminology associated with care and nurturing that would not be already feminized. The paradox lies in keeping the old language codes and usage disregarding their particular actions. Women in these families kept silent about their nonconformist role in public, whereas fathers presented themselves and were presented by their spouses as heroes. This conforms to the gender stereotype of visibility and invisibility in public.

The theme of public silence about private (re)arrangements concerning gender relations deserve more research attention. It can also reopen the question of whether these men, nurturing fathers in these families, have "the best of the two worlds" (Hochschild & Machung, 1990), fun with the kids and respect in the public sphere. Experiences described by their spouses, and some unreflected points from the fathers' own narratives indicate that this could be a legitimate statement. The plurality of family forms in "families where fathers nurture," however, presents a challenge to this pessimistic conclusion. Even though man's status as a caregiver in the private sphere does not automatically change the gender relations situation described as masculine domination, in many respects and in many actions these families do alter the status quo. At the least, they open new arenas concerning relevant issues connected to the parental position in society. Perhaps, in concurrence with the existing structures, men in nurturing status positions attract public attention, and thus may promote change also affecting mothers on parental leave, which is still by far the dominant group of caregivers.

Among the stimuli were: getting time of my own (several hours per week, sometimes a day without kids), spouse involved and sharing the housework as well as care, keeping in touch with paid work, and redefining the scope of what really needs to be done (cooking, cleaning, etc.).

Another aspect of silence or talk is (also) related to the public and private spheres. Even though environment- and family-friendly men performed certain chores at home, which do not comply with the stereotypical masculine role, they do so at their own will. They have the power to choose (see also Hearn et al., 2006). Nevertheless, involvement in daily chores of private life transgresses these boundaries. Some Czech sociologists have pointed to the fact that family arrangements with aspects of equal sharing of housework have existed in numerous households (Maříková, 2000; Možný, 1990). Nevertheless, families do not publicize these private issues—they are not the subjects of public talk. The aspect of private action and family discussion in contrast to public silence concerning equal division of labor in the home is sustained and reconfirmed also by "pub talk," discussions reassuring masculinity in the homosocial environment of men (also in sport clubs or at work). Here, public discourse around appropriate gender roles poses a manifest barrier to changes.

A similar situation surrounds the spouses of these men. In the case of families with men on parental leave the women also surpass expected spheres of action, and they often keep silent about their family arrangements in public. Even though we can expect that also for them, the private division of labor was a result of choice, the consequences of making it public would make them less heroic than the changing discourse regarding men involved in the daily care of children. Expectations concerning women's role are guarded very strictly, as are the men's, especially in "pub talk." The difference is in the aspect of the already predefined and stable status of women both in the private and public spheres, and the process of change concerning men's role in the private one, which is now strongly supported by public policies.

RELATION OF ENVIRONMENTAL PROTECTION AND CHILD CARE TO GENDER EQUALITY

The passage devoted to narration formulations was particularly meant to illustrate a broader process of reproduction and sustaining the gender order status quo. With reference to Bourdieu's (1998) concept of reversal of consequences and causes, these strategies illustrate the mechanism of "naturalization," that is, we consider certain things as natural, even though they are an outcome of historical processes of naturalization. Thus, for legitimizations of our actions, we use the internalized means available during the socialization process, and these are the essentializing factors, coming from the biological determinism of the dominant explanatory frame. This adopted form of dominance is perceived as natural, which then legitimizes its survival. According to Bourdieu (1998), people can only use explanatory tools offered by the dominant scheme, and this represents a form of symbolic violence. Examples from the empirical studies elaborated here illustrate the process of coping with the existing symbolic order, either on the level of talk or described practice, in incidents where its limitations were encountered and reflected.

Environment-friendly men declared openness to debates concerning gender equality, which still praises women for their reproductive capacities. They proclaim that "a woman does not belong to the kitchen stove," but they still protect her image as a mother. Partly in correspondence and partly in contrast to their proclamations, they leave the housework to their spouses, being often absent from home mending the world. They do reflect upon their absence from home once their children grow up, assessing it with self criticism. Family-friendly men in the nurturing status have entered the domain of "woman's work." Their actions are, in contrast to environment-friendly men, more in the realm of gender equal relations. Still, nurturing fathers stick to proclamations reconfirming the dual world of division of labor. Perhaps, this was presented as proof of their awareness of "normality" in spite of their everyday actions. The absence of a necessary causal link between child care and gender equality in the parental relationship also has been documented by other studies (Hearn et al., 2006).

Daily practices of environment-friendly and family-friendly men break the stereotype associated with conventional masculine gender roles. It is clear on the level of individual gender roles that their collage of identities (Šmausová, 2004) varies from context to context and floats in their life-paths representing the process of blending gender (West & Zimmermann, 1991). The borders of dual perception of the gender division of labor were also challenged—more so in the public sphere by the environment-friendly men and in the private sphere by the family-friendly men. Nevertheless, the symbolic order—"the gendered universum" (Harding, 1983)—restrains actors in certain aspects from a more radical change of meanings and hierarchical order associated with the so-called "normal" biographies, as they function at the same time as havens of security and well-tried tradition.

Contrariwise, nurturing as a stereotypical domain of mothers/women can also work in support of the status quo. The know-how associated with motherhood and legitimately attributed to women was guarded and protected in some interview passages. Perhaps as a sign of insecurity in other respects, we have noticed several incidents demonstrating exclusive competence of a mother to decide, judge, or reveal particular situations concerning care and situation-management. Breastfeeding was also used in a similar context. The power of symbols legitimizing the status quo and attempts to act self-confidently in new arenas was clearly revealed as a difficult task. Heroism and silence, gender blending, and sticking to a rigid but "traditional" well-tested dual division of gender are parts of the picture.

Environment-friendly men and fathers on parental leave can present a challenge to exploitative, misogynist forms of masculinities, but they can also reproduce and even take on forms that strongly support conventional, mainstream essentialist approaches to gender (protective forms of masculinity or curtailed equality in families where child care is shared but housework is not, etc.) supporting hierarchical gender relations. The mechanisms that work for change or sustaining the status quo are sometimes conflated. Easily made positive connections between "gender equality," "environment-friendly" and "family-friendly" attitudes, policies, and public discourse debates may thus be both inspiring and misleading.

NOTES

1. I am aware of the complex academic discussion concerning appropriate terminology used for references to the countries and their period in the recent history of the former Soviet Bloc (journals: *Europe-Asia Studies, Journal of Communist Studies,* and *Transition Politics*). Here, for simplicity and for personal inclination, I tend to use the most general term—totalitarian (Arendt, 1951), rather than postsocialist or post-Soviet. Based on the fact that the historical, cultural, and social context of that time is not the core of my analysis, and thus not a major terminological concern of mine, I decided to use the most neutral term, while also respecting the local discomfort caused by causal linkages of Czech and former USSR history.
2. See an earlier article dealing with this issue: Šmídová (1999).
3. My dissertation research (Šmídová, 2004), the empirical part of which was conducted in 1999–2000. In-depth interviews were conducted with seven men, and transcripts interpreted using primarily Silverman's (1997) methodological approach to qualitative data analyses. The main outcomes of the analysis were published in English as a chapter in *Men in the global world* (Novikova, I., & Kambourov, D. [Eds.] 2003) as Šmídová, 2003).
4. The project (2003–2004) consisted of interviews with five heterosexual couples followed by a focus group discussion among the mothers and fathers of these families 6 months after the first research contact. A team of sociologists and psychologists have conducted the transcript analyses.

REFERENCES

Acker, J. (1992). Gendered institutions. From sex roles to gendered institutions. *Contemporary Sociology, 21*(5), 565–569.
Arendt, H. (1996). *Původ totalitarismu.* Praha: Oikoymenh.
Badinter, E. (1992). *XY—de l'identite masculine.* Paris: Editions Odile Jacobs.
Bauman, Z. (2002). *Tekutá modernita.* Praha: Mladá fronta.
Beck, U. (1992). *Risk society: Towards a new modernity.* London: Routledge.
Bourdieu, P. (1998a). *La domination masculine.* Paris : Editions du Seuil.
———. (1998b). *Teorie jednání.* Praha: Karolinum.
Connell, R. W. (1995). *Masculinities.* Los Angeles: University of California Press.
———. (1999). A whole new world: Remaking masculinity in the context of the environmental movement. *Gender and Society, 4*(4), 452–478.
———. (2002). *Gender.* Cambridge: Polity Press.

Connell, R. W., Hearn, J., & Kimmel, M. (2005). *Handbook of studies on men and masculinities*. London: Sage.

Elshtain, J. B. (1999). Veřejný muž, soukromá žena. *Ženy ve společenském a politickém myšlení*. ISE Praha.

Frišová, M. (1993). Slúžtičky. *ASPEKT*, 1/1993, 4–6.

Funk, N., & Mueller, M. (Eds.). (1993). *Gender politics and post-communism. Reflections from Eastern Europe and the former Soviet Union*. London: Routledge.

Giddens, A. (1998). *Důsledky modernity*. Praha: Slon.

Harding, S. (1983). Why has the sex/gender system become visible only now? In S. Harding & M. B. Hintikka (Eds.). *Discovering reality: Feminist perspectives on epistemology, methaphysics, methodology, and philosophy of science* (pp. 311–324). Dordrecht: Riedel.

———. (Ed.). (1987). *Feminism and methodology: Social science issues*. Bloomington: Indiana University Press.

Havelková, H. (1997). Transitory and persistent differences: Feminism East and West. In J. W. Scott, C. Kaplan, & D. Keates (Eds.), *Transitions, environments, translations. Feminisms in international perspective* (pp. 56–62). London: Routledge.

Hearn, J., Oleksy, E. H., Kazik, J., Pringle, K., Müller, U., Lattu, E., Tallberg, T., Ferguson, H., Kolga, V., & Novikova, I. (2006). *European perspectives on men and masculinities*. Houndmills: Palgrave.

Hobson, B. (Ed.). (2002). *Making men into fathers: Men, masculinities and the social politics of fatherhood*. Cambridge: Cambridge University Press.

Hochschild, A., & Machung, A. (1990). *The second shift—Working parents and the revolution at home*. London: Pitkus.

Hølter, Ø. G. (2003). *Can men do it? Men and gender equality—The Nordic experience*. Copenhagen: Temanord, Nordic Council of Ministers.

IVVM. (1998). *Rozdělení činností v české rodině. Informace o výzkumu 98–07* [Division of housework in the Czech familyot]. Praha: Author.

Kimmel, M. (1987). *Changing men: New directions in research on men and masculinity*. Thousand Oaks, CA: Sage Focus Edition.

Maříková, H. (1999). Proměna rolí muže a ženy v rodině. In *Společnost žen a mužů z aspektu gender* (pp. 59–67). Praha: OSF.

———. (Ed.). (2000). *Proměny současné české rodiny (Rodina—gender—stratifikace)*. Praha: SLON.

May, L., Strikwerda, R., & Hopkins, P. D., (Eds.). (1996). *Rethinking masculinity: Philosophical explorations in light of feminism*. New York and London: Rowman & Littlefield.

Možný, I. (1990). *Moderní rodina, Mýty a skutečnosti*. Brno: Blok.

Novikova, I., & Kambourov, D. (Eds.). (2003). *Men in the global world: Integrating post-socialist perspectives*. Helsinki: Kikimora Publishers.

Parsons, T. (1951). *The social system*. London: The Free Press of Glencoe.

———. (1955). The American family: Its relations to personality and to the social structure. In T. Parsons & R. F. Bales (Eds.), *Family, socialization and interaction process* (pp. 3–33). Glencoe, IL: The Free Press.

Pateman, C. (1988). *Thesexual contract*. Cambridge: Polity Press.

Politika s ženami či bez žen? (1996). Praha: Nadace Gender Studies.

Pringle, K., et al. (2006). *Men and masculinities in Europe*. London: Whiting & Birch.

Scott, J. W., Kaplan, C., & Keates, D. (Eds.).(1997). *Transitions, environments, translations. Feminisms in international perspective*. New York and London: Routledge.

Segal, L. (1990). *Slow motion: Changing masculinities, changing men*. London: Virago.

Silverman, D. (2001). *Interpreting qualitative data: Methods for analysing talk, text and interaction.* London: Sage.

Šiklová, J. (1996). Jiný kraj, jiné ženy. Proč se v Čechách nedaří feminismu [Other place, different women. Why feminism is not popular in the Czech region?]. *RESPEKT, 13/1996.* 17.

Šmausová, G. (2002). Proti tvrdošíjné představě o ontické povaze gender a pohlaví [Against the stubborn concept of ontic gender and sex]. Sociální tudia, 7, FSS MU Brno: 15–27.

———. (2004). Normativní heterosexualita bez nátlaku k prokreaci? [Normative heterosexuality without pressure of procreation?]. *Gender, rovné příležitosti, výzkum.* Roč, 5, 2–3/2004,1–4.

Šmídová, I. (1999). Men in the Czech Republic (a few questions and thoughts on studying (some men). *Czech Sociological Review,* Praha, 7(2), 215–222.

———. (2003). Men in the Czech Republic (according to different men). In I. Novikova & D. Kambourov (Eds.), *Men in the global world: Integrating post-socialist perspectives* (pp. 159–175). Helsinki: Kikimora Publishers.

———. (2004). *Jiní muži* [Different men]. Dissertation. FSS MU Brno.

———. (2006). Nurturing fathers: Parenthood and gender relations. *Conference proceedings from the 20th Annual EFPSA (European Federation of Psychology Student Associations) Conference,* Špindlerův Mlýn.

Sociologický časopis. (1995). Praha: SoÚ AV, no. 1.

Sociologický časopis. (1997). Praha: SoÚ AV, no. 4.

Wagnerová, A. (1995). Emancipace a vlastnictví. *Sociologický časopis,* 31(1), 77–84.

West, C., & Zimmerman, D. H. (1991). Doing gender. In J. Lorber & S. A. Farrell (Eds.), *The social construction of gender* (pp. 125–147). London: Routledge.

Žena a muž v médiích [Woman and man in the media]. (1998). Praha: Gender Studies Foundation.

12 Experiencing Masculinity
Between Crisis, Withdrawal, and Change

Iwona Chmura-Rutkowska
and Joanna Ostrouch

INTRODUCTION

The most significant phenomenon defining the shape of modern times is the ongoing process of the individualization of human existence. Ulrich Beck defines this process as the disintegration of previous social forms and a decline of "normal" biographies, reference points, and roles, including those once connected with gender as well as those sanctioned by the state (2004). At the same time, traditional indicators and constraints necessary to construct individual biography are diminishing. According to Mirosława Marody and Anna Giza-Poleszczuk (2004), an individual person can or rather has to choose among numerous types of behavior confronting him/her at every single moment of life. Women are more inclined to (re)construct their roles by adopting features and behaviors previously designed only for men. In the case of males, however, the process of redefining their roles is much slower.

Recently, more and more attention has been drawn to the fact that men are poorly adapted to social changes taking place over the past few years in Poland. The reasons for this "crisis of masculinity" are numerous. In Dorota Pankowska's opinion (2005), the most important one is that in democratic countries the legal status of men and women has been equalized. Also, the intellectual superiority of men is questioned owing to the development of psychological research (see Bem, 2000). Other factors include: common access to education for women; the adoption of the most important benchmarks of men's roles by women (professional and social life) as well as certain stereotypes (independence, goal-oriented attitude); the diminishing importance of physical strength in favor of technology; and, finally, the lack of nontraditional role models presented to sons by fathers (Biddulph, 2004; Bly, 1993; Pankowska, 2005, p. 160). In addition, demands imposed on men by modern women are at times very unclear. Males are expected to be tender and gentle but at the same time bravely face difficulties. Women also want men to get involved in everyday chores and child rearing yet simultaneously earn a lot of money to support the family. As a result, masculinity has become relative, and there are many simultaneous and often contradictory types of masculinity, which create a "crisis" (Melosik, 2002).

PSYCHOLOGICAL AND SOCIO-CULTURAL CONTEXT OF RESEARCH

Research has focused on men between 35 and 40 years of age (i.e., the period specified in psychology as "saying goodbye to youth and entering adulthood"). The boundaries of middle age are not commonly agreed upon. Usually, however, various researchers place this stage of life between 35 and 60 years old. Entering this period lasts about 5 years and takes place exactly in the late 30s. Erik H. Erikson and Robert J. Havighurst as well as Barbara M. and Philip R. Newman deem it a phase of "middle adulthood"; according to Daniel J. Levinson it is a "culmination of early adulthood" and the "beginning of middle age," whereas Carl G. Jung believes that people turning 35 to 40 are in the middle of their existence (Brzezińska, 2000; Erikson, 1997; Oleś, 2000; Witkowski, 2000). These authors share a few common ideas—developmental tasks that need to be undertaken by people in this time of life. The most important are the following (Brzezińska, 2000, pp. 235–236; 2006; Oleś, 2000, 35–90):

- Establishing and maintaining a proper economic standard of life, "being productive" at work, and managing a professional career;
- Figuring out a responsible social attitude;
- Taking care of family, developing the ability to run a house;
- Taking care of and meeting the needs of young people, "generativity"— taking care of the younger generation, being able to adopt one's parental skills to changes in children's age (giving up control in favor of partnership), helping raise children to become happy and responsible adults;
- Taking care and developing relations and ties with a life partner;
- Changing relationships (adopting to the change) with aging parents;
- Learning how to spend free time in a way typical for adults in a given culture;
- Accepting and adapting to changes normal for middle age regarding physiological level and establishing one's place and accepting the fact that one belongs to the proper age category.

Crisis is a crucial moment in development and, if it finds a positive solution, it can result in a better quality of life. Such an outcome is always connected with some breakthrough (i.e., important change, new look at life, and different perspective on the past and future). The way of dealing with the crisis, which is the quality of developmental tasks delivered in a given period of time, depends on an individual's capacity (competences) established in previous stages of development, the cultural and social standards of fulfilling these duties, and the quality and intensity of support of the social environment a person can rely on when dealing with the previously mentioned tasks (Brzezińska, 2000, p. 237).

As already mentioned, the standards of developmental tasks and partly the strategies of dealing with crisis are defined by cultural context in which a person grows up and lives—a person's development depends both on biology and social environment (expectations, requirements, stereotypes, social and cultural standards, etc.). If we assume that the behavior of a grownup and the types of challenges he/she takes is significantly correlated with cultural gender, then both social and developmental standards, as well as strategies of (not) coping with developmental crisis have generic specificity (Mandal, 2000; Miluska, 1996). Therefore, one of the crucial questions we have asked ourselves is: How do men go through this stage of life?

By analyzing the social and cultural context in which a given person develops, we can determine not only the sources of pressure but also the reasons for their life failures. Thus, the cohort effect discovered in our research appeared to be very vital. This effect has resulted from the common experience of a rapidly changing social and cultural situation in Poland after 1989. All men under consideration here became adults (in 1989, men who are now 35–40 years old were then 18–23) in the crucial period, which meant rapid transformations of different levels of social life. As a consequence, this defined not only symbolic frames of socialization (values, norms, manners, etc.) but also a certain array of available resources and behaviors.

The childhood and teenage years of the men we have studied took place in the era of real socialism, one of growing political tension and social difficulties. The models of masculinity, femininity, relations between men and women, as well as those of family life to which young people had been exposed changed after 1989. It was a change for which they were not ready. During the period of real socialism, three sources impacted gender identity (Fuszara, 2002; Graff, 2001; Marody & Giza-Poleszczuk, 2000; Siemieńska, 1996). First was the official policy of the socialist state, within which the ideal of a generic role was created. Most influenced was the professional activity of women, triggered by the increasing demand for labor. Under a policy of keeping income at relatively low levels, the male ceased to be "head of family and breadwinner." Moreover, the position of females in the symbolic sphere rose thanks to common access to education. Therefore, women started to be better educated than men. The second source was a cultural tradition connected with the history of Poland, marked by fighting for freedom and close ties to Catholicism. What was characteristic for that period was the female role model of "Mother Pole" and the male one of national hero. The third source that influenced gender identity in those years was civilizational and cultural changes resulting from industrialization and urbanization.

Especially important seems to be the specific demographic situation in prewar Poland. Due to tragic historical events, the rural community dominated (70%), and after the war villagers migrated to cities bringing with them a strong patriarchal model of the family supported by traditional teachings of the Catholic Church. The long-standing place of women in the social hierarchy, "children, kitchen, church," was enriched by professional work. Even though men lost their high status as breadwinners, on the symbolic level they still were perceived as "the head of family." In relation to mental traditionalism, men's attitude toward chores and child rearing did not change. The challenging conditions of life created a model of relationship in which the woman was a "brave victim" with the man either a "big baby" or a "hardheaded patriarch" at her side. Our respondents were brought up in such a strong patriarchal model.

After 1989, a few significant changes took place. In the context of gender roles, the most important seem to be the following: cultural change constituting a wide range of possible patterns and lifestyles; the development of a goods and services market, which influenced new consumption pressures; and a sudden change in the labor market with a high unemployment rate on one hand and new possibilities in the area of a professional career and social promotion on the other. Professional success became one of the possible priorities in life. Obviously, for men this option was "natural," but for women it was associated with breaking out of their traditional roles (Marody & Giza-Poleszczuk, 2000; Philips, 2003).

Women are not the only ones to bear the cost of these changes. They are burdened with balancing many roles and dilemmas concerning their own identity (Ostrouch, 2006). Also, men have problems with their self-esteem; they take up bad habits, and the level of their frustration and aggression is ever-increasing. High unemployment rates, low grades for boys at school, escalating violence, premature death, and a suicidal tendency among men are signs of males "not being socially adjusted" (Biddulph, 2004; Dench, 1998; Golczyńska-Grondas, 2004; Goldberg, 2000).

The problem we have undertaken to explore is a part of current discourse on the formation of men's identity. Its main rationale is the obvious shortage of complementary/ reliable research on men in the Polish literature, as inquiry regarding gender identity mostly refers to that done on women (Fuszara, 2002; Siemieńska, 1996; Sikorska, 1996; Strykowska, 1992; Titkow, 2003; Titkow & Domański, 1995). Therefore, the objective of this study is to fill this gap, at least partially.

METHODOLOGY

The objective of our research was the reconstruction of masculinity role models in the awareness of contemporary men. Also, the study aimed to describe and analyze men's ways of thinking and acting in the context of the most important developmental tasks of midadulthood in different areas of life, private and public, as well as in that of symbolic patterns and models. We were interested in answering these questions: How do changes in defining womanhood influence men's lives and choices? How and to what extent is masculinity redefined? To what degree do males accept these changes? How do they perceive themselves in the context of "ideal" and "real" self?

Thus, it was important not only whether "men" feel like men, but also what meaning and definitions they attribute to being males and how these affect their lives. Definitions and ways of realizing masculinity referred to social and cultural contexts in which stereotypes and models of generic roles are stored and transmitted. In the research, we particularly focus on the developmental tasks and roles of father (who takes care of a child), son (who takes care of aging parents), life partner, and employee.

Taking into consideration the complexity (when it comes to content and meaning) of the phenomena constituting gender identity, we opted for a qualitative approach. The topics broached required analysis of not only behaviors and attitudes, but also feelings, values, norms, and evaluations concerned with being a man, phenomenological aspects that cannot be determined by measurements and quantitative results.

In order to solve the problem, a combined triangulation (triangulation of data and methodological triangulation) of two methods was applied: focus group and biographical interviews. Following the suggestion of Miles and Huberman (2000, p. 11), data from these consultations were analyzed on three equal levels: reduction (or condensation), which refers to such processes as selection, concentration, categorization, streamlining, separating, and processing data; representation (in the form of elaborated texts, graphs, and matrixes), which constitutes a set of information necessary to enhance clearness; and connecting the gathered information in order to draw conclusions, plus their verification.

We carried out individual biographic and focus group interviews with men 35 to 40 years of age, who were in relationships, lived with children, were homogenous education-wise, and worked in different professions. The interviews were recorded and then transcribed. In our analysis, we took into account the statements of our respondents as well as their behavior and way of interaction.

We would like to underline that for a better understanding of the analyses undertaken, it was essential to present interviewees' responses captured in their own language. In our opinion, no longer may men's experiences be concealed in numbers and percentages. Therefore, in our interpretations we gave voice to the men by employing many quotations, which show the atmosphere and context of their views and emotions as well as the change they experienced.

DISCUSSION

One of the developmental tasks of midadulthood is a change of relations with aging parents and the necessity to figure out new rules of functioning in the role of a son. On the basis of responses, one notices that in most cases ties with parents gets weaker as they age, but it is difficult to conclude about a conscious transformation into a new relationship. Men rarely spend time with their parents; sometimes they visit them, more often they speak on the phone. They stay in the relationship because of duty, often because of their own children, but they do not derive from it any positive energy or strength. One of the reasons for this could be general transformations in family structure. The multigenerational family, whose members used to live together, has transformed into a nuclear one due to choice:

> **Focus Group Interview 1:** My father is dead, mum lives near Poznan. We speak on the phone, we see each other on holidays.
>
> **FGI 1:** With my in-laws every second month for sure, I don't mind, and with my parents I talk on the phone.
>
> **Biographical Interview 4:** I try once a week because, well. . . to be honest, I also prefer this relationship children and. . . grandparents, closeness of grandparents with whom children might have everyday contact. Well, we try to meet on Saturday, Sunday even for a while. But besides that we meet less and less often, I mean we talk.
>
> **BI 5:** This is very little, this is very little amount of time. Practically none.
>
> When asked about the quality and forms of contacts with parents, men mostly refer to financial support from their parents or help in taking care of children, which they still expect from them(!):
>
> **FGI 1:** In my case my parents give pocket money and the children visit them. I don't have to give anything. But I don't want anything from them, they don't have to give me anything.
>
> **FGI 2 :. . .** because when they give something to the kids, or they buy something. But not only that, because sometimes they give some presents. Parents have two pensions and they have small needs. They don't buy themselves clothes unless their shoes wear out, then they buy new ones. But they don't buy themselves any clothes, they don't go to the cinema, they sit at home, watch TV. We also get something from them, some pots, don't know why but they buy.
>
> **FGI 2:** In my case it's not financial help but rather personal—for example, to stay with a kid.

The respondents have difficulty defining the meaning of their parents to their lives. They mostly refer to childhood or to an image of what parents should be to their children. They do not go to them with their problems; mostly they talk to them about their children, not about themselves. If they help their parents, it is usually in performing everyday chores:

> **BI 1:** I give her a lift, because she is already a woman about 74 years of age. So it is difficult for her, this kind. . . I'm always kind of at

service when it comes to transport. Before holidays I help her clean. I'm not connected with my mum now, nor I have never been connected with my parents with a so called. . . umbilical cord.

BI 2: I'm building a little house for her. I bring her beverages. I change her furniture. I arrange redecoration. I give her lifts and pick her up. . . everything which is connected with technical service for my mother, I do it.

BI 4: For sure they are role models. . . . and big ones. This is what we learn at home. . . . Respect, authority.

Only in a few statements can one notice a "reflexive" approach of respondents to their relations with parents. It is connected not only with showing concern about their everyday life but also their development in older years or emotional welfare:

BI 2: In the world I live my mum cannot have a decisive opinion because it's impossible. She suffers a lot because of that. I'm trying to sooth this pain somehow. Sometimes I adjust to this opinion, sometimes I suggest this opinion to make her happy.

BI 3: My mum wants to work for me. I'm thinking about it, maybe to, I don't know, to shorten this job. I would like to do this gradually, gently because I know that she feels needed because she is in a way my right hand and it is also important to me. . . mentally.

BI 4: My parents know they can rely on me and it makes me feel good that I help them. It is in my nature. . . . I enjoy helping other people. . . . It simply translates to. . . parents are the most important because it's family. I'll try to pull myself together and do what they expect me to do.

Functioning as a son in a new dimension and period of life beyond childhood is not easy. It takes time to think, for which most of the respondents are not ready. The lack of agreement with parents at this stage of life is perceived by respondents not only as a generational gap but also a consequence of rapid social and cultural changes currently taking place in Poland:

BI 2: My mum does not solve problems in a realistic way because in my mother's life there was a turning-point. The world has changed. My mum is rooted in a different world. My problems that I face today overwhelm my mother completely. . . . This is not just a generation gap. This is a difference of growing up, thinking in a different system, totally, because the transformation which took place in Poland is a transition which in other countries lasted for decades. It took us ten years. This is huge problem—huge diversity, not only an economic one but. . . mental one.

Modern Polish husbands also experience a number of contradictory feelings. Skills and strategies taught in the process of socialization, which should guarantee success in the labor market, do not ensure the same in domestic life. At the same time, they often become barriers to an open approach and the expression of feelings:

> **BI 1:** I don't know, hugging or. . . maybe. . . some simple stuff. . . , they don't require some. . . . I'm not the kind of emotional person to show my feelings like most men I suppose. It just isn't easy for me to do and it doesn't come easy. I guess for women it is much easier. From what I've heard. . . . Besides I'm contaminated with this upbringing I was given in my family home.

Success in family life depends on openness and sensitivity to the partner's needs, cooperation not competition (Golczyńska-Grondas, 2004, p. 60). Man's requirement for autonomy is often opposed to cooperative skills and trust, which are so necessary in a relationship. Our respondents were rather careful in showing feelings toward their partners. They felt somewhat embarrassed and referred to stereotypical impressions:

> **FGI 1:** Last time I told her that I loved her 15 years ago, it goes without saying.
> **FGI 5:** I don't say it to my wife. I mean I don't tell her directly that I love her or that she's beautiful 'cause for example I often tell my daughter don't stoop, stand straight, be as beautiful as your mother. It was time for her first high heel shoes and she couldn't walk in them, so: "look at your mum, how she does it, mum will teach you" and that's how I make my wife understand that she's the most beautiful woman. Most often they bought flowers, small gifts as an equivalent to expressing their feelings.

For them, love should mean, for example, holding hands on the street, helping with chores or doing the shopping together:

> **FGI 4:**. . . We've known each other for 14 years. Sometimes when we go for a walk I hold her hand. How many couples hold each other's hands after so many years? Mostly they just walk separately.
> **FGI 1:** I don't buy flowers, I don't make coffee but I wash the dishes, make dinner, it must be enough.

Most respondents claimed their relationships were based on partnership. They claimed to be involved in chores, taking care of and raising the children, but mostly with the permission or under the careful supervision of their wives. Nevertheless, the responses concerning the amount of time and kind of duties they performed led to the conclusion that there is a significant discrepancy between their declarations and everyday reality:

> FGI 2: I, for example, love to cook. On Saturday, Sunday I always cook.
>
> FGI 2: I have a wife who loves ironing so she wouldn't let me.
>
> FGI 4: My thing is that I cook and wash at the same time. Cooking I like. I don't like washing, but it's not a problem, because I just put everything into a washing machine, wait till it's clean and that's it. I don't like cleaning. I like to make a mess 'cause it's fun, but when it's time to clean it gets worse. When it comes to washing up the dishes—I do it, but hate it. When it comes to cleaning windows, I can buy new ones, but I won't clean them.

Similar discrepancies can be noticed in statements about respondents' attitudes toward their wives' jobs and their contribution to the finances of the relationship. A majority of them declared total support for their partners' desire or need to work. They also emphasized their approval for higher salaries of their spouses. Simultaneously, referring to everyday reality, they admired their wives for the ability to balance so many responsibilities, and they declared that they were more or less willing to stick to the dominant role of women in domestic life.

Research shows that the traditional division of tasks in a family has had an adverse impact on the emotional development of men and limits not only their growth as an aware partner, but also their ability to be good fathers. This becomes a reason for the physical and/or symbolic absence of the father at home, which further results in psychological disorders in the development of children, especially sons (Eichelberger, 1998):

> FGI 2: In my case, children rather talked to my wife, 'cause when I stayed at work for 12 hours, only Saturday and Sunday left, what should we talk about?
>
> FGI 2: When children were small, I worked so much that when I stayed with them on Saturday or Sunday because my wife had go out, they cried very hard, because they didn't know me. When I was leaving for work, they were still asleep, when I came back they were already sleeping.
>
> FGI 3: I also have some similarities but one thing my father overlooked in a way—he was not there when I was growing up. When I had to fight with my friends in the courtyard—when I needed him—he wasn't there. That's why I try to be with my son as often as possible to make him feel that his father is there. I teach him different things. Often I wanted my father to be there but he wasn't because he was at work.

The organization of social life and institutions makes it harder for a man and woman to be an employee and a parent at the same time:

> FGI 1: She was with the children when she had maternity leave, she didn't work for some time. She spent more time with the children than I did and it is still like that because she doesn't work so many hours. It doesn't change the fact that I have very good contact with my children. I also tried when they were little, very little to bathe them and play with them, go out for a walk, read books to them. But for sure my wife spends more time.
>
> BI 2: How do I balance work and family life? Very badly. Very badly. And I knew before the baby was born that I would have. . . huge. . . problem with it. I cope with it very badly, I feel very guilty that I cope with it badly and I still have the problem. . . how to change it.
>
> FGI 3: The children have a completely different attitude to me than to my wife. There is some distance. It's because of my job. I spend more time at work than at home. I come home, I go to bed. I don't feel like going out with them.

Moreover, men attempting to counter stereotypes, which assume concentration on a professional job, hiding emotions and fear of closeness, may lead to problems with being a good parent. The traditional model of a man—a father who is in charge of the family and guarantees proper status and behavior, who carries the name, fortune, and tradition and who is a link binding the family with the state and law—is being "corroded" (Delumeau & Roche, 1995; Flandrin, 1998). This is noticeable both in the respondents' opinions about fatherhood and in everyday reality:

> FGI 3: And why can't I bring up the children, am I worse or what? Why? There are bad fathers, there are bad mothers.
>
> FGI 2: I'm not the same to my son as my father was to me. He was overworked. I thought that he spent too little time with me. That's why I try to do it in the opposite way—I spend with my son as much time as I can. Although I don't have too much free time. To go for a walk, play football. I don't have too much but I try too make the most of it. As much as I can.

Although in a majority of Polish families women also work, culture and society still deems the man responsible for the financial status of the family. The socialization of boys continues to emphasize the success and money-oriented approach. Such an attitude becomes, then, a basic benchmark of "masculinity." Thus males, who at the cost of professional success—or work in general—get involved in child upbringing, are perceived not only as very unmanly but also may feel rejected and condemned (Fanning & McKay, 2003; Witkin, 1997). However, a modern father should be kind, open, gentle, honest, and interested in his offspring's problems. In raising children, one has to know how to give and support. Men are usually less prepared for this, which can be seen later on, for example, as a problem of showing one's feelings:

> FGI 2: Sometimes my son asks me: "Dad, do you love me?" and I tell him that of course I do. But since he's asking I guess something is wrong. I try to show him how I feel but he keeps asking.

Changing reality is also noticeable in men's professional lives. Susan Faludi believes that males socialized for work were deceived by society, "growing unemployment, lower wages, ever-increasing working hours and a fear of being fired, all these issues question the secure role of a 'bread winner' which used to belong to men" (see Giddens, 2004, p. 145). According to the author, modern males go through crisis and doubt about their own value and usefulness, and the professional expansion and growing independence of women does not improve this situation:

> FGI 3: It was a lot easier because only my father worked and he supported a family of five. Now I have a family of three and a son from my first marriage for whom I pay alimony and cannot just work myself because I would only earn enough to pay the rent and what about the rest.
>
> FGI 1: I think there is constant fear that we will lose this job and a woman often asks: "What's going on there?", "Are there any layoffs?", "Does the company still exist?" etc.
>
> BI 1: Nowadays it is sometimes easier for a woman to find a job, a well paid job. . . , for a man not necessarily. It's a big problem.

Since it is easier for men to find acceptance and self-esteem at work than in their private and family life, the atmosphere of insecurity when it comes to employment generates negative emotions, self-destruction, and pathologies more often among males than females:

> FGI 4: To scream or say something stupid and meaningless to the wife. Even when I don't know what she was actually asking about, just to get rid of her.
>
> FGI 4: Maybe not at my wife but sometimes I can scream at my children when I'm nervous, when something is wrong, when my son says something wrong, then I can scream.

The consequences of stereotypes and imposing patterns of masculinity are reflected in the process of male self-actualization. In the opinion of Dorota Pankowska (2005, p. 153), the role of a man prevents many from acting according to their "real self" and to bring their entire potential to life.

Entrapped in "duties" and fulfilling expectations, norms of behavior and specified types of life activities become insuperable barriers to self-actualization and pursuit of their own passions. What is poignant, the respondents were more willing to give up their own interests and self-development in favor of being good fathers over that of employees and husbands:

> BI 3: I used to ride a motorbike, I rode a bicycle a lot, and some physical activity helped a lot. And now, well. . . family, family. The house, I always have a lot of work here and at home with children.
>
> BI 5: Many times when going somewhere, to play some sports or to a stupid gym, there is always a guilty conscious. How is it, I have time but I don't have time for a child. My wife will understand but my child won't. . . .

The meaning of a professional career was perceived by the respondents in two ways, depending on their position in the social and professional structure. Those with a higher education, managerial positions, or owners of well-established companies emphasized the possibility of professional development, a will to create, not only for themselves but also for others:

> BI 4:. . . In order to satisfy your own needs, to be able to self-actualize. Besides I guess it is in human nature to work. I have such nature that I like to build. . . and I guess it is the main drive. . . at work.
>
> BI 2: Work. . . gives me some satisfaction. . . of implementing my visions, concepts. . . . There is also an economic aspect, when I work I can make my dreams, image of life come true. . . . A huge role in my work today is played by people I'm working with who believed me sometime ago and linked their fate to me, most of all the fate of their family.

Nevertheless, there were very few such responses. More often the respondents perceived their job as a duty, a way to support their family and satisfy basic needs. They clearly felt unhappy about the stage they were going through in their professional lives. They emphasized that they felt poorly paid, used, and frustrated, and in this way they also showed the reality of men in contemporary Poland:

> FGI 2: No. But I do piece-work, I have some influence on how much I earn. It is a hard job but. . . I earn as much as I did 10 years ago, when it comes to details. This money used to have higher value and now. . . . And besides employers in Poland treat their employees like slaves.
>
> FGI 2: We work longer, harder and for much smaller money than in the West.
>
> FGI 4: Supporting family is the most important.

FGI 4: I don't like my job, I mean I don't like it, it doesn't give me any satisfaction but it gives me money and some freedom.
FGI 3: You treat a job as a necessary evil. You go there because you have to. Days look alike. You don't think, you don't figure things out. You are not effective at work.

A desire to adhere to the traditional imperative of masculinity and aloofness, as described by the respondents, may be "lethal" not only for males' personality but also their health. Not only bravado when driving a car or riding a motorbike, combined with ignoring traffic regulations (speeding, not fastening the seatbelts, ignoring other protective measures), but also addictions pose a threat to men's well-being. Polish men, thrice as often as Polish women, die because of serious injuries and poisoning; they die four times more often in car accidents and five times more frequently because of suicides and self-inflicted wounds (Ostrowska, 1996, p. 42). In the case of road accidents, males are more often both culprits and victims. Moreover, men get involved in great numbers of fights and other situations hazardous to life. Unlike females, they also tend to drink and drive. In Polish society, there exist a general permissiveness toward and tolerance for addicts—men (Hulewska & Ziarko, 2002).

Traditional men's behavior such as resisting pain, avoiding the doctor and ignoring his advice, as well as drinking large amounts of alcohol is connected with self-destruction from the medical point of view. According to H. Goldberg, the reason for such comportment is a common belief that taking care of oneself is not manly. In many cases, males lose contact with their bodies due to socialization, which teaches a boy not to react to signals sent by his organism (e.g., exhaustion), because indifference to one's health is perceived by Polish culture as "manly" (Goldberg, 2000, p. 39; Melosik, 2002):

BI 2: Men yes because they think the are immortal, that they are so strong, probably yes, probably they ignore a lot, they don't want to admit they are weak. . . . Whereas they lead completely different. . . they drink alcohol more often, they drink a lot of alcohol. All negative factors of life they accept. . . .
BI 5: For three years? I've been thinking about it myself. I've noticed I feel worse and worse. Always some pain in my chest, always something. . . . But I never pay attention to it.

Zbyszko Melosik thinks that contemporary men find themselves in a sort of "socialization trap" (2002, p. 180) since they do not know who they have to be and what characteristics they should work on. However, contemporarily all people seem to be in such a trap, without regard to gender. The difference is that it is men, not women, who are at the beginning of the process connected with a "freedom crisis."

CONCLUSIONS: CRISIS, WITHDRAWAL,. . . CHANGE?

Problems connected with the social mechanisms of creating cultural gender are an important theoretical and practical issue for education. According to humanistic concepts in psychology, stereotypes associated with gender pose a threat to self-actualization, life opportunities, and the ability of an individual to develop—both men and women. As research has shown, in the aftermath of pressure to differentiate roles of women and men, the number of life choices made by them is reduced. Nevertheless, in the field of pedagogy there is still no thorough idea or deep and systematic research regarding mechanisms and effects of socialization in accordance with gender stereotypes, especially in the ever-changing social and cultural reality of Poland.

Steve Biddulph claims that the vast majority of modern men "pretends to live." which is detrimental not only to them but also to their families and relatives (2004, pp. 11–13). They are not clearly aware who they are but manage to learn very quickly that they have to pretend. The author emphasizes that as a society we are half-way there—after the emancipation of women there comes a time for men. According to Goldberg (2000), males, by gaining self-awareness, would have a chance to create new physical and emotional models, thus enriching and prolonging their lives.

According to Ulrich Beck and Anthony Giddens, getting men involved in fulfilling a "traditional" model of masculinity, which results from autonomic decisions, hinders creating their own biographies as individual projects. Such situations take place mostly among men of the lower social classes, ones poorly educated, from rural areas, or unemployed, or in pathological families (Golczyńska-Grondas, 2004). Changes in the social system of gender roles, even though they create tensions, become necessary as well as offer a chance for males to increase their self-awareness and create their own lives in line with their individual needs, not with those of the dominant culture or structure.

The results of our analysis prove that for men all areas of life are to a large extent "insecure" and full of conflict. The prevailing strategy of dealing with this situation is withdrawal. An analysis of respondents' statements shows that contemporary men "do not know how to" create their role in present day Poland, and they seem to locate the way of experiencing their masculinity somewhere between crisis, withdrawal, and the need for change.

REFERENCES

Beck, U. (2004). *Społeczeństwo ryzyka. W drodze do innej nowoczesności.* Warszawa: Wydawnictwo Naukowe Scholar.
Bem, S. (2000). *Męskość. Kobiecość. O różnicach wynikających z płci.* Gdańsk: GWP.
Biddulph, S. (2004). *Męskość.* Poznań: Dom Wydawniczy Rebis.

Bly, R. (1993). *Żelazny Jan. Rzecz o mężczyznach.* Poznań: Dom Wydawniczy Rebis.

Brzezińska, A. (2000). *Społeczna psychologia rozwoju,* Warszawa: Wydawnictwo Naukowe Scholar.

————. (Ed.). (2006). *Psychologiczne portrety człowieka. Praktyczna psychologia rozwojowa.* Gdańsk: GWP.

Delumeau, J., & Roche, D. (Eds.). (1995). *Historia ojców i ojcostwa.* Warszawa: Oficyna Wydawnicza Volumen, and Wydawnictwa Szkolne i Pedagogiczne.

Dench, G. (1998). *Pocałunek królewny. Problem mężczyzn.* Warszawa: Wydawnictwo IFiS PAN.

Eichelberger, W. (1998). *Zdradzony przez ojca.* Warszawa: Wydawnictwo Do.

Erikson, E. (1997). *Dzieciństwo i społeczeństwo.* Poznań: Dom Wydawniczy Rebis.

Fanning, P., & McKay, M. (2003). *Być mężczyzną we współczesnym zwariowanym świecie.* Gdańsk: GWP.

Flandrin, J. L. (1998). *Historia rodziny.* Warszawa: Oficyna Wydawnicza Volumen.

Fuszara, M. (Ed.). (2002). *Kobiety w Polsce na przełomie wieków. Nowy kontrakt płci?.* Warszawa: Instytut Spraw Publicznych.

Giddens, A. (2004). *Socjologia.* Warszawa: PWN.

Golczyńska-Grondas, A. (2004). *Mężczyźni z enklaw biedy. Rekonstrukcja pełnionych ról społecznych.* Łódź: Przedsiębiorstwo Specjalistyczne ABSOLWENT.

Goldberg, H. (2000). *Wrażliwy macho. Mężczyzna 2000.* Warszawa: Diogenes.

Graff, A. (2001). *Świat bez kobiet. Płeć w polskim życiu publicznym.* Warszawa: W.A.B.

Hulewska, A., & Ziarko, M. (2002). Zachowanie zdrowotne kobiet i mężczyzn—raport z badań. In A. Hulewska, A. Jasielska, & M. Ziarko (Eds.), *Interdyscyplinarne studia nad płcią. Od polaryzacji płciowej ku depolaryzacji rodzajowej* (pp. 15–29). Poznań: Wydawnictwo Fundacji Humaniora.

Mandal, E. (2000). *Podmiotowe i interpersonalne konsekwencje stereotypów związanych z płcią.* Katowice: Wydawnictwo UŚ.

Marody, M., & Giza–Poleszczuk, A. (2000). Być kobietą, być mężczyzną—czyli o przemianach tożsamości związanej z płcią we współczesnej Polsce. In M. Marody (Ed.), *Między rynkiem a etatem. Społeczne negocjowanie rzeczywistości* (pp. 44–74). Warszawa: Wydawnictwo Naukowe Scholar.

————. (2004). *Przemiany więzi społecznych.* Warszawa: Wydawnictwo Naukowe Scholar.

Melosik, Z. (2002). *Kryzys męskości w kulturze współczesnej.* Poznań: Wydawnictwo Wolumin.

Miles, M. B., & Huberman, A. M. (2000). *Analiza danych jakościowych.* Białystok: Trans Humana.

Miluska, J. (1996). *Tożsamość kobiet i mężczyzn w cyklu życia.* Poznań: Wydawnictwo Naukowe UAM.

Oleś, P. K. (2000). *Psychologia przełomu życia.* Lublin: Towarzystwo Naukowe KUL.

Ostrouch, J. (2006). Kobieta nieustannie (u)wikłana. *Acta Universitatis Nicolai Copernici. Socjologia Wychowania, XVI(378),* 121–128.

Ostrowska, A. (1996). Zdrowie i samopoczucie a społeczna sytuacja kobiet. In J. Sikorska (Ed.), *Kobiety i ich mężowie. Studium porównawcze* (pp. 29–58). Warszawa: IFiS PAN.

Pankowska, D. (2005). *Wychowanie a role płciowe.* Gdańsk: GWP.

Phillips, A. (2003). Przestrzeń publiczna, życie prywatne. In R. Siemieńska (Ed.), *Aktorzy życia publicznego. Płeć jako czynnik różnicujący* (pp. 24–50). Warszawa: Wydawnictwo Naukowe Scholar.

Siemieńska, R. (1996). *Kobiety: nowe wyzwania. Starcie przeszłości z teraźniejszością.* Warszawa: Instytut Socjologii UW.
Witkin, G. (1997). *Stres męski.* Poznań: Dom Wydawniczy Rebis.
Witkowski, L. (2000). *Rozwój i tożsamość w cyklu życia. Studium koncepcji Erika H. Eriksona.* Toruń: WIT-GRAF.

13 Bent Straights
Diversity and Flux Among Heterosexual Men

Michael Flood

INTRODUCTION

New formations of sexuality are emerging among young heterosexual men. There are signs of diversity, and flux, in the sexual cultures of such males, shaped by wider shifts in gender and sexual relations. This chapter maps some of the clearest examples of diversity and flux among them, as part of a wider project on young men's sexual and social relations with women.

Overview of This Research

The wider project in which I am engaged is a critical analysis of the sexual cultures of young heterosexual men. My primary aim is to document the cultural understandings and social relations, which shape the sexual practices and involvements of such males aged 18 to 24, drawing on in-depth interviews and focus groups with 90 of them from a variety of backgrounds and settings. The term "sexual cultures" embodies a recognition of the cultural and collective constitution of sexual relations, and refers to clusters of norms, beliefs, and practices associated with particular settings, contexts, or communities. The project is oriented toward improving young men's, and young women's, sexual and reproductive health.

Mapping: What We Know so Far

From a now substantial scholarship, we know that certain forms of gender and sexuality are dominant (culturally celebrated and socially sanctioned) in any context, while others are stigmatized, silenced, or punished. Constructions of gender and sexuality vary among young heterosexual men in different cultures and countries. At the same time, there are themes that appear again and again in diverse contexts. I outline them before focusing on questions of diversity and change. Very briefly, some aspects of dominant constructions of masculinity and heterosexuality identified in the literature include:

- The notion of male sexuality as an uncontrollable or barely controllable force (Kippax, Crawford, & Waldby, 1994, p. S318; Richardson, 1997, p. 161; Wilton, 1997, p. 34);
- Women's sexuality as passive, and an absence of the naming of girls' and women's sexual desire, pleasure, or sexual entitlement (Fine, 1993, p. 35);
- The organization of heterosexual sex around men's sexual needs and men's sexual pleasure, including the definition of "real" sex as penis-in-vagina intercourse (Foreman, 1998, p. 22; Wight, 1994; Wilton, 1997, p. 34);
- The homosocial policing of young men's sexual and social relations with women, including patterns of male–male competition, surveillance, and discipline (Flood, in press; Holland, Ramazanoglu & Sharpe, 1994, p. 14), associations between sexual experience, and masculine status (Wilton, 1997, p. 34), and so on;
- Women as the gatekeepers and guardians of sexual safety and health, with responsibility for both their own and men's sexual behavior (Richardson, 1997, p. 161; Wilton, 1997), while masculinity is associated with risk-taking and constructed as stoic, brave, and aggressive (Primary Health Care Group, 1996, pp. 13–14);
- Male emotional insensitivity (Doyle, 1989, pp. 148–160), unequal divisions of emotional labor in heterosexual relationships and a reliance on women's emotional work (Strazdins & Broom, 2004), and feminine investment in discourses of "love" and "romance" (Duncombe & Marsden, 1993; Rosenthal, Gifford, & Moore, 1998);
- Heterosexual male ambivalence toward girls or women: On the one hand, boys may show contempt for femaleness and the stereotypical qualities of femininity, and conflate male femininity and homosexuality, and on the other hand, they also treat girls as objects of sexual desire, fascination, and fixation (Mac an Ghaill, 1994, pp. 102, 164);
- Sexual control and knowledge as the property of men, based on cultural equations of masculinity, activity, and knowledge on one hand, and femininity, passivity, and innocence on the other (Waldby, Kippax, & Crawford, 1993, p. 255);
- A sexual double standard and the policing of female sexual reputation (Hillier, Harrison, & Warr, 1998, p. 26; Holland, Ramazanoglu, Sharpe, & Thomson, 1996, p. 242; Kitzinger, 1995; Stewart, 1999);
- Norms, particularly among a minority of young men, in which sexual violence is seen as legitimate or desirable (National Crime Prevention, 2001, pp. 64–70), victims are blamed, and consent is ignored or violated;
- Homophobia and heterosexism: definitions of masculinity against or in opposition to homosexuality (as well as femininity) (Connell, 1995, p. 78; Flood, 1997; Kinsman, 1987), a homophobic policing of boys'

and men's performances of gender, and the daily enforcement of compulsory heterosexuality. (Rich, 1980)

There is evidence that such constructions have shifted over the past several decades. My own PhD research documented a number of configurations of sociosexual meaning and practice among young heterosexual men, which are at odds with the depictions of masculinity and masculine sexuality in much of the literature (Flood, 2003b).

DIVERSITY

There has been a tendency in some queer and lesbian feminist writing to paint heterosexual social and sexual relations as homogenous and indeed monotonous, in contrast to the diversity and vibrancy of nonheterosexual life. However, given the widespread recognition of sexual diversity, it is problematic to assume that heterosexual sexual cultures, whether in the West or elsewhere, are characterized by homogenous sexual subjectivities and relations (Herdt, 1999, p. 100).

There are good reasons to think that heterosexual sexual cultures are both heterogeneous and dynamic. If a sexual culture is defined in terms of shared sexual conduct and sociosexual norms, then it is likely that there are multiple heterosexual sexual cultures based on divergent sexual practices and understandings, shaped by forms of social differentiation, institutional locations, and so on.

Specifically, we are likely to see forms of diversity associated with axes of social differentiation, diverse peer cultures, particular settings and contexts, and nonmainstream sexual relations and communities.

Axes of Social Differentiation and Sexual Practice

Multiple forms of social differentiation and categorization, such as class, race, and ethnicity, are likely to structure young men's social and sexual relations. In the first instance, these axes of difference are related to varying patterns of sexual activity, as simple demographic data attest. Among youths, the average age of first intercourse varies with class, education, culture, and ethnicity (Roker & Coleman, 1998, p. 7). Female students from non-English-speaking backgrounds in Australia are less likely to be sexually active than their Anglo counterparts (Lindsay, Smith, & Rosenthal, 1997, p. 26). Young people who adhere to religious values, whatever the religion, also are less likely to be sexually active (Moore & Rosenthal, 1998, p. 46). Those in rural locations are more likely to be sexually active than urban youth, and this is especially so for women (Lindsay et al., 1997, p. 26). Finally, homeless youth practice higher levels of risky sexual behavior and do so with more partners (Hillier, Matthews, & Dempsey, 1997).

Multiple and Diverse Peer Cultures among Boys and Young Men

Research among boys and young men in schools documents the existence of multiple and contradictory masculinities and male peer groups with different masculine subjectivities and practices. British and Australian research has revealed diverse subcultures and identities among boys in schools (Connell, 1989, 1993, 1996; Mac an Ghaill, 1994, 1996; Martino, 1999; Martino & Pallotta-Chiarolli, 2003). Scottish research found that young men in male-only peer groups espoused norms of a predatory male sexuality and sexual double standard, while in mixed-sex groups these were largely absent, and the men expressed ideals of companionate relationships (Wight, 1996). Mac an Ghaill (2000, p. 205) shows that while some young men cultivate females' attraction through their consumption of fashionable clothes, hairstyles, and music, as well as display their competence at forming heterosexual relationships, other young men celebrate a sexual prowess based instead on "extreme perversity, violent misogyny, and a racialized sexuality."

There are likely to be further diversities in the sexual relations of youth cultures associated with particular bodies of music, fashion, and cultural consumption, from goth (Wilkins, 2004) and skater scenes, to punk and straight edge (Haenfler, 2004), to rural Bachelors' and Spinsters' Balls.

Sexual Cultures Associated with Particular
Sports, Workplaces, or Social Circles

Among young heterosexual men, local sexual cultures may be constituted through collective participation in particular sports, workplaces, or social circles. For example, the 2004 allegations of sexual assault by professional rugby league and AFL players suggested that at least some of them participate in a local sexual culture defined by homosocial bonding and tight group loyalties, heavy drinking, and participation in group sex.

Australian research on gay and homosexually active men has begun to pay attention to the ways in which ethnic or cultural identity, family, class, and community construct and in turn are constructed by sexuality and a gay community (Connell, Davis, & Dowsett, 1993; Pallotta-Chiarolli, 1998). It is likely that class, and the sexual cultures of particular workplaces, also shape young heterosexual men's sexual relations. For example, a national survey of over 2,500 male TAFE apprentices in the occupational streams of hairdressing, automotive studies, and commercial cookery found systematic differences in sexual practices, use of condoms, and attitudes toward HIV, depending on these males' vocational choices (Grunseit & Kippax, 1996). Men in the traditionally masculine stream of automotive studies were less likely than those in commercial cookery to have used condoms at last intercourse and had more negative attitudes toward them.

Another dimension of sexual diversity among young heterosexual men concerns their participation in nonmainstream sexual relations, milieux, or communities, such as swinging, sadomasochism, and so on.

Nonmainstream Sexual Relations and Communities: Swingers, S&M, and So On

"Swinging" refers to organized recreational sex among mixed-sex couples, premised on emotional monogamy and physical nonmonogamy (Bergstrand & Williams, 2000). Swinging represents perhaps the only heterosexual equivalent to gay male "beats" and sex on premises venues. Overlapping with swinging are communities and sexual relations centered on polyamory, "the love of many people at once" (Society for Human Sexuality, n.d.), and those centered on BDSM (bondage and discipline and/or sadomasochism): sexual interests or practices involving the use of restraint and/or mock or real punishment or power-based role playing (Ellard, Richters, & Newman, 2004, p. iii).

An Australian national survey of 19,307 people aged 16 to 59 years found that among respondents with a sexual partner in the last year, 2% of men and 1.4% of women had engaged in BDSM or DS in the last year, and 4% of men and 3.7% of women had been involved in role playing or dressing up (Richters, Grulich, de Visser, Smith, & Rissel, 2003, p. 185). Group sex in the last year was reported by 2.3% of men and 0.6% of women (Richters et al., 2003, p. 185). Such rates of participation among the general population are considerably lower than those among particular subpopulations, such as men who have sex with men. While only small numbers of heterosexual men and women participate in such sexual relations, this is another dimension to potential diversity among young males.

FLUX: SHIFTS IN HETEROSEXUAL MEN'S SEXUAL CULTURES

Heterosexual Sexual Cultures also Dynamic

Heterosexual sexual cultures also are dynamic. They are influenced by, and themselves impact, other social changes. There is evidence of change in both young men's and women's sexual practice and in the social and cultural factors that are their context.

Shifts in Children's and Young People's Sexual Lives

We know that there have been at least four shifts in young people's sexual lives over the last few decades. First, children in Western countries are now starting puberty and adolescence earlier and staying in it for longer than ever before. The average age of puberty is now 10 to 10–1/2 for girls, and

11–1/2 to 12 for boys (Roker & Coleman, 1998, pp. 4–5). Second, the average age of first intercourse has declined. In Australia, one third of students in Year 10 and just over half of those in Year 12 have had vaginal intercourse, with steady increases since 1997 and 1992 (Smith, Agius, Dyson, Mitchell, & Pitts, 2003, p. 2), and higher percentages have experienced passionate kissing and sexual touching. Third, there has been a generational change in sexual "styles." Younger people engage in a significantly wider variety of sexual behaviors than older people, including oral sex and heterosexual anal intercourse (Moore & Rosenthal, 1998, pp. 47–48). Fourth, youths now have a greater number of sexual partners, and over a lifetime will have substantially more of them than did their parents (Moore & Rosenthal, 1998, p. 50). However, this is not a simple story of steady increases in Australian youths' sexual activity over time. The numbers of sexual partners reported by Year 12 students has declined over the past decade, although they have increased among those in Year 10 (Smith et al., 2003, p. 35).

Gender Convergence—Closing the Sexual Gap

There are various signs of a convergence in men's and women's sexual and intimate practices and understandings. A series of gender differences have been documented in relation to sexuality, reflecting intersecting constructions of gender and sexuality. In brief, men think about sex more often than women, are more likely to fantasize when masturbating (and their fantasies are more likely to involve sex with strangers, often more than one at a time, involving a variety of sexual acts), are more intercourse-focused, place less value on sex with emotional commitment, have a greater interest in one-night stands and sexual infidelity, and experience more pleasure during sex (Kimmel, 2000, pp. 223–227). Males also are significantly more likely than females to view pornography frequently and to be sexually aroused by, and have favorable attitudes toward it (Lo & Wei, 2002, p. 16; Walsh, 1999, p. 779).

However, such gender gaps are closing in some Western countries. For example, there is less cultural emphasis on the need for women to preserve their virginity until marriage. There has been some gender convergence in rates and motivations for masturbation, the proportions who have had sex, ages of first intercourse, numbers of sexual partners, and interest in sexual variety (Kimmel, 2000, pp. 227–232). A large Australian survey finds that men's and women's attitudes toward a range of sexuality-related topics are similar, although there are substantial differences with regard to sexual explicitness in films and sex between men (but not between women; Richters & Rissel, 2005, pp. 29–33).

Aspects of this convergence represent the movement of women's sexualities closer to men's, rather than the reverse (Kimmel, 2000, p. 232). At the same time, there are some signs of shift among males toward more traditionally feminine forms of sexual and intimate engagement. For example, while men traditionally are said to be emotionally constipated and hostile to discourses of love and romance, some young men in my PhD research emphasized their investments in narratives of trust, intimacy, and monogamy. They were ambivalent about "love," but often relied on "trust" as their primary strategy in protecting themselves against sexually transmitted infections and HIV. Other qualitative research, for example in the United Kingdom, has explored boys' investments in verbal exchanges of romantic love (Redman, 2001), while in an American study among heterosexual men, narratives of sexual conquest and a sexual double standard sat alongside those of romance and sexual intimacy (Seal & Ehrhardt, 2003). Similarly, Australian research has noted a "gender convergence" in young people's reasons for having sex, with "love, caring and affection" the main motives (Moore & Rosenthal, 1993). As Seal and Ehrhardt (2003, p. 314) suggest, it may be that "men's interpersonal scripts for heterosexual courtship, romantic, and sexual interactions are in a state of transition" (2003, p. 314).

At the same time, there are still important gender differences and inequalities, for example, in relation to pleasure in sex. A recent national survey of 20,000 people aged 16 to 59 years in Australia found that 90% of men, and 79% of women, report that the sex in their regular relationship is "very" or "extremely" pleasurable (Richters & Rissel, 2005, p. 62). Five percent of females say that the sex is slightly or not at all pleasurable, compared to 1% of males. More than a quarter of women (27%) said that they did not find sex pleasurable (as did 6% of men), suggesting that many females are having sex that they do not like or really want (Richters & Rissel, 2005, p. 90). Perhaps the starkest gender difference is in relation to forced sex. One in five Australian women (21%) has been forced or frightened into doing something sexually that they did not want to do (96). The same is true of one in twenty men (5%; Richters & Rissel, 2005, p. 96).

There have been profound changes in the wider social forces, which may shape sexual cultures among young men and women. Focusing on young heterosexual males, there are at least six developments in Australia with implications for their sexual relations: changes in family structure and patterns of fertility and childrearing, new technologies used to mediate and foster sexual relations and communities, the growing acceptance of norms of gender equality, cultural "pornographication," an increased assertion of young female sexual desire and agency, and new discourses of "queer" and "metrosexual" masculinities.

Changes in Family Structure and Patterns of Fertility and Childrearing

Shifts in both family structure and the circumstances and timing of fertility have transformed the contexts for young men's sexual and social relations with women. Overall rates of marriage have declined, nonmarital cohabitation has increased, and divorces have risen. Both females and males are becoming parents at progressively older ages, having fewer children in total, and more of them outside marriage (Flood, 2003a, pp. 5–11). In addition, mothers' labor force participation has increased, offspring depend on their parents to a greater extent and live with them for longer, and there is increased unemployment and labor mobility and insecurity (Sanson & Lewis, 2001, p. 4; Weston, Stanton, & Soriano, 2001).

Such changes mean that young men (and young women) are experiencing a much longer period of sexual experimentation and partner change after the initiation of sexual activity and prior to cohabitation, marriage, and parenting, and the circumstances of such involvements themselves are increasingly diverse and fluid.

Shifts in family structure have been accompanied by a growing emphasis among fathers on their role as providers of emotional support to their children (Russell et al., 1999, pp. 32–33). However, the culture of fatherhood has changed much faster than the conduct in Australia. Despite the proliferation of imagery and rhetoric centered on the nurturing father, there has been virtually no change in the gender division of child care in couple households over the year 1986 to 1997 (Baxter, 2002, pp. 409–410). Many young men continue to expect that such responsibility will be primarily that of their partners (National Crime Prevention, 2001, p. 74; Singleton & Maher, 2004; White, 2003). In a survey of Australian youth aged 12–20, 25% of males but only 10% of females agreed that "Women should be responsible for raising children and doing housework" (National Crime Prevention, 2001, p. 74).

The Development of Internet Media and Internet-based Relations and Communities

There have also been changes in the means through which sexual interactions and relations are carried out and negotiated. The Internet is facilitating new possibilities for these activities and enabling emergent sexual communities to cohere. We know very little about what role Internet chat, online communities, and other technologies and digital contexts may be playing in shaping new forms of such interaction.

In addition, other technologies such as the mobile phone now are used by young people for social and sexual interaction.

The Growing Acceptance of Norms of Gender Equality

There also have been shifts in the cultural norms that structure young men's involvement in sexual relations. One significant example is the growing acceptance of gender equality, in the wake and presence of feminism and other social changes.

There is no denying that young men are less supportive of gender equality than young women. In a recent Australian survey of 5,000 young people aged 12 through 20, 37% of young males agreed that "Men should take control in relationships and be head of the household," compared to 12% of young females (National Crime Prevention, 2001, p. 74). At the same time, boys and young men are likely to have better attitudes toward gender equality than older generations of males, at least if patterns in Australia follow those documented in the United States.

Survey data from the United States show that both women's and men's attitudes toward gender equality have improved over the past 30 years, although the latters' have changed more slowly, and, as a result, the gap between females' and males' outlooks attitudes has widened (Ciabattari, 2001, pp. 574–575). Improvement in men's views reflects two processes. First, as individual males' attitudes improve, those of cohorts of men also change positively over time. Second, younger generations of men have less conservative positions than older ones. Similar processes are likely in Australia.

Significant pockets of resistance remain among boys and young men to gender equality, just as they do among older males (Ciabattari, 2001, p. 576). There has been more progress on some issues such as women's participation in paid work than on others such as interpersonal violence or domestic inequalities.

A Sexualized Cultural Environment: Pornographication and "Raunch Culture"

Today's young people are growing up in a cultural environment that is vastly different from that experienced by their parents and grandparents as youth. Late 20th-century Western cultures saw a proliferation of sexual imagery and an explosion of popular sexual debate (Levine, 2002, p. 4). Contemporary youth experience levels of "sexualization" in society higher than ever before, in the form of sexualized media representations and everyday interactions (Goldman, 2000, p. 11). Thus has been an increased sexualization or "pornographication" of mainstream media and culture (McNair, 1996, p. 23). There is greater testing and blurring of boundaries between pornography and mainstream media and art, an adoption of the language and visual codes of pornography, and endless "sex talk" in popular culture (Attwood, 2002, p. 98; Levy, 2005, pp. 1–3, 17–28).

Such a process brings both positives and pitfalls. While it facilitates sexual knowledge and diversity, it also intensifies exposure to forms of sexualized content, which some argue encourage sexism or violence.

For antipornography feminist writers, pornography "sexualizes and normalizes inequalities" and "makes violence sexy" (Russell, 1993; Russo, 1998, p. 18). What is objectionable is not pornography's sexual explicitness, but its abusive, hierarchical, objectifying, and degrading portrayal of females and female sexuality (Jensen & Dines, 1998, pp. 65–66; MacKinnon, 1994, p. 87). Other feminist and nonfeminist authors argue that there is great diversity in pornographic imagery and that the vast range of sexual images should not be characterized solely in terms of violence gainst women (Snitow, 1988, p. 14). They also posit that male and female iewers interpret representations in complex, selective, and ambiguous ways (Strossen, 1995, pp. 145–154); that diverse meanings may be attributed to the same scenes and sexual acts; that pornography can have positive effects and meanings; and that the usual criticisms of pornography cannot be applied simply to the gay male version of it (Thomas, 2000, pp. 63–64). Nevertheless, in most mass-marketed heterosexual pornography, "sex is divorced from intimacy, loving affection, and human connection; all women are constantly available for sex and have insatiable sexual appetites; and all women are sexually satisfied by whatever the men in the film do" (Jensen & Dines, 1998, p. 72). Heterosexual pornography's "narrative of female nymphomania and male sexual prowess" (Jensen & Dines, 1999, pp. 77–78) does not cater to all men's desires, nor are its appeals exclusive to males, but it works in a symbiotic relationship with common constructions of masculine heterosexual sexuality.

At the same time, one can also find very different texts about heterosexual men at least at the outer reaches of the pornographic universe. For example, the sex instruction video *Bend Over Boyfriend* teaches women how to give their male partners anal pleasure, in particular through anal intercourse with strap-ons or dildos (Taormino, 2000). Such a text violates, literally, a common principle of masculine heterosexuality: A man should only be the penetrator, never the penetratee.

Raunch Culture

Levy (2005) describes aspects of the pornographication of culture in terms of the rise of "raunch culture." In it, women make sex objects of themselves and others, there is a cultural expectation that women will exhibit their bodies, female empowerment is signaled only by overt and public sexuality, and sexuality itself is recognizable in the codes of pornography and prostitution (Levy, 2005, p. 26).

Speculating on what this might mean for young heterosexual men, this pornographication invites them into sexual interactions modeled on those enacted by the male clients of pornography and prostitution, such that they engage with women only as objects, as breasts and buttocks, and value them only for their conformity to narrow codes of sexual availability.

An Increased Assertion of Young Female Sexual Desire and Agency

Alongside the sexualization of popular culture, there are also signs of a growing assertion of sexual desire and agency by young women. Qualitative research in Australia documents that some young females challenge the imperatives of heterosexual femininity by divorcing sex from love; expressing sexual desire and agency; making lusty demands for sexual pleasure; and pursuing one-night stands, casual sex, older male partners, and nonmonogamous relationships (Stewart, Mischewski, & Smith, 2000, pp. 413–416).

Such practices are an important challenge to dominant norms of female sexual passivity and propriety. They may also interact with normative shifts among heterosexual men. In an American study among 100 heterosexual males, largely blue-collar and African-American, there was growing acceptance of female-initiated courtship, and of female-initiated sex, at least within steady loving relationships (Seal & Ehrhardt, 2003). However, narratives of female desire and sexuality remain constrained by the policing and inequalities of the sexual double standard and an ethic of female sexual servicing. For example, young women may feel sexually agentic enough to perform oral sex on young men, but this may reflect interpersonal and social pressure as much as it does personal desire, and they rarely receive oral sex in return. Turning this around, young heterosexual males may benefit sexually from young females' participation in raunch culture, but experience little obligation to adopt more equitable divisions of sexual pleasure.

New Discourses of "Queer" and "Metrosexual" Masculinities

I conclude by exploring perhaps the most visible aspect of new formations of male heterosexuality, "queer" and "metrosexual" masculinities.

New formations of sexuality are emerging among heterosexual men, informed by constructions of "queer" and "metrosexual" masculinities and other alternatives. Some straight men express alliance with gay men or question the binary of heterosexual and homosexual, or proclaim themselves to be "wusses" and "sissies," or take up egalitarian roles in their heterosexual sexual relations, or adopt a feminized preoccupation with personal grooming. Such developments signal a weakening of longstanding constructions of heterosexual masculinity.

The "metrosexual" was defined by *The New York Times* as "a straight urban man willing to embrace his feminine side." While such "embracing of femininity" might have heralded men's radical critique of gender divisions, this potential was quickly coopted by commercial imperatives. Metrosexuality has come to signify merely a commitment to personal grooming and cosmetics. Clothing and lifestyle companies have moved to create and capture this new market of men interested in such traditionally feminine products. The feminization of male tastes can mean that men become what women once were expected to be: vain, shallow, and status-conscious. This "New Man's" sensitivity is transformed into consumerism, creating an ideal subjectivity for the marketplace, a narcissistic and receptive consumer (McMahon, 1998, p. 155, citing Ehrenreich).

Popular culture too shows instances of either the blurring of hetero/homo boundaries among men or their comic transgression. In the television program "Queer Eye for the Straight Guy," it is gay males who have the cultural and personal capital with which to teach heterosexual men how to be attractive to women. In "Playing It Straight," a woman chooses a man from among 14 contestants, all acting straight but some of whom in fact are gay (Abernethy, 2004). In promoting the program, the Fox website showed a Gay-O-Meter with a needle flashing back and forth between "Breeder," "Metrosexual," "Sensitive," "Questionable," "Effeminate," and "Flaming" (Brioux, 2004). Take another Fox program, "Seriously, Dude, I'm Gay," in which two straight men live "the gay lifestyle" for a week, completing daily challenges, which test their ability to pass for gay, and then standing before a panel of gay judges to convince them of their gayness and thus win $50,000.[1]

Perhaps a more substantial challenge to homophobic constructions of heterosexual masculinity is represented by those straight men who draw on gay culture or who "act gay." I am thinking of those males described by some as "queer heterosexuals," "straight queers," or "straight with a twist" (Curiel, 2001), "straight fairies" who are "adamantly hetero but seemingly gay" in terms of their appearance, interests, and mannerisms (Lloyd, 2004). Such men are not merely "allies," "antihomophobic," or "gay-friendly," but attracted to and comfortable in queer culture and indeed often mistaken for gay. There is at least a perception that straight men increasingly are adopting the styles, clothing, and bodies first popularized by gay men, and the time lag between gay innovation and straight appropriation is shortening (Colman, 2005). Some heterosexual men are sporting looks that until recently might have been read as gay (and probably often still are by some). These males may be indifferent to having their sexual orientation misread (Colman, 2005), and this certainly indicates their distance from the powerful and defensive hostility traditionally offered by heterosexual men in response to such perceptions.

This gay-friendly straightness points to the weakening of heterosexual men's traditional hostility toward male homosexuality and a blurring of the boundaries between gay and straight. It reflects the growing visibility, strength, and cultural cachet of gay and lesbian culture, to which young heterosexual men have responded variously with hostility, interest, or participation. At the same time, notions such as "queer straights" have been criticized as akin to men calling themselves feminists or middle-class white people appropriating black street culture (Curiel, 2001).

CONCLUSION

I hope that I have left you with some sense of the significant forms of diversity, and change, evident among young heterosexual men. Young males' sexual practices and relations are heterogeneous, shaped by local contexts, peer cultures, and multiple axes of social differentiation. Their sexual relations are in a state of flux, as sexual practices, the intimate relations within

which these take place and the narratives, discourses, and cultural formations that give them meaning all shift. I have noted a number of ways in
which those of us with a more activist bent might see "progress": increasing norms of gender equality, assertions of female agency, and destabi-
lizations of rigidly heterosexual and masculine identities. At the same
time, as I also have noted, many heterosexual men's social and sexual
relations with women continue to be organized by gendered power centered on male privilege, and some new cultural formations do little to
undermine these. It is an open question as to what kind of movement we
will see next.

NOTES

1. "Fox's new reality special: Straight men convince everyone they're gay. . . ."
   The Empty Closet, June 3, 2004. New York: Gay Alliance of the Genessee
   Valley. http://ec.gayalliance.org/articles/000345.shtml (accessed September
   9, 2004).

REFERENCES

Abernethy, M. (2004, March 22). The gay deceivers, again. *PopMatters*. Retrieved
    September 28, 2005, from http://www.popmatters.com/tv/reviews/p/playing-it-
    straight.html
Attwood, F. (2002). Reading porn: The paradigm shift in pornography research.
    Sexualities, 5(1), 91–105.
Baxter, J. (2002). Patterns of change and stability in the gender division of house-
    hold labour in Australia, 1986–1997. *Journal of Sociology, 38*(4), 399–424.
Bergstrand, C., & Williams, J. B. (2000). Today's alternate marriage styles: The
    case of swingers. *The Electronic Journal of Human Sexuality* http://www.ejhs.
    org/volume3/swing/body.htm.
Brioux, B. (2004, March 11). She had a gay old time. *Toronto Sun*.
Ciabattari, T. (2001). Changes in men's conservative gender ideologies: Cohort and
    period influences. *Gender & Society, 15*(4), 574–591.
Colman, D. (2005, June 19). Gay or straight? Hard to tell. *The New York Times*.
Connell, R.W. (1989). Cool guys, swots and wimps: The interplay of masculinity
    and education. *Oxford Review of Education, 15*(3), 291–303.
———. (1993). Disruptions: Improper masculinities and schooling. In L. Weis &
    M. Fine (Eds.), *Beyond silenced voices: Class, race, and gender in United States
    schools*. New York: State University of New York Press.
———. (1995). *Masculinities*. Sydney: Allen & Unwin.
———. (1996). Teaching the boys: New research on masculinity, and gender strate-
    gies for schools. *Teachers College Record, 98*(2), 206–235.
Connell, R. W., Davis, M. D., & Dowsett, G. W. (1993). A bastard of a life: Homo-
    sexual desire and practice among men in working-class milieux. *Australian and
    New Zealand Journal of Sociology, 29*, 112–135.
Curiel, J. (2001, June 24). A straight embrace of gay culture—with a twist. *The San
    Francisco Chronicle*.
Doyle, J.A. (1989). *The male experience* (2nd ed.). Iowa: W. M. C. Brown.

Duncombe, J., & Marsden, D. (1993). Love and intimacy: The gender division of emotion and "emotion work": A neglected aspect of sociological discussion of heterosexual relationships. *Sociology, 27*(2), 221–241.

Ellard, J., Richters, J., & Newman, C. (2004). *Non-gay sexual subcultures: A content analysis of Sydney sex contact publications.* Sydney: National Centre in HIV Social Research, University of New South Wales.

Fine, M. (1993). Sexuality, schooling, and adolescent females: The missing discourse of desire. In L. Weis & M. Fine (Eds.), *Beyond silenced voices: Class, race, and gender in United States schools.* New York: State University of New York Press.

Flood, M. (1997, April). *Homophobia and masculinities among young men (Lessons in becoming a straight man).* Presentation to teachers, Professional Development Training, O'Connell Education Centre, Canberra. Retrieved April 27, 2005, from http://www.xyonline.net/misc/homophobia.html

———. (2003a, November). *Fatherhood and fatherlessness* (The Australia Institute, Discussion Paper No. 59).

———. (2003b). Lust, trust and latex: Why young heterosexual men do not use condoms. *Culture, Health, & Sexuality, 5,* 353–369.

———. (2008). Men, sex, and homosociality: How bonds between men shape their sexual relations with women. *Men and Masculinities, 10,* 339–359.

Foreman, M. (Ed.). (1998). *AIDS and men: Taking risks or taking responsibility?* London: Panos Institute and Zed Books.

Goldman, J. (2000). Sexuality education for teenagers in the new millennium. *Youth Studies Australia, 19,* 11–17.

Grunseit, A., & Kippax, S. (1996, November). *Tech's mechs: Male apprentices, masculinity and HIV.* Annual Conf Australas Soc HIV Med. .

Haenfler, R. (2004). Manhood in contradiction: The two faces of straight edge. *Men and Masculinities, 7*(1), 77–99.

Herdt, G. (1999). Clinical ethnography and sexual culture. *Annual Review of Sex Research, X,* 100–119.

Hillier, L., Harrison, L., & Warr, D. (1998). When you carry condoms all the boys think you want it: Negotiating competing discourses about safe sex. *Journal of Adolescence, 21,* 15–29.

Hillier, L., Matthews, L., & Dempsey, S. (1997). A low priority in a hierarchy of needs: A profile of the sexual health needs of homeless young people in Australia. *Sexuality, Homelessness and Young People Project (Part One).* National Centre in HIV Social Research, Centre for the Study of Sexually Transmissible Diseases, La Trobe University.

Holland, J., Ramazanoglu, C., & Sharpe, S. (1994). *Wimp or gladiator: Contradictions in acquiring masculine sexuality* (WRAP/MRAP Paper 9). London: Tufnell Press.

Holland, J., Ramazanoglu, C. Sharpe, S., & Thomson, R. (1996). Reputations: Journeying into gendered power relations. In J. Weeks & J. Holland (Eds.), *Sexual cultures: Communities, values and intimacy.* Hampshire & London: Macmillan.

Jensen, R., & Dines, G. (1998). The content of mass-marketed pornography. In G. Dines, R. Jensen, & Russo, A. (Eds.), *Pornography: The production and consumption of inequality.* New York: Routledge.

Kimmel, M. S. (2000). *The gendered society.* Oxford University Press.

Kinsman, G. (1987). *The regulation of pleasure: Sexuality in Canada.* Montreal/New York: Black Rose Books.

Kippax, S., Crawford, J., & Waldby,C. (1994). Heterosexuality, masculinity and HIV. *AIDS, 8*(suppl. 1), S315–S323.

Kitzinger, J. (1995). I'm sexually attractive but I'm powerful: Young women negotiating a sexual reputation. *Women's Studies International Forum, 18*(2), 187–196.

Levine, J. (2002). *Harmful to minors: The perils of protecting children from sex.* Minneapolis: University of Minnesota Press.

Levy, A. (2005). *Female chauvinist pigs: Women and the rise of raunch culture.* Melbourne: Schwartz.

Lindsay, J., Smith, A. M. A., & Rosenthal, D. A. (1997). *Secondary students, HIV/ AIDS and sexual health.* Melbourne: Centre for the Study of STDs, Faculty of Health Sciences, La Trobe University.

Lloyd, C. (2004). Straight fairies. *Salon.* Retrieved September 9, 2004, from http:// www.salon.com/weekly/fairies960729.html

Lo, V., & Wei, R.(2002). Third-person effect, gender, and pornography on the internet. *Journal of Broadcasting & Electronic Media, 46*, 13–33.

Mac an Ghaill, M. (1994). *The making of men: Masculinities, sexualities and schooling.* Buckingham: Oxford University Press.

———. (1996). What about the boys? Schooling, class and crisis masculinity. *Sociological Review, 44*(3), 381–397.

———. (2000). Rethinking (male) gendered sexualities in education: What about the British heteros? *Journal of Men's Studies, 8*, 195–212.

MacKinnon, C. (1994). *Only words.* London: HarperCollins.

Martino, W. (1999). "Cool boys,", "party animals," "squids" and "poofters": Interrogating the dynamics and politics of adolescent masculinities in school. *British Journal of Sociology of Education, 20*(2), 239–263.

Martino, W., & Pallotta-Chiarolli, M. (2003). *So what's a boy? Addressing issues of masculinity and schooling.* Open University Press.

McMahon, A. (1998). Blokus domesticus: The sensitive new age guy in Australia. *Journal of Australian Studies, 56*, 147–158.

McNair, B. (1996). *Mediated sex: Pornography and postmodern culture.* London & New York. Arnold.

Moore, S., & Rosenthal, D. (1993). *Sexuality in adolescence.* London: Routledge.

———. (1998). Contemporary youths' negotiation of romance, love, sex, and sexual disease. In V. de Munch (Ed.), *Romantic love and sexual behaviour: Perspectives from the social sciences.* Westport: Praeger.

National Crime Prevention. (2001). *Young people and domestic violence: National research on young people's attitudes and experiences of domestic violence.* Canberra: Crime Prevention Branch, Commonwealth Attorney-General's Department.

Pallotta-Chiarolli, M. (1998). *Cultural diversity and men who have sex with men: A review of the issues, strategies and resources.* Sydney: National Centre in HIV Social Research, Macquarie University.

Primary Health Care Group. (1996). *Draft national men's health policy.* Canberra: Department of Community Services and Health.

Redman, P. (2001). The discipline of love: Negotiation and regulation in boys' performance of a romance-based heterosexual masculinity. *Men and Masculinities, 4*(2), 186–200.

Rich, A. (1980). Compulsory heterosexuality and lesbian existence. *Signs, 5*(4), 631–660.

Richardson, D. (1997). Sexuality and feminism. In V. Robinson & D. Richardson (Eds.), *Introducing women's studies: Feminist theory and practice.* Hampshire & London: Macmillan.

Richters, J., Grulich, A. E., de Visser, R. O., Smith, A. M. A., & Rissel, C. E. (2003). Autoerotic, esoteric and other sexual practices engaged in by a representative sample of adults. *Australian and New Zealand Journal of Public Health, 27*(2), 180–190.

Richters, J., & Rissel, C. R. . (2005). *Doing it down under: The sexual lives of Australians.* Sydney: Allen & Unwin.

Roker, D., & Coleman, J. (1998). Introduction. In J. Coleman & D. Roker (Eds.), *Teenage sexuality: Health, risk and education.* Amsteldijk, The Netherlands: Harwood Academic Publishers.

Rosenthal, D. A.,Gifford, S., & Moore, S. M. (1998). Safe sex or safe love: Competing discourses? *AIDS Care, 10*(1), 35–47.

Russell, D. E. H., & Trocki, K. (1993). Evidence of harm. In D. E. H. Russell (Ed.), *Making violence sexy: Feminist views on pornography.* New York & London: Teachers College Press.

Russell, G., Barclay, L., Edgecombe, G., Donovan, J., Habib, G., Callaghan, H., & Pawson, Q. (1999). *Fitting fathers into families: Men and the fatherhood role in contemporary Australia.* Canberra: Commonwealth Dept of Family and Community Services.

Russo, A. (1998). Feminists confront pornography's subordinating practices: Politics and strategies for change. In G. Dines, R. Jensen, & A. Russo (Eds.), *Pornography: The production and consumption of inequality.* New York: Routledge.

Sanson, A., & Lewis, V. (2001). Children and their family contexts. *Family Matters, 59,* 4–9.

Seal, D.W., & Ehrhardt, A. A. (2003). Masculinity and urban men: Perceived scripts for courtship, romantic, and sexual interactions with women. *Culture, Health & Sexuality, 5*(4), 295–319.

Singleton, A., & Maher, J. (2004). The "new man" is in the house: Young men, social change, and housework. *Journal of Men's Studies, 12*(3), 227–240.

Smith, A.M.A., Agius, P.,Dyson, S., Mitchell, A., & Pitts, M. (2003). *Secondary students and sexual health: Results of the 3rd national survey of Australian secondary students, HIV/AIDS and sexual health.* Melbourne: Australian Research Centre in Sex, Health & Society, La Trobe University.

Snitow, A. (1988). Retrenchment vs. transformation: The politics of the antipornography movement. In Caught Looking, Inc. (Eds.), *Caught looking: Feminism, pornography and censorship.* Seattle: The Real Comet Press.

Society for Human Sexuality. (n.d.). *The swing community: A profile.* Retrieved April 27, 2005, from http://www.sexuality.org/swinging.html .

Stewart, F. (1999). "Once you get a reputation, your life's like. . . wrecked": The implications of reputation for young women's sexual health and well-being. *Women's Studies International Forum, 22*(3), 373–383.

Stewart, F., Mischewski, A., & Smith, A. M. A. (2000). "I want to do what I want to do": Young adults resisting sexual identities. *Critical Public Health, 10*(4), 409–420.

Strazdins, L., & Broom, D. H. (2004). Acts of love (and work): Gender imbalance in emotional work and women's psychological distress. *Journal of Family Issues, 25*(3), 356–378.

Strossen, N. (1995). *Defending pornography: Free speech, sex, and the fight for women's rights.* London: Simon & Schuster.

Taormino, T. (2000, March 1–7). Bend over, boys! *The Village Voice.* Retrieved April 30, 2005, from http://www.villagevoice.com/people/0009,taormino,12883,24.html

Thomas, J. A. (2000). Gay male video pornography: Past, present, and future. In R. Weitzer (Ed.), *Sex for sale: Prostitution, pornography, and the sex industry.* New York: Routledge.

Waldby, C., Kippax, S., & Crawford, J. (1993). Cordon sanitaire: "Clean" and "unclean" women in the AIDS discourse of young men. In P. Aggleton, P. Davies, & G. Hart (Eds.), *AIDS: Facing the second decade.* London: Falmer Press.

Walsh, A. (1999). Life history theory and female readers of pornography. *Personality and Individual Differences, 27*, 779–787.

Weston, R., Stanton, D., Qu, L., & Soriano, G. (2001). Australian families in transition. *Family Matters, 60*.

White, N. R. (2003). Changing conceptions: Young people's views of partnering and parenting. *Journal of Sociology, 39*(2), 149–164.

Wight, D. (1994). Boys' thoughts and talk about sex in a working class locality of Glasgow. *Sociological Review, 42*(4), 703–737.

———. (1996). Beyond the predatory male: The diversity of young Glaswegian men's discourses to describe heterosexual relationships. In L. Adkins & V. Merchant (Eds.), *Sexualising the social: Power and the organisation of sexuality* (pp. 145–170). Hampshire & London: Macmillan.

Wilkins, A. C. (2004). "So full of myself as a chick": Goth women, sexual independence, and gender egalitarianism. *Gender & Society, 18*(3), 328–349.

Wilton, T. (1997). *Engendering AIDS: Deconstructing sex, text and epidemic.* London: Sage.

Contributors

Rosi Braidotti is Distinguished Professor in the Humanities and the founding Director of the Center for the Humanities at Utrecht University in the Netherlands She has published extensively in Continental philosophy, poststructuralism and feminist theory, epistemology, social theory, and cultural studies. Her books include: *Patterns of Dissonance* (Cambridge, Polity Press, 1991); *Nomadic Subjects: Embodiment and Sexual Difference in Contemporary Feminist Theory* (New York: Columbia University Press, 1994); *Metamorphoses: Towards a Materialist Theory of Becoming* (Polity Press, 2002); *Transpositions: On Nomadic Ethics* (Polity Press, 2006). She has coedited: *Between Monsters, Goddesses and Cyborgs,* with Nina Lykke (London: Zed Books, 1996); *Thinking Differently. A European Women's Studies Reader* with Gabriele Griffin (Zed Books, 2002). She is a member of the editorial board of *Signs, Differences, Theory; Culture & Society; The European Journal of Women's Studies,* and many other journals.

Judith Butler is Maxine Elliot Professor in the Departments of Rhetoric and Comparative Literature at the University of California, Berkeley. She received her PhD in Philosophy from Yale University in 1984. She is the author of *Subjects of Desire: Hegelian Reflections in Twentieth-Century France* (Columbia University Press, 1987); *Gender Trouble: Feminism and the Subversion of Identity* (Routledge, 1990); *Bodies That Matter: On the Discursive Limits of "Sex"* (Routledge, 1993); *The Psychic Life of Power: Theories of Subjection* (Stanford University Press, 1997); *Excitable Speech* (Routledge, 1997); *Antigone's Claim: Kinship Between Life and Death* (Columbia University Press, 2000); and *Hegemony, Contingency, Universality,* with Ernesto Laclau and Slavoj Zizek, (Verso Press, 2000). In 2004, she published a collection of writings on war's impact on language and thought entitled *Precarious Life: Powers of Violence and Mourning* with Verso Press. That same year, *The Judith Butler Reader* appeared, edited by Sara Salih, with Blackwell Publishers. A collection of her essays on gender and sexuality, *Undoing Gender,* appeared with Routledge in 2004 as well. Her most recent book, *Giving* *an Account of Oneself*, appeared with Fordham University Press (2005) and considers the partial opacity of the subject, and the relation between critique and ethical reflection. She is currently working on essays pertaining to Jewish Philosophy, focusing on pre-Zionist criticisms of state violence. She continues to write on cultural and literary theory, philosophy, psychoanalysis, feminism, and sexual politics.

Iwona Chmura-Rutkowska is currently an assistant professor in the Faculty of Educational Studies, Department of Sociology of Education, Adam Mickiewicz University in Poznań, Poland. She earned her doctoral degree in 2003 under the tutelage of Professor Zbigniew Kwiecinski, at the Adam Mickiewicz University. Dr. Chmura-Rutkowska is an expert in social education sciences including gender studies. Her interests concern social-cultural sources and the formation mechanisms of a gender identity, with a special focus on the family, mass media, and education/ schooling influences.

Michael Flood is a Lecturer in Sociology at the University of Wollongong, Australia. He conducts research on men and masculinities, male heterosexuality, violence, and sexual and reproductive health. He is a coeditor of the *International Encyclopedia of Men and Masculinities*, and the author of academic papers on such areas as men and masculinities, heterosexual men's sexualities, men's violence, homosociality, fatherhood and "fathers' rights," antiviolence mobilizations, and youth and pornography. Dr. Flood also has been involved in a variety of activities such as profeminist educator, speaker, writer, and activist on issues of men and gender. In particular, he is involved in community advocacy and education work focused on men's violence against women.

Agnieszka Graff is Assistant Professor in the American Studies Center, University of Warsaw, and coeditor of *The Americanist: Warsaw Journal for the Study of the United States*. Her current research concerns the rhetorical strategies of feminism in the United States. A scholar and activist, she has published extensively on gender in Polish public life in both scholarly and political journals and the mainstream press. Best known in Poland for her book *Swiat bez kobiet* [World without Women] (2001; 2003), she has recently published in English: "A Different Chronology: Reflections on Feminism in Contemporary Poland," in *Third Wave Feminism* (edited by S. Gillis, Palgrave 2007); "We Are (Not All) Homophobes: A Report from Poland, *Feminist Studies*, Summer 2006; "The Land of Real Men and Real Women: Gender and EU Accession in Three Polish Weeklies," in *Global Empowerment of Women* (edited by C. Elliott, Routledge, 2008).

Jeff Hearn is Professor of Gender Studies (Critical Studies on Men), Linköping University, Sweden; Professor, Swedish School of Economics, Helsinki,

Finland; and Professor, University of Huddersfield, United Kingdom.. His many authored and edited books include: *The Gender of Oppression* (1987), *"Sex" at "Work"* (1987/1995), *The Violences of Men* (1998), *Gender, Sexuality and Violence in Organizations* (2001), *Handbook of Studies on Men and Masculinities* (Sage 2005), *Men and Masculinities in Europe* (Whiting & Birch 2006), and *European Perspectives on Men and Masculinities* (Palgrave Macmillan 2006). He has been Principal Contractor, EU FP5 Research Network "The Social Problem and Societal Problematisation of Men and Masculinities," and acted as Sub-Network Coordinator, EU FP6 "Coordination Action on Human Rights Violation."

Sally Hines is a lecturer in Sociology in the School of Sociology and Social Policy at the University of Leeds, United Kingdom. Her research interests fall within the areas of identity, gender, sexuality, and the body. Her work is particularly concerned with transformations in gendered, sexual, and embodied identities. Her current work explores social/cultural change and transgender visibility and citizenship in relation to recent legislative shifts regarding sexuality and gender. She has published articles in *The Journal of Gender Studies, Sociology, Critical Social Policy* and *Sociological Research Online*. Her recent book, *TransForming Gender: Transgender Practices of Identity, Intimacy and Care*, is published by Policy Press (2007).

Anikó Imre is Assistant Professor of Critical Studies in the School of Cinematic Arts of the University of Southern California. She taught at the University of Washington before completing a 3-year postdoctoral fellowship at the Amsterdam School of Cultural Analysis, where she participated in a collaborative project on globalization, the media, and the transformation of identities in the new Europe. She has published articles on media and globalization, feminism, nationalism, postcoloniality, education and the East European transitions in *Screen, Camera Obscura, Framework, Third Text, CineAction, Signs,* and various book collections. She is editor of *East European Cinemas*, published in Routledge's Film Readers series (2005), and coeditor of *Transnational Feminism in Film and Media*, part of Palgrave's Comparative Feminist Studies series (2007). Her book, *Identity Games: Globalization and the Transformation of Post-Communist Media Cultures*, is forthcoming with MIT Press.

Karin Lenke holds a master's degree in Political Science and a bachelor's degree in Gender studies, both at Lund University, Sweden. In 2005 through 2006, she was a research assistant and a Marie Curie fellow for Gender Graduates at Lodz University, Poland. She specializes in critical examinations of social policy, especially the ways that parenthood is organized politically and socially in relation to sex/gender, (hetero) sexuality, and biologist essentialism.

Kateřina Lišková is Assistant Professor in the Gender Studies program, Faculty of Social Sciences, Masaryk University, in the Czech Republic. Her research focuses on gender, sexuality, and the social organization of intimacy. She has recently received her PhD in sociology for her dissertation entitled "Feminist Anti-Pornography Discourse: A Sociological Analysis," to be published in 2009.

Elżbieta H. Oleksy is Professor Ordinarius of the Humanities at the University of Łódź and University of Warsaw. She is Founding Director of the Women's Studies Center and Dean of the Faculty of International and Political Studies, both at the University of Łódź. She has published extensively in cultural studies/visual culture and gender studies. Her books include: *Gender and Citizenship in a Multicultural Context,* coed. (Peter Lang, 2008); *Tożsamość i obywatelstwo w społeczeństwie wielokulturowym,* ed. (Polish Scientific Publishers, 2008); *Men and Masculinities in Europe,* coauthor (Whiting & Birch Publishing, 2006); *European Perspectives on Men and Masculinities. National and Transnational Approaches,* coauthor (Palgrave Macmillan, 2006); *Representing Gender in Cultures,* coed. (Peter Lang, 2004); *Gender in Film and the Media. East-West Dialogues,* coed. (Peter Lang, 2000); *Kobieta w krainie Dixie. Literatura i film* (Łódź University Press, 1998).

Joanna Ostrouch is in the Faculty of Social Sciences and Arts, Department of Philosophy and Sociology of Education, University of Warmia and Mazury, in Olsztyn, Poland. She runs seminars and gives lectures on sociology of education, social inequality and exclusion, and social pathology. Her research interests concern social and cultural aspects of gender and learning, different dimensions of family relations in the context of gender socialization and education, and balancing work and family life; she has authored and edited four books and over thirty articles. She prefers biographical and life-history approaches in researching gender. Ostrouch is involved in different international research projects and has also been a convener of European Society for Research on the Education of Adults (ESREA) Network on Gender and Adult Learning since September 2007.

Iva Šmídová is Assistant Professor in the Gender Studies Program, Department of Sociology, Faculty of Social Studies, Masaryk University, Brno, Czech Republic. She is a cofounder and, since 2005, also the Head of the Gender Program there. She teaches courses on the Gendered Structure of Society and Critical Studies on Men and Masculinities. Her recent research projects deal with the relationship between educational tracks in reproduction of gendered anticipations of chances on the Czech labor market; fatherhood beyond child-delivery (early parenthood); and alternative masculine social identities (doctoral thesis on "Different Men" defended in 2004). She also has been involved in several research projects at the European level, collaborated with Czech feminist NGO's, and initiated the foundation of Gender Center (2000) and Children's Corner (2004) at her home faculty.

Lisa Smyth is a lecturer in Sociology at Queen's University Belfast. Her research interests are in the fields of gender, reproduction, national and cultural identities, moral politics, feminism, and intimate citizenship. Her book, *Abortion & Nation: the Politics of Reproduction in Contemporary Ireland* (Ashgate, 2005), examines the shifting dynamics of abortion politics in the Republic of Ireland since the early 1980s. She has also published work on the cultural politics of sex education and abortion debates in Northern Ireland, as well as on pro-breastfeeding campaigns. She is currently working on the moral grammar of women's reproductive lives and is planning a study on the gendered dynamics of public space in contemporary Belfast, as part of a large ESRC-funded project on Conflict in Cities and the Contested States.

Marek Wojtaszek is currently completing his doctoral dissertation in the American and Mass Media Department at the University of Lodz, Poland, where he earned his Masters' degree (2004) in International Relations. He did a 1-year (2004–2005) research stint at Utrecht University, the Netherlands, in women's studies, and in 2006 through 2007, he was a researcher at Central European University in Budapest, Hungary. His research accounts for his critical engagement with feminist poststructuralist philosophies, gender, and visual studies, as well as Gilles Deleuze's and Félix Guattari's philosophy. He has published articles on cinematic representation and gender. He has been engaged in the European project *Coordination Action on Human Rights Violations* (since 2006), researching gendered violences and their sociological roots, extant epistemological and methodological frameworks. Also, he collaborated with Hungarian Civil Liberties Union in Budapest (2006), contributing to the development of the international project on *Sex Workers' Advocacy* and constructing its global network. For many years, he has been cooperating with the Women's Studies Center at the University of Lodz on their various international projects. He teaches gender studies courses.

Index